THE TEACHING OF CALVIN

THE TEACHING OF CALVIN

A Modern Interpretation

BY

REV. A. MITCHELL HUNTER, M.A.

CARDROSS

Wipf & Stock
PUBLISHERS
Eugene, Oregon

Wipf and Stock Publishers
199 W 8th Ave, Suite 3
Eugene, OR 97401

The Teachings of Calvin
A Modern Interpretation
By Hunter, A. Mitchell
ISBN: 1-57910-217-4
Publication date 2/17/1999
Previously published by Maclehose, Jackson & Co., 1920

TO
MY TRUE HELPMATE
IN LIFE, IN MINISTRY,
AND IN THIS BOOK.

CONTENTS.

INTRODUCTION.

Rapid spread of Calvinism—comparison with Lutheranism—Calvin an aristocratic democrat—the master-mind of his age—his passion for righteousness—no crabbed Puritan—the secret of his life. - - - - - - pp. 1-5

CHAPTER I.
THE INSTITUTES.

Calvin's systematic mind—the growth of the Institutes—its reception—Calvin no doctrinal weathercock—influence of the work. - - - - - - - - pp. 6-14

CHAPTER II.
THE COMMENTARIES.

Biblical exposition the key to spiritual liberty—significant order of Calvin's Commentaries—his qualifications as an expositor—lucidity and self-restraint—honesty, sincerity and good sense—independence and fidelity—defects—experimental value. - - - - - - pp. 15-33

CHAPTER III.
SOURCES OF HIS THEOLOGY.

Heir of the past—attitude to ancient creeds—Scripture the ultimate and sole authority—illegitimacy and futility of speculation. - - - - - - - - pp. 34-44

CHAPTER IV.
THE DOCTRINE OF GOD.

The Fatherhood of God—the divine sovereignty—Calvin's agnosticism—arbitrariness of God—God and nature—miracle—the glory of God. - - - - - pp. 45-58

CONTENTS

CHAPTER V.

THE HOLY SCRIPTURES.

Their supreme and final authority—its grounds—the Church's affidavit—the witness of the Holy Spirit—the Canon the exclusive and inclusive Word of God—inerrancy of Scripture—indispensability—consistency—sufficiency—no needful truth outside and all needful truth within—principles of interpretation—torturing Scripture—self-interpretative—the norm and touchstone of truth. - - - pp. 59-87

CHAPTER VI.

PREDESTINATION.

Predestination and Providence—place of the doctrine in Calvin's system—its historical antecedents—its grounds—presuppositions—reprobation—relation of Christ to the doctrine—and of faith—the proof of election—perplexities—predestination and sin—is freewill a reality?—necessity and spontaneity—supra- and sub-lapsarianism—subsequent denunciations of the doctrine—its inspiration of heroism and consecration—" whosoever will—." - - - pp. 88-129

CHAPTER VII.

PROVIDENCE.

Yes and No—providence and contingency—man and nature—prayer and miracle—God and moral evil—providence and prudence—and moral responsibility—practical value of the doctrine. - - - - - - - - pp. 130-146

CHAPTER VIII.

THE CHURCH.

Outside the Church no salvation—visible and invisible Church—marks of the true Church—Calvin and foreign missions—efforts after Protestant and Catholic union. - - pp. 147-160

CHAPTER IX.

THE SACRAMENTS.

Diverging Protestant views—what are sacraments?—value of the Sacraments—how efficacious—the Word and the Holy Spirit—is participation necessary to salvation?—relation

CONTENTS

to election—the benefits conferred—infant baptism—the Lord's Supper—Protestant splits—where is Christ?—how is He partaken of?—insoluble mystery. - - - pp. 161-185

CHAPTER X.
CHURCH AND STATE.

Relation of Church and State in Geneva—Luther's and Calvin's views of relationship—Calvin's compromise and its issues.
pp. 186-194

CHAPTER XI.
CHURCH ORDER AND WORSHIP.

Necessity of Church order—principle of accommodation—the Church's right to self-government—place of the laity in the Church—Presbyterianism—election and work of ministers, elders and deacons—centrality of the sermon in church services—ordinances—bells—liturgies—examples of Calvin's prayers. - - - - - - - - pp. 195-216

CHAPTER XII.
DISCIPLINE.

Indispensability of discipline—the danger of moral disorders—the Libertines—examples of disciplinary measures—excommunication and anathema—can the State claim spiritual powers? - - - - - - - - - pp. 217-224

CHAPTER XIII.
INTOLERANCE AND SERVETUS.

Defence of intolerance—the heretic a criminal—an expiatory monument—Servetus and his life story—his views—a compound of heresies—a theological anarchist—a herald of modernity—collisions with Calvin—Calvin's complicity in his execution and his impenitence—extenuations. pp. 225-249

CHAPTER XIV.
LEGISLATION.

Calvin a great statesman—and legislator—a democratic aristocrat—his code of laws and their vindication—details of legislation—Calvin as a political economist. - - pp. 250-266

CONTENTS

CHAPTER XV.

ATTITUDE TO ART, MUSIC AND SCIENCE.

Was Calvin unmusical and unaesthetic ?—reasons for meagreness of indications—his poetic temperament and effusions—a lover of nature—appreciative of art—musical sympathies—pioneer of congregational singing—psalms or hymns ?—psalm tunes—part-singing—organs—Scottish Psalmody—Copernicus—astrology—Calvin's no and yes—his clairvoyance and credulity. - - - - - - - pp. 267-289

CHAPTER XVI.

THE ESSENCE OF CALVINISM.

Has Calvinism a future ?—What is Calvinism ?—Calvin not primarily a theologian but a man of God—His loyalty to Scripture as the sole authoritative determinant of doctrine—not a pathfinder or innovator—the essence of Calvinism—the letter and the spirit—the purgative influence of Calvinism—directive of legislation—the heart and soul of religion—the inspirer of Christian socialism—and of enlightened progressive democracy—champion of the ideal of Christian unity—the God of Calvinism the hope of the world. pp. 290-301

INDEX. - - - - - - - - - - 302

INTRODUCTION [1]

THE principal intention of this volume is to provide a discussion of the distinctive features of the doctrinal ecclesiastical and legislative system identified with Calvin, based not merely on his epoch-making work, the *Christian Institutes*, but on a comprehensive survey of his writings of all descriptions, commentaries, treatises, and especially letters, as well as of his practical achievements in the domain of civic politics. Those doctrines which he held in common with other Christian Churches have received only such attention as is necessary to show how they fit into the whole severely logical structure.

Few people have so stamped their name upon the world as Calvin. It was not that he merely gave wide vogue to a system of ideas; he poured into the veins of multitudes a new spirit, inspired their hearts with a new religious passion, galvanised them into a new moral life, and started them in ardent pursuit of new ideals. Already in his own day the theological and ecclesiastical system with which he was identified had received the distinctive name of Calvinism. By dint of a red-hot propagandism inspired by the fiercest absolute conviction of the truth of what he taught and its fitness to provide a doctrinal basis for the whole Reformed world, he speedily gave currency to his views and ideas over a wide area of Europe. The map provided at the end of Professor Lindsay's *History of the Reformation* graphically presents the extent of their spread by 1580, only sixteen years after Calvin's death. A large proportion of Switzerland and the German provinces with

[1] The author would like to acknowledge very gratefully the service rendered by Prof. H. R. Mackintosh, New College, Edinburgh, in giving encouragement as stimulating as his suggestions were wise and helpful.

all Scotland and Holland display the colour assigned to Calvinistic Churches, while France is streaked all over with it, as are also Hungary and, in less degree, Moravia, Bohemia and Poland. England was profoundly influenced by Calvinistic thought, while even Russia, immobile under the rule of the Greek Church, and Spain, terrorised by the Inquisition, felt the pulse of the spirit that streamed from Geneva. The influence of his Academy reached far and deep. Thousands of students from all countries must have sat on its benches under his tuition and carried back into their own lands the ideals, principles and doctrines with which they were there saturated.

The grip which Calvinism took of the world soon far exceeded that of its rival, Lutheranism. The deepest reason is to be found in the fact that it answered more completely to the needs of the times. The day of democracy was dawning throughout Europe and the form and spirit of Presbyterianism was much more in consonance with a growingly wide-spread temper of mind than the monarchical episcopalian spirit of Lutheranism. Calvinism fell into step with the trend of political evolution, while Lutheranism, with its principle of non-resistance and obedience along with its conservative tendency in political economy, perpetuating the division between the social classes, strove to hold back the rising tide of democracy. As Calvinism developed individualism by its doctrine of predestination and safeguarded morality by making conduct and character the proof and test of election, so it stimulated the spirit of socialism by its insistence upon communal responsibility and its demand that the general good should take precedence of all private interests. It exalted the worth of labour and raised the status of the labourer. It gave scope, opportunity and freedom for the education in all men of that capacity for taking part in the direction of national and civic affairs which has resulted in the new modern world, in the transformation of political institutions, and in civil constitutions which bar out autocracy. Calvin along with Rousseau may be said to have laid the train of the French Revolution in its beneficent aspect, and to have been the ultimate inspirer of that Declaration of the Rights of Man proclaimed in the United States of America and echoed vociferously by France in the time of its remaking.

Aristocratic in his deepest sympathies, Calvin was democratic in his fundamental convictions but autocratic in their practical application. With God as his constant referee, he too often treated the world as his football and kicked it hard, not always so judiciously as to propel it towards its goal. If he would have made a front-rank statesman, he would also have given efficient service as a police-court magistrate or an inspector of nuisances, his mind being both telescopic and microscopic, panoramic and parochial. Though accessible to all, he does not appear to have been on affectionate or intimate terms with any who belonged to the 'masses.' They served him; he ruled them. The 'masses' were quite conscious of this haughty attitude of distance and aloofness, and while they mostly gave him their obedience, they never gave him their hearts. There was justice in the comparison his staunch friend Farel used to draw between him and Moses; both maintained their power by the respect they extorted, not by a love which they could not win.

It may be said with confidence that, if Calvin was excelled in this or that department of learning, he was indisputably the master-mind of his age in respect of the encyclopaedic range of the subjects with which he could deal as an expert. In exegesis, dogmatics and polemics, as well as in the more restricted spheres of ecclesiastical organisation and civil legislation, he moved with equal ease and claimed equal authority. Like Augustine, he wrote more than another can well read. In addition to what survives, there is evidence that whole works were lost during their transmission to friends for review. To his unfailing flow of thought and easy command of appropriate language he added a memory which seemed to forget nothing and had the power of instantly summoning up all its resources. Minute details came at its call as promptly as important facts. He could marshal dates, pertinent examples, illustrative passages in church history, corroborative quotations from the Fathers, useful contributions from the classics, after an effortless fashion which provokes wonder and excites envy. Of over four thousand letters already published (only a portion of the sum total) many are practically lengthy essays or treatises. Over two thousand of his sermons have been preserved (not half of all he preached), and of those published it would be hard to find one trashy or thin. The brain that could forge such a mass of literature must have been an engine of enormous power and resource.

Zeal for righteousness was as a burning fire in Calvin's bones, and the supreme purpose of his life was to procure its realisation in himself and in society. To condone moral slackness or smile indulgently on peccadilloes was to play fast and loose with what gave value to spiritual being. Better to suffer a hundred deaths, he once wrote, than to swerve a hairbreadth from the straight line. Whether he was actually given at college the nickname of " the accusative case " or not, the strictness and severity of his conduct (as though he were descended from a long line of maiden aunts, whimsically says Professor Lindsay) were a constant rebuke to his less well-behaved fellow-students in a time of common loose-living. Nevertheless it is unjust to picture him as a kill-joy ; at college he joined freely in innocent pleasures and laughter, and frequently in his writings he insists upon the human right to enjoyment. His own favourite pastime was a game resembling billiards which he played of an evening at one of the clubs organised by him in Geneva. Once he took a real holiday of a few days, and it is with schoolboyish zest that he arranges to enjoy it with Viret. No one who reads his description of their experiences on the shores of the lake will accuse him of being without appreciation of the charms of nature.

Whatever Calvin was or was not, he was a man to whom religion was the very breath of life. His piety was as profound as it was constant. All that was best, noblest and most influential in him (Rénan calls him the most Christian man of his generation) is traceable to its true source in a heart that was wholly given to God. Never has a more genuinely consecrated life been lived than his. Morning by morning he returned to the business divinely assigned him from the secret presence of the Most High. His seal symbolised the man and mirrored his life,—a hand stretched out as to One invisible offering a bleeding heart, with the motto,

' I give Thee all; I keep nothing back for myself.' His sense of discharging a divine mission was so strong as to place him among the race of prophets who identify themselves with God. That was partly the secret of his power. The danger for such a man, consciously the divine instrument, is that he may habitually claim God as his inspiring authority and hearty ally in all his activities. Such a sublime assurance increasingly charged him with a sensitive and passionate egotism which either bred or intensified his most intractable faults. Yet with all these faults none ever deserved more the reverential tribute posthumously paid him by the Council of Geneva when it declared that "God had impressed upon him a singularly majestic character." In virtue of achievement and of character impartial judgment will agree that Calvin takes rank amongst the noblest as well as the greatest sons of men.

CHAPTER I

THE INSTITUTES

I

It has been said with the usual amount of accuracy attaching to an epigram that "the watchword of Luther was war, that of Calvin, order; the one stormed, the other furnished the citadel of truth." It would be more in accordance with fact to recognise that they were both warriors and to say that, while both were also furnishers, one crowded in the furniture confusedly, the other put it carefully into its proper place. But the contrast cited, so far as it is true, reflects not only the differing natures of the men, but the differing circumstances of their work. Luther and Calvin could not have changed places; they could not have done each other's business. Calvin had too little of the bludgeon in him, Luther too little of the truncheon. But they belonged to successive generations, and in a generation or less men sometimes grow older by the space measured by a world-revolution. With the beginning of the sixteenth century, the Reformation was practically an accomplished fact. Europe was split into two irreconcilably hostile ecclesiastical camps. A Protestant Church was in being, vitalised by a new spirit, conscious of its mission, clear as to its principles. But it was more or less inchoate both as regards its organisation and doctrine. There was a good deal of go-as-you-please and *laissez-faire* in the various centres of its existence. There was no co-ordination of parts, no accepted consensus of creed, no model of ecclesiastical structure. If there was to be any firmly established Protestant Church, it must be founded not on a miscellaneous rubble collection of ideas and views, but on a solid, symmetrical, sharply defined body of determinative doctrine. Luther had cleared the ground and provided the rough material; there was now required a man less of originative than of architectonic mind to shape and build that material into its proper place and so fashion an organised Church, defined by its ordered system of belief.

Providence provided Calvin for that task. He was the complement of Luther, and his work was the completion of Luther's. It would be difficult to imagine a man better fitted both by nature and education for the work that remained to be done. The distinguishing feature of his mind was the quality which cannot tolerate unrelatedness and untidiness in the constituent elements of accepted belief. They must be systematised into an orderly, harmonious, and self-consistent body of truth. Nebulosity to Calvin was as distasteful as confusion. Predominant in him was the logical faculty, whose native quality had been early applied and developed in the incessant disputation of the college of Montaigu. It was indeed a powerful instrument, in whose decisions Calvin came to have such an arrogant confidence that, while claiming the right to dissent from Luther or any one else, he exhibits surprise that any one can differ from himself.

Instances of Calvin owning himself in the wrong are hard to find, such was his mental surefootedness and complacent intellectual self-righteousness. Champion of faith and confessed foe of reason, he was essentially a rationalist. Given truths and principles as premises, all inferences that seemed to follow logically must be true. Sentiment had no right of criticism. Truth must command implicit allegiance even though it outrage those feelings of the soul which are profound because instinctive. Calvin allowed little for the logic of the heart. There is much truth in Brunctière's estimate: " Just as he would have reasoned on the properties of a triangle or of a sphere, so Calvin reasons on the attributes of God. Everything that does not conform to the exigencies of his dialectic, he either contests or rejects. Cartesian before Descartes, rational proof, incontrovertible logic are for him the sign and proof of truth. He would not have believed if belief did not support itself by a syllogism in proper form. From 'an affair of the heart,' if I may so put it, Calvin has transformed religion into 'an affair of the intellect.'"

Such a view must be qualified, however, by the recognition that Calvin's logical faculty was not always in play. Indeed he lived from two centres, the one purely intellectual, the other essentially religious. Sometimes his heart escaped from the control of his head, and he wrote out of the gathered knowledge of a rich religious experience. The systematic theologian gave place to the preacher who spoke as the Holy Spirit moved him, regardless of consistency, concerned only to reconcile men to God. More and more as he grew older, he doffed the robe of the professor and spoke as a man to men, accepting the views of freewill and human ability on which common men base their lives, breaking through the iron chain of system and becoming all things to all men, if by any means he might save some.

All this receives ample illustration in the Institutes. Ostensibly written to instruct enquirers after truth in Protestant doctrine, Calvin was doubtless obeying the imperious instinct of his nature in systematically arranging and logically relating the contents of his new faith. The first edition is predominantly an intellectual *tour de force*. Successive editions exhibit the working of a heart growing in spiritual maturity and richer in human sympathies. Its harsher doctrines, if they are brought into greater relief, are at the same time toned down by the eager assertion of the divine righteousness, wisdom, and goodness, on which ultimately he would fix the eyes of all, in the assurance that the poignant mysteries involved have a bright side next to God.

II

The Institutes, says Brunetière, constitute almost the whole of Calvin ; to know him you have need only of the Institutes. That sounds encouraging until one proceeds to follow the implied advice, when it becomes evident that this road to knowledge is by no means a shortcut or else that there is a great deal of Calvin to know. For the

Institutes is a very elaborate and bulky treatise, not to be read at a reviewer's sitting, and demanding prolonged and repeated study for anything like real acquaintance, much less mastery, of its contents. But if the reader think amazedly that this is the product of the brain of a young man of twenty-six, he is giving its author more than his due of credit. The Institutes in its primary, original form was a slender volume well within the mental compass and application of ordinary readers. Its 514 octavo pages contained six chapters, dealing successively, and at no excessive length, with the themes of the Apostle's Creed. Its success assured Calvin that it was fulfilling its purpose, and thereupon he began a work of revision, amounting later to reconstruction, elaboration, and expansion, which continued up till within a few years of his death. Released from his early humanist studies, consecrated from young manhood to Biblical and historical science, he rapidly accumulated stores of sacred knowledge which he kept pouring unstintedly into his great masterpiece, providing additional illumination, illustration, and proof of those parts which he perceived to require strengthening in view of the subsequent controversies in which he became engaged. Three years after the first edition was issued at Basel from the printing press of Platter, its six chapters were expanded into seventeen in a second edition which appeared in Strasburg under the pseudonym of Alcuin (an anagram on his name), probably that its study might not be forbidden in Roman Catholic countries where already he was a well-known and well-hated man. Four years thereafter there appeared a third edition with twenty-one chapters, the volume being in folio form with 509 pages, at least six times the bulk of the first edition.[1] After various issues, what is accepted as its final, authoritative form was published in 1559 at Geneva. In this the whole work was practically recast and rewritten, an undertaking which

---

[1] A Latin couplet at the end of the preface to the last edition runs :
>Quos animus fuerat tenui excusare libello,
>Discendi studio, magnum fecere volumen.
>(" The zeal of those whose cause I undertook,
>Has swelled a short defence into a book."
>   Beveridge's translation.)

must have involved enormous labour. Calvin himself says in a letter of July 1st, 1559, in which he announces its forthcoming publication, that it is " rewritten and so altered as to have almost the appearance of a new work." That he took such infinite pains with it proves his own sense of its first importance to which he gives expression in the same letter,—" it holds the principal and by far the most conspicuous place amongst all my lucubrations."

III.

It might have been thought a presumptuous thing for a young man of twenty-six to constitute himself *the* authority on Protestant doctrine and dogmatically set forth what was to be believed on many points regarding which there was much current uncertainty and confusion and even fierce controversy. But the tone of assurance was just what was needed to solidify nebulous ideas and precipitate wavering opinions into definite convictions. Not a voice took exception to it or threw suspicion upon the work because of the comparative youth of the author. Its timeliness, undeniable power, clearness, grasp, and mature unction, silenced all objections on that score. Recognised by the Protestant world to be the word that had been urgently needed, fitly spoken, it received nothing less than an enthusiastic welcome, to which Calvin himself in long after days looks back with humble wonder and devout gratitude. Bucer acclaimed it as a great gift of God to the age, extolling the work as paving the way to the unification of the Church and the reconciliation of contending views. Would that we had many Calvins! cried the learned Saint-Merthe of Poictiers as he laid the volume down. Nor was it a nine days' wonder, attaining a mere cometary success ; admiration and appreciation grew as its fame spread. It sank ever deeper roots in the regard of the Reformed Church and exerted an ever stronger influence upon the moulding of its doctrine and organisation.

The effects of its publication were both immediate and immeasurable. It was soon translated into practically all European tongues, Italian, Spanish, German, Dutch,

Hungarian and Greek, and even into Arabic. An English edition appeared in a few years, Thomas Norton doing the same excellent service for Calvin which he did for Plutarch. So large was the sale of the French edition, issued in 1559, that a number of presses working in different places could scarcely keep pace with the demand. A Hungarian poet and scholar paid it the unusual compliment of celebrating it in verse, daring to say that there had been no such work since the time of the apostles. The chorus of praise has never since ceased and has been joined in by men of all theological complexions. The jurist Salmasius declared that he would sooner have written that one book than all the mighty tomes of Hugo Grotius, and Grotius was both a great lawyer and a great man. Sir Thomas Pope Blount [1] thought that this man was worth all who could claim to be called great theologians, and that whoever did not read Calvin would be considered an ignoramus by students, while still more ignorant was one who belittled him, and most ignorant of all he who learnt nothing from him. A professor of Göttingen (Dr. Müller) told his students that any one of them should sooner forget to take his dinner than omit to read Calvin's Institutes. Strongest contemporary evidence of all to its recognised value perhaps is given in the prompt action of the Sorbonne, who caused it to be burnt by the hangman and prohibited its perusal or spread under the severest penalties. Martyrs were cross-examined as to whether they were infected with their errors by this poisonous book. By Roman Catholics it was styled the Koran of the heretics, an evidence of its position of authority in the Protestant world.

IV

Beza is the originator of the assertion, echoed in almost every characterisation of the Institutes, that the views expressed by Calvin in the first edition remained unchanged to the end. Unlike Augustine, who published a book of retractations, and Luther and Melanchthon who had well-

---

[1] Author of a widely-circulated Censura celebriorum Autorum (1690).

marked earlier and later phases, Calvin never found reason to revise, much less repudiate, any of the doctrines for which he stood forward as champion and defender on his first entry into the theological arena. In large degree that is true; the essential substance of his system remains unaltered through all the controversies, discussions, and experiences of twenty-three years. The mental furniture of the worn-out man of fifty-six, ripe in spiritual experience, was the same as that of the young man with soul still flushed by the glow of his conversion. The text of his confession of faith was stereotyped from the time of its adoption. The later editions of the Institutes are no more than expansions of the first, certain doctrines receiving greater prominence and emphasis or more elaborate illustration and application. Never does Calvin act the critic of himself as Ruskin does in later editions of *Modern Painters*, exposing puerilities, exploding fallacies, calling attention in trumpet tones to mistaken views or false judgments. Calvin betters his work, but never corrects it. The doctrines which constitute the framework of his belief remain entirely unaffected. In regard to these, Calvin consistently exhibited an imperviousness to the influence of other views which amounted to a claim to the divine inspiration which confers infallibility. He could not conceive of himself as being wrong in these primary matters; he took it for granted that he was right, and he could not understand how any intelligent and honest man did not see with his eyes. The disagreement of those he esteemed was a grief to him,—he did not like to see his friend exposed to the danger incurred by embracing error. If he submitted to have his views overruled or set aside, it was never because he found reason to depart from them, but always because of considerations of expediency or policy.

It might not be reckoned a virtue in Calvin that he should have exhibited this unchangeableness. His justification is to be found in this, that these doctrines were not to him matters of opinion, convictions reached by the exercise of pure reason, but articles of faith plainly and unmistakably taught in Scripture. Holy Writ was the sole source of his beliefs, and he could not in loyalty to Scripture

THE INSTITUTES

depart a hairbreadth from the truths which the Holy Spirit had shown him to be therein contained. His wonder was not that others should disagree with him but that they should disagree with Scripture, so absolutely certain was he of having had revealed to him the truth, the whole truth, and nothing but the truth.

V

The doctrine of the Institutes will fall to be considered in subsequent chapters. Here it will be sufficient to indicate the kind of influence it exercised. That was as profound as its circulation was wide. It was issued at a critical time for Protestantism, when the shackles of ecclesiastically imposed doctrine had been completely struck off, and emancipated minds found themselves without any definite rule of faith or systematic body of belief by which they could live. There will always be many who delight in such absence of hedges. But absolute freedom of thought is a luxury which soon palls upon the man who realises that he can arrive of himself at no certainty. Epochs occur, too, when freethinking is the prelude to freeliving, and intellectual liberty fruits in moral licence. There were all too evident signs of that tendency being abroad in the generation which immediately entered upon the original Reformers' labours. The Libertines of Geneva found their counterpart elsewhere. On the other hand, many serious, earnest souls, who had dared to break free from the old ecclesiastical tyranny, must have felt timidly conscious of being left without that authoritative spiritual guidance which the bulk of men desire and need. They required something to take the place of these concrete supports to their faith which the Roman Church had so liberally supplied. The Reformation declared every believer to be a priest towards God, independent of the help of other mortals in securing the blessings of the Christian salvation. But the mental habit of reliance upon a clergy is not easily got rid of. It is easier to accept the assurance of a visible person, claiming authority to give it, than to lay hold of it for yourself directly from the hand of an unseen God. The situation clamoured for a man who could provide that on which mind and heart could rest, in quietness and confidence. To meet this clamant need Calvin was surely sent of God. As Prof. Lindsay says, "What the *Christian Institution* did for the sixteenth century was to make the unseen government and authority of God, to which all must bow, as visible to the intellectual eye of faith as the mechanism of the mediaeval Church had been to the eye of sense."[1] That was an immense service, for which all subsequent Protestant generations, however they may depart from the doctrine contained, should never cease to be grateful. To have prevented the ranks of Protestantism from becoming a mere rabble without a unifying creed and rule of life; to have marshalled so large a part of it under one common confession; to have pulled up an excited liberty when on the point of taking the bit in its teeth; to have given the spirit of revolution marks to steer by, ground on which to fight, an aim and a hope; to have provided a standard for the testing of that which claimed credence; to have given clear definition to the body of convictions and beliefs from which the Protestant Church drew its life, that was to raise a rampart against the old Church which all its power could never henceforth break down, and to ensure room and time for the new Church to grow into the mature strength by which a multitude which cannot be numbered have been brought to life, and peace, and God.

[1] Lindsay, *Hist. Reform.* ii. 157.

CHAPTER II

THE COMMENTARIES

I

THE greatest gain of the Reformation (because on it all others depended and by it were consolidated) was the putting of the Bible into the hands of the people and enabling them to read and appreciate it for themselves. It came like a new revelation to them, and revelation, as ever, worked revolution. Translations into the vernacular had been already published sporadically with results ominous to the Church that frowned upon them.[1] But to make Scripture speak in the people's tongue was not enough; that still left them without any proper understanding of much in it. Doubtless there was sufficient that was lucid and luminous to provide the hungry soul with fat things and guide the wayfarer into paths of peace. But if all Scripture was given for our edification and instruction, then it must constitute a serious deprivation to be unable to excavate some of its treasures of wisdom and knowledge. Here alone was sound building material for

[1] A very strong prohibition against the vernacular Scriptures was issued in the time of the Albigenses, early in the thirteenth century. An Austrian inquisitor, towards the end of that century, reports that he had heard and seen a certain country clown who repeated the Book of Job word for word, and several who knew the New Testament perfectly. The Waldenses, Picards, Hussites all had renderings in their own tongues. Wiclif's English translation was published about 1382. A large number of German versions of the whole Bible (no less than from fourteen to seventeen) came out in the end of the fifteenth century and the beginning of the sixteenth. The earlier editions were independent productions, but the later ones gradually assimilated to a certain type which ultimately took the shape of the German Vulgate. (*v.* Lindsay, *Hist. Reform.* i. 147, ff.).

the soul to be found, and its very existence was a summons to take advantage thereof. Here too were the armoury and the ammunition for the emancipated mind wherewith to fight its battles against heresy and superstition and ecclesiastical tyranny. If the world was to be released from its dependence upon the Roman Church and established firmly on the foundation of the Word of God, it needed above all things to be provided with the necessary helps to that end by those competent to give them. To this essential work all the leading Reformers devoted themselves with an industry and thoroughness which speedily left no excuse for ignorance or perplexity to protest its helplessness.

Amongst all who contributed to the work of popular enlightenment, Calvin easily takes rank as chief. He might be said to have made it the main business of his life to open up Scripture to the common people. From beginning to end of his crowded career there were but short intervals when he did not have a Commentary on the stocks. From one book he passed to another without haste and without rest. In view of the multiplicity of other claims upon his time and thought and energies, his expository work,—a labour requiring peculiar detachment and concentration of mind with swift and sure command of material,—is monumental in its witness to his amazing capacities, quick penetration, and an insight that worked almost like an instinct. If he did occasionally cut knots and evade difficulties, something must be allowed for the high pressure under which he constantly worked due to his urgent sense of the common needs clamouring to be satisfied. The grateful acclamation with which his successive volumes were received must have made him aware that he was meeting a deeply and widely felt want, and that in no more fruitful way could he employ his powers. Through his Commentaries he addressed an ever enlarging public in many lands and spoke by the mouths of thousands of other pulpits. From the rostrum of his study he commanded an audience which even Luther failed to reach. It was no wonder if he gave himself with tireless industry to a task so rewarding and so influential in promoting the aims he had at heart.

THE COMMENTARIES

II

His expositions did not follow any systematic course. The order of the books taken up would seem to have been determined at first by his view of their degree of importance as specially normative and formative of Christian thought and doctrine. The Ep. to the Romans was dealt with first of all, then the Epp. to Cor., Gal., and Ephes. Afterwards he was mostly guided by the appropriateness of some book to meet a pressing current need of the Church,—perhaps the danger of invasion by some new heresy or of perversion by an old error still clinging to it. For the inspiration and consolation of the French Protestants passing through the fires of persecution, he turned to Daniel and Jeremiah. It is characteristic and significant of him that he should deal with all the Epistles before he tackled the historical sections of the N.T. It was not till thirteen years after he had published his Comm. on Rom. (1539) and while in the concluding decade of his life that he put pen to his Comm. on Acts (1552), afterwards turning his attention to the Synoptic Gospels and lastly to the Gospel of John. He had already overtaken most of the N.T. before he entered upon the field of the O.T., characteristically starting with Isaiah (1551). His masterly work on the Psalms did not appear till 1557, four years after he had completed his labours on the N.T. Whether his studies on the O.T. coloured his mental outlook in later years or whether he found in them support and confirmation for the views with which he had identified himself, it would be difficult to decide. But that he was so predominantly engaged with the ancient oracles cannot have been without its influence upon him. Calvin, however, did not succeed in traversing the whole ground of Scripture, failing to overtake Judges, Ruth, Samuel, Kings, Esther, Nehemiah, Esra, Proverbs, Ecclesiastes and the Song of Solomon. He candidly confessed himself baffled by the book of Revelation, acknowledging that he was altogether unable to comprehend the meaning of the very obscure writer of that book.[1]

[1] The order of publication of the Commentaries was: New Testament—Romans 1539, Corinthians 1547, Galatians, Ephesians, Philippians, Colossians, Pastoral Epistles 1548-9, Hebrews, Thessalonians, James 1549-50, Catholic Epistles 1551, Acts 1552, lastly the

For the proper appreciation of Calvin's Commentaries in their varying quality and manner, it must be realised that a considerable amount of their material was first given to the public in pulpit discourses. They were originally popular expositions, suited to the capacity and needs of the ordinary hearer, as *e.g.* those on the Minor Prophets, Ezekiel, and Deuteronomy. The dates on which they were issued from the press do not uniformly represent the order in which Calvin himself studied the books, but rather the order determined by what he regarded as the public needs and their appropriateness to the existing situation. The Gospel of John was the first expounded in his quasi-professoriate at Strasburg, followed by 1 Cor., though the lectures on the latter, reduced to Commentary form, were published six years before those on the former. Calvin too did not himself write out all the Commentaries in the seclusion of his study. Some of them were notes of his pulpit expositions taken down and expanded by one or other of his students or successive secretaries and given a rapid revision by himself. He himself tells us how the Comm. on Isaiah was produced. The composition of the work was Des Gallars' (his secretary at the time), " for as I have little time for writing, he jots down to my dictation and arranges his materials afterwards at home. I then make a revision of it, and wheresoever he has missed my meaning, I restore it." If allowance required to be made for imperfections, it might be generously given in view of the secretary's remark in his Preface to this volume that Calvin seldom got peace to expound even two or three verses at a time, so engaged was he with business, not his own but the Church's and other people's.

III

It may be confidently affirmed that there was no one of that age so qualified for the work of a commentator as

Synoptic Gospels and John 1553. Old Testament—Isaiah 1551, Genesis 1554, Psalms and Hosea 1557, the remaining Minor Prophets 1559, Daniel 1561, Job and Jeremiah 1563. After his death the Commentary on Joshua and the lectures on Ezekiel were published partly by Beza, partly by Budaeus and Joinvilliers his secretaries. He expounded in Bible studies Deuteronomy and 1 Samuel.

THE COMMENTARIES 19

Calvin, both by reason of his possession of the peculiar mental gifts necessary for success and in respect of his scholarly acquirements.[1] With an extraordinarily tenacious memory, with an intellect of equally remarkable associative power, anything in the nature of a Concordance was for him almost unnecessary; he could summon at command relevant text to illuminate text and passage to illustrate passage. There are few who have so united mastery of the whole realm of theology, perfect acquaintance with the whole range of Scripture, and a knowledge of the original tongues such as gave him the right to speak with authority on linguistic difficulties. The learned Joseph Scaliger, the value of whose praise is in proportion to the scantiness of its bestowal, (" he scarce thought any man worth his commending," says Bayle), gave unstinted admiration to Calvin's Commentaries. He pronounced their author to have been " the greatest wit the world had seen since the Apostles." If the Reformer started this responsible business of providing reliable expositions at an age when others are but amateurs in scholarship, it was not because of any audacity which exaggerated its competency. He takes his place amongst the world's most genuine intellectual precocities, the rapid blossoming of whose powers was equalled by the strength with which they flowered. At the age of twenty-two, asserts a Roman Catholic writer of his own age, Calvin was the most learned man in Europe.

The *sine qua non* of a trustworthy commentator is such an intimate knowledge of the original tongues as enables him to exercise an independent judgment and fits him to estimate the value of the work of his predecessors. Before Calvin commenced his task which assumed such prodigious dimensions, he had given that thorough study to Hebrew

---

[1] The opinion of Arminius, the founder of the theological school opposed to Calvinism, is specially noteworthy. " After the Holy Scriptures, I exhort the students to read the Commentaries of Calvin, for I tell them that he is incomparable in the interpretation of Scripture; and that his Commentaries ought to be held in greater estimation than all that is delivered to us in the writings of the ancient Christian fathers; so that, in a certain eminent spirit of prophecy, I give the preeminence to him beyond most others, indeed beyond them all. . . . But to all this I subjoin the remark that they must be perused with cautious choice, like all other human compositions."

and Greek which established his right to enter the lists, if need be, with those who ranked as the highest authorities. He had enjoyed the tuition of scholars of European reputation, and extorted their highest respect by an ardent acquisitiveness aided by a leechlike retentiveness which speedily put him in possession of all they had to teach. Self-confidence is not always proof of corresponding fitness, but one in Calvin's position would not have dared to pronounce so dogmatically as he frequently does on thorny points involving linguistic difficulties without the assurance of being in possession of that knowledge which made it safe for him so to speak. He did not hesitate to cross swords with the redoubtable Erasmus, prince of N.T. exegetes of his day and pioneer in N.T. higher criticism; and modern scholarship has endorsed Calvin's view on many not unimportant passages. He had much of that special sense of the exegete of high rank which enables him to ferret out the meaning of words whose exact significance can only be arrived at by a combination of happy conjecture and industrious comparison of other instances or parallels. He reaches correct conclusions regarding many Hebrew and Greek words to which only the wider knowledge of modern learning has been able confidently to assign a definite meaning. Often he successfully uses Hebrew to illustrate ambiguous Greek terms in the N.T. No doubt in this he frequently took his cue from predecessors in the same field, but always he spoke as their peer, offering reasons that evidence the constant use of an independent judgment. One thing Calvin could never be, and that was an echo. If he accepted suggestions, it was not because of the weight of any authority behind them but because they commended themselves to him on grounds convincing to himself.

There is abundant evidence of the unsparing study he devoted to the work, but the proofs are often only apparent to those competent to appreciate them. Many a simple sentence or modest paragraph is the precipitate of investigation which left no materials for decision unexamined. No one has been more successful in concealing the immense amount of preliminary labour he undertook to prepare himself for his task. He was not concerned to win a reputation for scholarship; he was content if he "made it

THE COMMENTARIES

plain." He knew that it was not the raw material but the finished product of thought which was of interest and value to the reader for whose instruction he catered. "How much sweat I have poured out (in the work of preparation) it is not necessary to dilate upon," he remarks in the Preface to his Comm. on the Harmony of the Gospels. Any self-conscious display of learning was abhorrent to him. " I do not ambitiously gather these things which may serve for a vain brag." There was not, of course, the same extent of literature to consult as has now made Biblical exegesis the domain of specialists. Nor did he have the critical apparatus at his hand which is now in our possession with its precise, methodical laws and rules. Textual criticism with its work of collection and collation was in its mere infancy. But Calvin overlooked or ignored no means that were available to get at the truth of Scripture, industriously consulting such MSS. as were then procurable.[1] Even without modern helps, he frequently arrived at conclusions by a species of intuition, just as Sir Isaac Newton would leap to results without any preliminary process of difficult calculation.

The fact that Calvin's Commentaries have not ceased to be widely and respectfully consulted is sufficient evidence of the regard which they won and held. They have something of the timeless in them. Inevitably bearing the impress of their age, they are far less tinctured by its spirit than those of any commentator of previous centuries. They contain such a very large element of thought applicable to life universal as gives them in considerable measure a perpetually modern tone. If Shakespeare is "full of quotations," as an old farmer judged, commentaries of later days have been unashamedly, if unconfessedly, "full of Calvin." To quote many of them, as it has been said, is to quote him. The profound estimation in which his exegetical work has been held in other communions than his own receives emphatic witness from Hooker who asserted that "the sense of Scripture which Calvin alloweth " was held in the Anglican Church to be of more

---

[1] In his commentary on 1 Cor. vii. 29, there is an instance of a change of mind regarding the exegesis of a passage as the result of seeing a MS. which had not previously been before him.

force than if "ten thousand Augustines, Jeromes, Chrysostoms, Cyprians were brought forth." Such amazing deference can only be explained by qualities which commend the Commentaries as offering, with a large measure of success in matter and form, what satisfied the needs of Biblical students concerned only to discover the truth.

There have been few able to move so freely and surely in the intricate by-ways of the O.T. as in the broader highways of the New. The mind that could enter so sympathetically into that of an Isaiah or a John, that could make the Psalms "sing their song twice over" and plumb the depths of Paul's dark thought, must have had a singular sweep and an astounding equipment. Calvin was equally at home in the region of doctrine and of experimental religion. He brought to the task head and heart harmoniously yoked together. His best work in the O.T. was that on the Psalms, humanity's Book of Confessions, while his best in the New Testament was that on the Epp. of Paul, storehouse of exalted thought. He revelled in the one as he did in the other. If the one challenged and fed his mind., the other stimulated and comforted his soul. He was spiritual brother to David and such others as utter thoughts that arise in all but which few tongues can express, while he was in profound sympathy with Paul in his eager desire for the assurance of faith that is imparted only by knowledge of the divine mysteries to which Christ is the key.

IV

Calvin's aspiration after lucidity moved him to abjure philosophical discussion and also to condemn and reject ingenuities and refinements of exegesis which only bewildered and "darkened counsel." For indulging in such gymnastics he does not spare even Augustine. In reference to Eph. iii. 18, he remarks, "Augustine is quite delighted with his own acuteness, which throws no light on the subject. Labouring to discover some kind of mysterious allusions to the figure of the Cross, he makes the breadth to be love, the height, hope, the length, patience, and the depth, humility. That is very ingenious and entertaining, but

THE COMMENTARIES

what has it to do with Paul's meaning ? not more certainly than the opinion of Ambrose, that the allusion is to the figure of a sphere." Of Augustine's comment on John i. 16, he tartly remarks, " This is piously and judiciously said, but has nothing to do with the point."

Calvin avoids discussions which would only puzzle the average intelligent reader unfurnished with knowledge necessary to their proper understanding. He declines to embark on purely speculative ventures which might divert the thoughts from the true spiritual intention of a passage or lead the mind away from profitable meditation and personal application. The history of the Church shouted warnings against the danger of being enticed up tempting alleys of elusive ideas in pursuit of possible solutions of stubborn and disconcerting perplexities. What it was necessary or good for us to know, God made sufficiently plain ; what He did not want us to know, we could very well do without. The Scripture had no commission to satisfy an idle curiosity or an impertinent inquisitiveness which desired to look into the secret things that belong to the Lord God. The limits imposed by Holy Scripture were the limits of safety ; to trangress them was to trespass upon provinces of mystery which divine wisdom intended so to remain. That wisdom had shown itself justified by the course pursued by those who had broken through its hedges and ventured often where angels feared to tread. Examples such as these times themselves afforded in disturbing abundance, Servetus, Gruet, Gentilis, and all those others who had been intoxicated to the point of delirium by the spirit brewed by the Renaissance, exhibited how the speculative fever, once in the blood, uncontrolled by the Holy Spirit, induced an intellectual ambition, a spiritual recklessness, a looseness towards the essentials and fundamentals of Christian belief which were palpably demoralising, rabidly infectious, and gravely perilous to the health of the Church and its soundness in the faith once committed to the saints.

Against the habit of reading allegories out of every jot and tittle of Scripture he set his face like a flint, regarding that practice as puerile instead of clever, and as " offering nothing solid nor firm." He dubs it an audacity akin to sacrilege to twist the Scriptures thus and "wanton with them as with a plaything." Therein he agreed with Luther who called it "a monkey-game" (Affenspiel), though it must be admitted that both occasionally slipt into something suspiciously like it. Calvin's repudiation was the expression of a reaction from a practice, carried sometimes to ridiculous lengths, which turned the Scripture into a conjurer's hat out of which anything might be brought, the more surprising, the more clever. It did not bind him to avoid that method altogether in his own exposition,—to do so would have been to condemn the example of such as Paul. He would only resort to it when any edifying meaning could not be discerned on the surface and the whole passage frankly invited the extrication of truth or teaching from the wrappings of the word. The thing was not to look for riddles or cryptograms where the face-meaning was sufficient of itself, but to be on the outlook for riddles divinely intended on the principle of not laying pearls before swine. Moreover, Calvin's approval of brevity and his professed practice of it would incline him to see in teachings given in figurative language a like exemplary divine economy of words.

V

Calvin did much to free exposition from the spell of scholastic methods. The field of the Bible had come to be treated too much as a playground for ingenuities of interpretation or as an area rich in deposits of hidden treasures of mystery. Exposition was an exercise in fanciful conjecture and the excavation of meanings juggled in and then triumphantly unearthed. To many of the scholastic commentators the Bible was largely a "salted mine." If Calvin may not be absolved from yielding to the temptation of discovering proof or support of favourite dogmas where impartial candour would discern something more related to life than to doctrine, at least he led the way in bringing to the task a mind disposed to take out of the Word only what was strictly and really contained, not what the expositor surreptitiously inserted. He exposed himself to the accusation of even his own brethren in respect of resolutely declining to endorse the time-honoured use of certain texts as decisive confirmation of primary articles of faith. If these articles were true and based upon the Bible revelation, they were bound to be taught with sufficient clearness in passages whose pertinency could not be questioned without their having to be corroborated by others which had really nothing to do with the matter and which only exegetical torture would compel to say what they had no commission to say. The doctrine of the Trinity did not require to be buttressed by such standard proof-texts as Gen. i. 1, etc. A pillar that has no true base is a weakness instead of a strength to a structure otherwise strongly upheld. Elementary tactics dictate to enmity the attack upon points which cannot be defended, and the looker-on or neutral is apt to measure the strength of the antagonist by the number of successes he scores upon these points. Calvin recalled apologists and defenders of the faith to the strategical inadvisability of the misuse and misapplication of Scripture. Every passage or verse made to say something other than what it really had to say was a hostage to the enemy. The more honestly you deal with Scripture, the less will you be embarrassed to establish securely the doctrines that are really therein contained.

That was a principle much in need of being driven home. An exegesis governed by an apologetic or dogmatic interest had been in vogue since the days of credal construction, and the Fathers appealed to many a proof-text fantastically irrelevant. The appetite grew with what it fed on, and mediaeval commentators revelled in discoveries which dishonoured the Bible by making it a field extensively productive of mares' nests. Calvin rescued faith from a precarious condition of extreme vulnerability to the new renaissance spirit which looked at things immemorially sacred with shrewd, searching eyes that paid no deference to hoary traditions nor respect to great names.

All through the Commentaries we come upon striking evidences of the sincerity and honesty of purpose which animated Calvin in his exposition. The impartial humanist in him often overcame the prejudiced theologian, and that in not a few surprising instances. He refuses to regard John vi. 46 as proving Christ's sinlessness or complete innocence, insisting that Christ's intention is to assert that "nothing could be brought forward to show that He was not a faithful servant of God." (He compares Paul's boast in 1 Cor. iv. 4.) Christ's object is to give authority to His ministry, and He is concerned to defend His doctrine rather than His person. So in regard to John x. 30, he charges the ancient theologians with giving a wrong interpretation to the passage from a desire to prove that Christ was ὁμοούσιον[1] with the Father; whereas our Lord is not disputing concerning the unity of the substance but emphasising His agreement with the Father. His attitude to the whole Gospel of John is quite modern in that he declines to place it on the same historical level as the Synoptics. He was blamed for selecting so few proofs of the Trinity from the O.T.; but what did not help to convince himself, he would not use in the attempt to convince others. He does not hesitate to admit when he is baffled. *E.g.* he acknowledges his inability to solve the problems of the Second Coming raised by the appertaining passages in Acts i., quite candidly saying, "it is better that I should leave untouched what I cannot explain"—an example to those who determinedly squeeze some sort of meaning out of the obscurest Scripture.

Living as he did in an atmosphere strongly impregnated with the controversial spirit, fighting the battle of dogmas on whose successful assertion the justification of Protestantism depended, it was little likely that even Calvin, with the sincerest intentions and the best will, should have proved free from dogmatic bias and prepossession in his exposition of passages temptingly applicable to current topics. Sometimes you must meet your foe with his own kind of weapon; if you use it according to his practice, he at least cannot complain of your not playing the game. The Roman controversialist was not nice or scrupulous in his choice of the Scripture with which he backed his contentions. To meet him on his own ground was to be led unconsciously in the eagerness of the fray to adopt his

---

[1] Of the same substance.

methods in some degree. Imitation is as often the result of the despotism of example as it is the sincerest flattery. If Calvin found no support for his opponents' views in passages they instanced and relied upon, he found sufficient for his own in passages whose significance for this purpose they had not recognised. It was inevitable that Calvin should take every opportunity of discussing points at issue between Protestant and Roman Catholic. But the pertinency of the text he uses as support or proof is often less apparent than the ingenuity with which he makes it appear relevant.

Not a few reviewers credit Calvin with a courageous refusal to evade difficulties. While that is largely true, it is undeniable that he frequently altogether ignores them, whether it is that he declines to tackle or fails to see them or thinks it unnecessary for his purpose to take account of them. Also, where he does acknowledge and apparently proceed to overthrow them, he frequently steals furtively round them, ingeniously conveying the impression that they have been left behind demolished. Calvin indeed often exercises an extraordinary mesmeric influence upon the judgment of the reader who gives himself into his hands and puts himself under his control, compelling a meek assent to whatever he asserts with such a triumphant air of authority. The evasions he practises may not be conscious; they may have been genuine efforts to solve the difficulty involved; we must accept as sincere his death-bed assertion that he had never knowingly twisted or misinterpreted a single passage of Scripture. But such a man as he, writing with the eyes of the world upon him and conscious of his responsibility in view of the dependence of so many upon his guidance and illumination, must have felt compelled sometimes to produce an explanation or solution which could be made to appear satisfying and which he himself may have believed to be so. A logical mind such as his, working with certain definite and commanding ideas and principles assumed to run through the whole divine economy and to be consistently expounded and illustrated in Scripture, is subject to its own temptations, subtle and persistent, and may be unconscious of its own yieldings. An assumed conclusion is apt to make it argue in a way whose specious plausibility conceals from itself its erroneousness.

But of this sort of thing there is very little in Calvin compared to the sagacity and good sense which seldom desert him and which make him such a trustworthy and surefooted guide and interpreter. He usually tracks the thought with a sleuthhound's pertinacity and runs down the meaning with a quickness and certainty that are sometimes positively uncanny. Regarding ambiguous passages on whose interpretation nothing of moment depends, he is ready to agree to differ; he will force his opinion upon no one. With an admirable candour and an instinctive fairmindedness he lays before the reader the alternatives and leaves him to choose, though not concealing his own preference. And Calvin's preference is something to be respected; there are few commentators who in matters of no doctrinal moment have exercised greater sanity and balance of judgment and penetrated so straightly and surely to the mind of the writer.

VI

Calvin's Commentaries are no rehash of previous writers; they are independent and individual, bearing the clear stamp of his own mentality. He had great respect for the work of the Fathers and kept it constantly before him in preparing his own, but it was a respect that was emancipated from submissive acceptance of the views of even the greatest amongst them. His admiration for even an Augustine never gets the better of his critical discrimination and his resolute fidelity to the plain meaning of Scripture. He is as prompt to disagree with Augustine as with any of the Popish small-fry, whom he contemptuously regards as "ignorant of many things, frequently at variance with each other and sometimes even inconsistent with themselves." (Pref. to Instit.) His primary concern was to set forth the truth or meaning in Scripture which the Holy Spirit had discovered to himself.

With an immense reverence for the *litera scripta*, Calvin was generally free from the exegetical method of taking the text word by word which often results in an inability to see the wood for the trees. Keenly alive to the importance of discovering why exactly such and such expressions were used, he did not allow his attention to be focussed on phrases and words to the detriment of his appreciation of the significance and bearing of the whole passage in which they were imbedded. He was saved from many of the grotesque solecisms and wildly-astray interpretations of the meticulous scholastic by insisting upon the determination of the most reasonable construction to be put on ambiguous words in view of the whole ascertainable intention of the writer and in full view of their historical background. It was his complaint against Luther that he was not careful to examine the exact sense of Scriptural words or the circumstances of the history behind them, but was satisfied if he could derive from the text some useful or fruitful lesson. To Calvin, the interests of truth must be set before the interests of edification ; the truth will always yield the truest edification. He gave the lead to the sane methods of exegesis which have brought such a proper understanding of sacred Writ as was not possible under those which had formerly been generally applied. He paved the way indeed to such a scientific examination of Scripture as has laid the axe to the root of much of his own dogmatising and has deprived the Bible of that attribute of uniform and unquestionable authority on which he based his whole system. It could not be prosecuted long before the evolution in Scriptural thought and the various levels of its doctrine became apparent and the indiscriminate use of the Bible as a reservoir of proof-texts was increasingly seen to be unjustifiable.

It is not to be expected that Calvin anticipated all that modern exegesis has done to illumine Scripture. He left many dark corners into which the knowledge he possessed was insufficient to shed light. He passed over much whose significance has been discovered only by later study aided by the laborious accumulations of an army of scholars, while he magnified much to which the modern sense of perspective has given an inconspicuous place in the background. But credit should be given to him and his fellow-labourers for initiating the work of later scholarship which has been so enormously fruitful in the elucidation and proper estimation of the Word of God. Calvin was doubtless handicapped by the lack of a terminology such as is current coin now, expressive of ideas familiarised and made definite by discussion. In consequence, there is often in his exposition a vagueness and allusiveness as well as elusiveness, a mere adumbration of ideas. The thought is there in his mind but he lacks the words to convey it with precision and force. A humanist scholar by disposition and training, it must have been a real self-denying ordinance which made him abjure the peculiar pleasure of scholarly disquisition unconcerned by thought of proper edification. Recognising that there was a place for academic work of the kind in which his own was deliberately defective, he did not ask others to do what he had done. Theirs might be a different commission from his and its discharge equally necessary for the better understanding of Scripture, especially if they were engaged in the responsible business of settling those questions regarding the originals on whose correct decision depended the trustworthiness of the teaching given to the people. He encouraged Beza to publish his Commentary on the N.T. as supplementing his own in the region of philological discussion.

The omissions in Calvin's Commentaries find their reason and their excuse in the practical aim which he constantly set before himself. He is the exemplar of the experimental commentator. The pressing need of the times was to set life in the light of Scripture for guidance, warning, and comfort. True ideals had been falsified by the introduction and imposition of other standards of life and behaviour set up by ecclesiastical authority. The regulations laid down by the Church had indeed become controlling principles of conduct to the subordination of Scripture. On what lines God intended life to be lived, what examples and directions, what aids of grace, what inspiring promises and assurances, what supports of faith and stimulants of hope He had given, these were the things which Calvin was intent to declare. The value of Scripture as of dogma was to him its value for the practice of life. In his view, what the head learnt was only of worth for

THE COMMENTARIES

the help it gave to the heart. An abstraction was for him of as little interest and worth as a speculation.

VII

With all the outstanding good qualities which can heartily be attributed to the Commentaries, they are notably lacking in others which alone can make such a form of literature appetising reading. Keeping close to brown earth, they seldom capture a glint of the blue sky. If anything could prove that Calvin was no true poet, as he once imagined himself to be, it would be these volumes. They are the result of the application of a predominantly prosaic mind to the interpretation of "winged words." It is the theodolite applied to evaluate the glory of a mountain, the hammer of an analytical geologist employed to reveal the beauties of a scintillating opal. He advances with pedestrian tread, shedding a clear and welcome light on this passage and on that, but how much of it a cold light! Now and then he flashes into fire, the fire of indignant denunciation or of scathing condemnation; here and there he warms into a glow, as his heart responds to the uplifting thought of his mind. But on the whole, it is all so remorselessly severe, often so flatly and thinly beaten out as to leave one with the feeling of getting little nourishment from an abundant meal. But it would have been wonderful if it had been otherwise, with such an almost incessant stream of commentary flowing from an ever facile pen which seldom faltered and seldom found reason to correct itself. Chained to the ordinary levels of life by the demands made upon him, true to his purpose of providing not nectar for the gods but plain food for the common man, such romance and poetry as were in him received little chance of blossoming in the atmosphere of hard-driven, breathless activity which required the exercise mostly of sober business sagacity and political acumen. It is not surprising, then, if his Commentaries are mostly as a full-flowing, unexciting river of clear though not always appetising waters rather than a sparkling stream with delicious pools of plenty that satisfy the thirsty or tired wayfarer, hurrying here with swift flow, if there it lags lazily caught in a shadowed shallow, scintillating here in the light of the sun, if there it is dull as ditchwater. Sometimes one feels as if the exposition were almost mechanically ground out, though one is seldom allowed to forget that it is by a machine of wondrous power and under constant control.

Calvin was a man obsessed by a few great ideas and doctrines, clearly perceived and obstinately held. His range of thought is not really wide, though the prodigious amount of his writing might deceive one into thinking so. Resourceful in varied treatment of his governing ideas, unashamedly reiterative of them, amazingly fertile in their application, he often imparts the feeling of a certain mechanicalness of handling, like that of a juggler working with his familiar plates and balls, doing his feats with a skill which practice has made second nature. Not that he ever fails to give earnest and concentrated thought to the matter in hand, but like the poet who "lisped in numbers for the numbers came," he expounds in a way that may be almost foreseen and predicted. His thoughts form themselves kaleidoscopically into new patterns which, analysed, discover the same familiar constituents and elements. One feels at times as if he had to whip his jaded mind to resume the jog-trot of repetition. Certainly to work through some of his commentaries is to be conscious of intermittent weariness and of that feeling of rapid satiety which results from too much of the same food, and also of that impatience which comes of hearing the same thing over and over again.

VIII

The chief virtue perhaps of Calvin's Commentaries is that they are suffused with the native and profound piety of his own soul. There is nothing of the coldly academic temper or the personal aloofness which so often rob Biblical exposition of all real spiritual helpfulness. He sought to feed men with the same nourishment as he had himself received from the Lord's hand.[1] What was bread

---

[1] " If my readers derive any fruit or advantage from the labour I have bestowed in writing these Commentaries, I would have them to under-

THE COMMENTARIES

of life to him he thankfully passed on, distributing it mostly with a soberness of mien that hid the strong emotion of a heart which he seldom wore on his sleeve. What the Bible was to himself, he succeeded in making it for multitudes,—a light for the daily path, a shelter from the storm, and an unfailing storehouse of comfort and assurance. Nowhere was he so much at home, nowhere could he so find rest, as in its green pastures and by its still waters; and he would shepherd others where the Lord had shepherded himself. By Psalm, prophecy and sacred story, by Gospel and epistle, was his table continually furnished. His Commentaries were in some wise the tale of the great things the Lord had done for him. Spiritual experience gave vision to book-learning, and the mind that thought and the hand that wrote were controlled by a soul that dwelt amongst the things which angels would fain look into. It is this personal quality instilled into his exposition of the Bible, conducted as it ever was with his eye on common life and its unchanging needs and in consultation with his heart, that gives the freshness of interest and appeal which has exempted it from the common fate of finding a neglected grave on the dusty, forlorn bookshelf. Never does he allow the pure scholar in him to oust the preacher entrusted with the cure of souls. The Scripture is meant for doctrine and for life, but whatever be the doctrine that he finds, he turns it round to show the side with which it touches life. Not merely to instruct but to edify, not to gain a scholar's victory but to defeat a pernicious error, not merely to plumb the depth of a divine thought but to lift the aspiring soul on the height of it a little nearer God,—that is Calvin's aim, and that, in wonderful degree, is his achievement.

stand that the small measure of experience which I have had by the conflicts with which the Lord has exercised me, has in no ordinary degree assisted me, not only in applying to present use whatever instruction could be gathered from these divine compositions, but also in more easily comprehending the design of each of the writers." (Pref. to Comm. on Psalms.)

CHAPTER III

THE SOURCES OF HIS THEOLOGY

I

Though Calvin himself would have asserted that his theology had only one source and fountain, namely the Scriptures, it requires no minute study of his works to see that he was strongly acted upon by other influences. Behind his doctrine was not only revelation but philosophy, though he never espoused any philosophical system. He was a Scriptural theologian who brought to his study ideas coined in the mint of patristic metaphysics or mediaeval scholasticism which operated upon his mind with a strength of which he was quite unconscious.

It must always be kept in mind that Calvin emphatically disclaimed being a leader in theological revolution or a pioneer in untrodden paths of thought. It was not as if in breaking so cleanly and finally with the Church of Rome he cast all its doctrine and lore into the dustbin of outworn and discarded things. He claimed to be in the direct line of descent from all true Christian thinkers of previous ages. When the Italian Blandrata suggested that in view of certain criticisms he had made upon Justin and Tertullian he should cast overboard the teaching of the Fathers and provide a better worked out system in its place, Calvin regarded that as an attempt to make him suspect of the whole of orthodox Christendom. There was none who had studied the Fathers more closely than he or had more thoroughly assimilated their doctrine. If he did not do unquestioning obeisance to the authority of even an Augustine, he made hearty acknowledgment of what he owed to such master-minds in teaching and suggestion. He wielded his patristic knowledge with the ease of a master swiftly discomfiting Roman champions who presumed on the ignorance of Protestant opponents to make the Fathers chorus in their support. On one occasion at a public discussion held at Lausanne, a Romanist declared that the Protestants expediently ignored the Fathers as they could get no support from them for their contentions. If he counted on such a charge remaining unanswered by reason of the inability of any one present to offer immediate refutation, he "forgot Goschen." Calvin at once stood up and without the slightest hesitation out of the treasures of his marvellous memory poured forth such a stream of convincing quotation from patristic works as overwhelmed both the confident aggressor and the astonished audience. There was indeed in that age of scholastic learning no one more skilled in its use than he.

II

In the same considered respect he held the Creeds of the Ancient Church moulded by these Fathers, and to their doctrine he substantially subscribed. The Apostles' Creed formed the framework of the Institutes in its original form. Indeed it may be said that the basal doctrines contained in that work were not so much what he had drawn directly from Scripture as what had become already the theological furniture of his mind, provided by the Ancient Symbols of the Christian Church. He accepted these as correctly summarising the essential and fundamental truths of Scripture. They provided him with his terminology and the foundation stones of the structure of his thought. His view coincided with that of the second Helvetic Confession (1560) which declared that "the Reformed faith is in harmony with the true Catholic faith of all ages, especially the ancient Greek and Latin Church." In one of his letters he asserts that "as they (the Symbols) have been received by the approving judgment of the whole Church, they ought to be considered as beyond controversy."[1]

[1] Letter Oct. 8, 1539.

He hated heresy with all his soul, and heresy to him was practically what did not square with the teachings of the classical Creeds, especially the Apostles' and the Nicene. His quarrel with the Roman Church was due to its having become a hothouse of heresies of all kinds. The mischievous results of departure from the recognised standards were illustrated on the other hand by the Libertines whose conduct was the practical counterpart and outcome of a philosophy which was a resurrection of all the worst ancient heresies.

In spite of many sayings indicating his emphatic approval of these master-creeds, he often adopts a critical attitude which betrays an independence of mind that refused to be put into the straightjacket of traditional formulae or to be fettered by " dead hands." When challenged by Caroli to clear himself of the suspicion of Arianism by signing these Symbols, he flatly and resolutely declined on the professed ground that he would not thereby give his accuser an occasion of triumph in his attacks on the ministry. But there was more behind his refusal than that. He was not prepared to put his signature to a Symbol such as the Athanasian which had not been regularly approved by any legitimate Church Council. To the authority of the Nicene Creed he bowed with apparently submissive respect as the official and deliberate expression of the faith of the whole Church. Yet even in regard to it he was not affected by such a reverence as to disarm his critical scrutiny.

There was in Calvin's mind an instinctive aversion to the fine-spun logomachies of those who sought to put the mysteries of the Godhead into concise, precise and comprehensive definitions. (Cf. Inst. I. ii. §§14, 15.) He saw that what was intended to clarify often only beclouded. To go beyond what could be intelligibly grasped was not to strengthen faith but to bewilder and perplex the mind. In his own catechisms, definition is often given in the shape of description sufficient for adequate apprehension of the truth or doctrine. He spoke of God and things unseen in language level with common human experience and understanding. There is truth in the assertion that he gave the death-blow to scholastic theology not by attacking it,

THE SOURCES OF HIS THEOLOGY

but by inaugurating a new theology distinguished from the old not only by its spirit and method but by its style, a theology which expressed itself in the concrete terms of psychology and never escaped from the grasp of the understanding, the large residuum of mystery being recognised and simply acquiesced in without attempt at elucidation. The meticulous fashion in which the clauses of the Ancient Creeds were drawn up stirred his native impatience with anything that savoured of needless verbiage or that was in his view unnecessary for the sufficient statement of the truth. In his answer to Caroli in 1545, he betrayed the inner disposition of his mind behind all his protestations of implicit acceptance when he called the expression of the Nicene Creed, Deum de Deo, Lumen de Lumine, Deum verum de Deo vero, a " battalogia (redundancy) rather fit for singing than as a formula of confession, in which to repeat a syllable is absurd." Many years afterwards, in 1563, it is true, in his Brief Admonition to the fratres Poloni, he acknowledges that in these very words the Fathers were guarding against a possible dogmatic error. He himself by that time had had considerable experience of creed-making and recognised its difficulties. Yet this attitude to these Ancient Symbols as to the Fathers themselves, a combination of reverent acceptance and critical independence, exhibits itself throughout his writings.

A characteristic instance is provided in his treatment of the doctrine of the Trinity, a doctrine not explicitly asserted in Scripture, but the precipitate of theological reflection upon statements of Scripture. Zwingli, faithful to his a priori method, while accepting the dogma, gives it a minor place in his system or at least allows it to remain in the hazy background. To Calvin, however, it was an article of faith which formed an integral part of the credal foundations of the Church. In a letter regarding Gribaldi,[1] he calls it " the chief article of our faith." His logical mind

[1] May 2, 1557. Gribaldi was a learned lawyer of Padua who had to leave that town on embracing the Reformed doctrine. He renounced, however, the doctrine of the Trinity, and on frequent visits to Geneva, succeeded in impregnating the Italian congregation there with his views. Sentence of banishment was pronounced against him at the instigation of Calvin.

recognised its profound importance as providing a strong scaffolding for the doctrine of the Incarnation with all its implicates. His sense of its importance increased as time went on, as is evidenced by the fact that in the second edition of the Institutes he uses the word Trinity sparingly, but in the last edition copiously. Nowhere is there to be found a discussion of the doctrine more comprehensive, balanced, sane, clear, and acute in its criticisms than that given in the final form of his great work. It is written out of a burning conviction as to its centrality as an article of faith, and is an earnest attempt to set forth with such plainness and simplicity as may be attained in dealing with such an elusive and mysterious theme the utmost that fidelity to Scripture compels us to believe. With due acknowledgment of their patristic sources he avails himself freely of terms which enable him to state the doctrine precisely and positively. What must be accepted as truth according to Scripture he carefully fences off from what must be regarded as dangerous error. His judgments with regard to the great anti-Trinitarian heresies of early days coincide absolutely with the pronouncements of the majorities in the Councils which formed the Creeds. He speaks as the inheritor and guardian of their dogmatic legacies. That which they constituted orthodoxy he heartily accepts as the orthodoxy by which the Church should abide. Yet in his controversy with Caroli it must be admitted that both his conduct and his words gave ground for the suspicion that he was not sound on this central doctrine. When he and Farel prepared a confession of faith for submission to the conference sitting on the matter, it was at once noted that it did not contain the words Trinity or Person. On being challenged they grounded their refusal to insert them in any such document on their objection to faith being bound by words or syllables when the matter was sufficiently clear. There were those, too, they contended, who had scruples about using these particular words and they must be respected. At the same time Calvin appealed to the Institutes as proving that he did hold and teach the substance of the doctrine. On Caroli's demanding that he should sign the Apostles' and Athanasian Creeds he emphatically declined, giving as his reason that he would not by his example risk the introduction of a kind of tyranny into the Church which might result in any one being branded as a heretic who would not speak in the words or according to the will of another. Nevertheless his attitude excited such suspicions regarding his orthodoxy that some of the Reform leaders such as Bullinger, Myconius, and Capito intervened to allay the prevalent uneasiness by drawing up a document in which they approved of the use of the terms in dispute and characterised as absurd the refusal to employ them. Thereupon with an ill grace Calvin consented to remove suspicion by subscribing a confession in which these words were explicitly used.[1]

From such an incident it is evident that with all his respect for these ancient Symbols and his frequent reference to them in support of his contentions, he yet reserved to himself the right to break away from their control and take his own way. He was not prepared to let them set limits to the excursions of later theological thought under the guidance of Scripture and the Spirit, nor to assign them a finality beyond which Christian thought might not go. With Bullinger, the author of the Second Helvetic Confession, he asserted that the constant growth in knowledge of the Word of God gave the right to improve upon confessional statements of the Christian faith.[2]

[1] "It is a common prayer, Holy Trinity, one God, have mercy on us! It displeases me, and savours throughout of barbarism" (*Ep. ad Polon.* 746). Calvin's attitude in this matter becomes clearer from subsequent utterances. It was not that he objected to the use of the terms Trinity and Person. He cordially recognised that the Church was impelled by the strongest necessity to use them to the end that "the truth might be made plain and transparent and maintained against calumniators who evade it by quibbling, and to prevent that ambiguity of expression which is a kind of hiding-place to ungodly men." But he was indisposed to *force* any one to subscribe to a formula stated in these terms. He expresses the wish, indeed, that these names were buried provided all would concur in the belief that the Father, Son, and Spirit are one God, and yet that the Son is not the Father, nor the Spirit the Son, but that each has its peculiar subsistence. "I am not so minutely precise as to fight furiously for mere words." He points out that the Fathers disagreed widely and often contradicted each other flatly in the controversies raised by the use of non-Scriptural terms, largely because of their lack of clear definition, as *e.g.* in the case of the word "Substance" in relation to the Godhead.

[2] Schaff's *Creeds*, ii. 404.

It was in consistency with this attitude that he was not content simply to incorporate the Oecumenical Creeds in the constitution of the Reformed Church as its sufficient standards. The form of these summaries of doctrine was distasteful to him with their scholastic definitions and their very limited range of dogmatic statement. Much in Scripture too had become plain since their composition, and what Scripture unequivocally asserted must become constitutive articles of faith in the Christian Church. A Creed should offer clear and full instruction on what the Church stood for. It should leave indefinite what the Scripture leaves so, but state unreservedly what the Scripture indubitably asserts. True piety depended on right and full belief; where the head does not lead, the heart will not follow. His complaint against the Augsburg Confession, drawn up to reconcile the contending Protestant bodies, was that it was " obscure in its conciseness and mutilated by the omission of some articles of capital importance." [1] Because of its indefiniteness in some particulars, it was " neither flesh nor fish." [2] To him it was essential that a Creed should state without equivocation and with plainness of speech what beliefs were held in common by the members of a Church, otherwise there would be continual disturbance amongst them. His own experience had driven home this conviction. The continual controversies in which he was embroiled resulted from the lack of any coherent, definite, clear-cut system of Protestant doctrine such as might constitute a referendum of orthodoxy. An orthodoxy there must be; Calvin's life-work might be said to be an unremitting endeavour to define what was to constitute orthodoxy in the Protestant Church. His first theological work, the first edition of the Institutes, was often called a Catechism. There was no business into which he entered with more zeal than the construction of Creeds, and it must be admitted that he brought to it a sanity and a self-restraint which have not always characterised the work of his followers. Precision he desired, but not the precision of finical elaboration which was more the concoction of the head than the expression of the heart. It is questionable if he would have approved

---

[1] Letter, Sept 10, 1561. [2] Letter, May 10, 1563.

THE SOURCES OF HIS THEOLOGY 41

of the extensive and minute Calvinistic confessions of a later day. He would probably have regarded them as a burden rather than a support to the Church, as a maze rather than a hedge. Those of which he was either in whole or in part the author have no such dimensions nor do they condescend to such particularity. They aim at sufficiency and are content with declaring on what the believing heart rests in quietness and confidence.

III

Calvin drew his whole theology then from Scripture and the classical authorities of the Ancient Church. It was a fixed principle with him that he would not go beyond what the express teaching of Scripture authorised.[1] Every doctrine that presented itself for acceptance had to submit to the test of the touchstone of the Word. If it could not approve itself by proven affinities to the body of revealed truth, if its guarantees were merely the *ipse dixit* of some bold adventurer in regions beyond the boundaries of the Word, he would have nothing to do with it and declined to stamp it with the hallmark of the authentic Christian faith. He would admit of nothing purely speculative within the system of Christian doctrine. Steadfastly he held to the principle that what God had not chosen to reveal we must not seek to know, and that what He had revealed was sufficient for all practical purposes and

---

[1] The number of proof-texts quoted in the Institutes from the various books of Scripture (sometimes consisting of two or more verses) may be found interesting both as indicating the bias of Calvin's mind and the thoroughness of his acquaintance with the Bible.

Old Testament—Gen. 72, Ex. 69, Levit. 16, Numb. 11, Deut. 68, Josh. 7, Judges 11, 1 Sam. 35, 2 Sam. 20, 1 Kings 27, 2 Kings 21, 1 Chron. 0, 2 Chron. 3, Nehem. 5, Esther 1, Job 25, Psalms 321, Prov. 50, Eccles. 7, Song of Songs 1, Isaiah 162, Jer. 77, Lament. 3, Ezek. 76, Dan. 21, Hos. 18, Joel 6, Amos 7, Obad. 1, Jonah 2, Micah 4, Habb 7, Zeph. 4, Hagg. 2, Zech. 9, Mal. 14.

New Testament—Mw. 159, Mk. 18, Lk. 79, Jn. 167, Acts 104, Rom. 184; 1 Cor. 141, 2 Cor. 62, Gal. 54, Eph. 78, Phil. 36, Col. 43, 1 Thess. 17, 2 Thess. 18, 1 Tim. 34, 2 Tim. 21, Tit. 14, Heb. 72, James 22, 1 Pet. 36, 2 Pet. 10, 1 John 35, 2 John 1, 3 John 0, Jude 2, Rev. 11 (all from the first two chapters), and from the Apocrypha 9. In all he quotes about 1300 proof-texts from the O.T. and 1400 from the N.T.

needs. The closed area of Scripture defined the total region of truth in which it was legitimate for us to wander. God made the Bible just that size because He had told us in its compass all that it was desirable for us to know. There is much in it which stimulates the spirit of curious enquiry : it suggests many questions to which no answer is provided. In that case we must be content without an answer. To pry into what was left mysterious, to seek to penetrate to depths left in dense darkness, was to transgress the appointments of God's will, whose concealment of these things must have been deliberate and purposive, otherwise they would have been revealed. Constantly in his Commentaries when dealing with a matter which stirs perplexity, amazement, or merely inquisitiveness, he diligently explores Scripture for possible enlightenment. If no explanation is to be found therein, he resolutely refuses to go a step farther in quest of probable solutions, while denouncing any who would venture beyond it in defiance of what he regarded as God's implicit prohibition contained in the mere fact that He gave us the Bible as it is, so much and no more.[1] The accusation that he regarded Christianity as " a dogmatic fallen from heaven " finds support in his demand that nothing should be included in Dogmatic which was not plainly contained in the pages of revelation. It was characteristic of Calvin that he always wished to feel firm ground under his feet. Temperamentally averse to flight into speculative regions, he would barter the whole world of conjectural possibilities or asserted logical inferences for one grain of the gold of truth divinely guaranteed.

Speculation he abhorred not only because it argued a kind of mutiny against God, but because it was so mischievous in its consequences. It set up an itch of inquisitiveness which resulted in a fever of irreverent and reckless enquiry. It centred interest in the fascinating bubbles of conjecture. It was apt to live in castles in the air, content no longer to occupy the sure dwelling-places of the humble and contrite heart. He had only too much experience of the danger of the soaring Icarus spirit. Controversy after controversy hinged on questions raised

[1] Instit. i. 13, 21, 29.

THE SOURCES OF HIS THEOLOGY

by men who would not submit to the restraints of Scripture but must needs seek to know more. So the spirit of restlessness and the disposition to assert one's own mental acquirements against the revelation of God were excited, and as a result dispeace and revolt were sown in the Church.

That speculation was futile, a vain groping in the dark, Calvin regarded as proven by the negligible gains of substantial truth in relation to God made by pre-Christian philosophy. He held in the highest admiration the writings of "the ancients" on such subjects as law, mathematics, medicine, these being the product of the intelligence given man for earthly things. But as for the pure knowledge of God and the mysteries of the Kingdom, they have nothing to teach; that can be won only by "another kind of intelligence." Occasionally there occur in them shrewd and apposite remarks on the nature of God, "though they invariably savour somewhat of giddy imagination." But with these minute particles of truth there are mingled "many monstrous falsehoods." These ancients are indeed "like a bewildered traveller who sees a flash of lightning glance far and wide for a moment, then vanish in the darkness of the night, before he can advance a single step." "To the great truths, what God is in Himself and what He is in relation to us, human reason makes not the slightest approach."[1]

Whether we sympathise with him or not in this attitude, it cannot be doubted that it was the wisest that could be adopted in that age for the future of religion. On no other ground could a new Church be firmly established. When men were set free from the paralyzing spell of the Roman Church, when they breathed the intoxicating air of a new liberty of thought, many were apt to assert a licence which brooked no restraint and rejoiced to plunge into orgies of mental dissipation. From the prisons of tradition they flung themselves into the hedgeless fields of free thought. They claimed to think as they pleased. It was a resurrection of Sophists. The Libertines of Geneva were examples of a multitude who wedded free thinking to

---

[1] Instit. II. ii, § 18.

free living and detested control in mind or in morals.[1] They adopted a philosophy that harmonised with their life and loudly vindicated it. No Church was possible under these conditions, an organised body of men dominated by one ideal and welded together by one definite faith. The whole religious future of the world depended on the immediate formation of such a body. A society uncemented by a common religious belief, uncontrolled and undirected by an accepted code of divine law would have no cohesion, no unifying soul, no guarantee of persistence. Unrestricted licence of thought would be as fatal to wholesome life as ungoverned licentiousness of conduct. With his practical sagacity Calvin recognised that, and he took the one means open to him to master the tendency to it and prevent its escaping from all control. The way of free speculation was the way to social disintegration and damnation.

[1] Sin is an illusion, the Libertines said, and salvation consists in the deliverance from the phantom of sin. "What you or I do," said one of their spokesmen, Quinton, "is done by God, and what God does, we do, for He is in us."

CHAPTER IV

THE DOCTRINE OF GOD

I

CALVIN'S entire system is built upon his doctrine of God. His views on Atonement, on the Sacraments, and on matters ecclesiastical, are either derived from it or shaped and coloured by it. The consideration of this doctrine, then, is a necessary introduction to the proper understanding of his teaching on these and other subjects. Calvin himself was, if not a God-intoxicated, at least a God-possessed man. His whole mind, heart and life were vitalised, governed and suffused by his thought of God. Of no man could it be more truly said that he set God ever before him.

It is unnecessary to set forth in detail what views he held regarding the Divine nature and character in common with all Christian teachers. No one has ever spoken or written with more warmth of genuine feeling about the Fatherhood of God and all that it implies of love and care and compassion. An unwonted tenderness of tone steals into his voice when he pours out his heart upon that theme. There is no greater error than to think that that great doctrine was alien to his mind and heart. Calvin was a true child of God whose love was the light and soul of his life. God's perfect goodness, directed by unerring wisdom, carrying out its purposes with omnipotent power, was a postulate of all his thinking. He had been no dull pupil of Jesus Christ, but rejoiced to believe that in seeing Him he saw the Father also. To Calvin the true knowledge of God was summed up in the knowledge of His fatherly love ratified by the experience of it. It is by His love that God seeks to draw us to Himself " that we be not forced," for He wishes to be freely loved by us. Calvin had a vivid and profound sense of the Divine majesty, but, while seeking to communicate it to others, he would not set it before them as the supreme object of their contemplation; that would be to plunge them into an awe that was mingled with terror. The principal thing was to be sure of His paternal goodness. Calvin had little sympathy with the endeavour to command obedience by the appeal to fear. While he did not abjure that method altogether, the disciple not being above his Master, his sermons prove that he aimed at winning men to trustful devotion. There is no lack of the wooing note in his preaching. Ever he seeks to root faith in the grateful recognition of God's goodness to us in Providence and grace. Is He not the Fountain of all good?

The difficulty is to reconcile these hearty convictions with assertions regarding God which seem to argue that there were two lines in his thinking about Him. In the one he descended upon the world from a conception of God which might find support in Christ but which did not start from Him; in the other he ascended from Christ to God or rather with Christ to God. It is the dominance of the former way that shapes his whole system. His master-thought was indeed that of the sovereignty of God, but it is essential to apprehend how exactly he conceived it.

While their views practically agreed, Calvin repudiated the a priori method by which Zwingli reached his conclusions. The God whom he posited was not the fruit of the speculation which was his peculiar abhorrence, but a Being not merely depicted in Scripture but reflected in life and religious experience. The survey of history and the world with the questioning of his own experience revealed to him ever-present features and elements which required for their explication a certain view of God, and finding that in consonance with Scripture, he selected it as the point from which His relation to the world must be primarily regarded. His early sympathy with the principles of Stoicism and the subsequent saturation of his mind with the congenial teaching of Augustine disposed him to see in the sovereign will of God the reason for things being exactly as they are. He entered the sphere of theological thought with the doctrine of predestination deeply imbedded in his heart. It would be difficult to say whether his idea of God imposed upon him his doctrine of predestination or, rather, his acceptance of predestination as explaining life forced upon him his idea of God.

Though the sovereignty of God dominates Calvin's thought and forms the citadel into which he retreats whenever hard pressed by antagonists, yet he conceives of it as acting through various attributes, or, as it were, from different centres of His Being. He represents the sovereign divine will as operating now as justice, now as mercy or love or wrath, as though any one of these might be isolated from the rest for the time being, and other centres or springs of action in God become quiescent, inactive. The various impressions he gives us of God's activity produce the sense of a composite photograph in which the features are so blurred as to represent no definite personality. He shows signs of being uneasily conscious of this himself, protesting, as he frequently does, that there must be some point of view, could we only reach it, from which the appointments of each of these various attributes might be reconciled with the demands of the rest, or rather that, did we know all of God, we should see that there was no inner contradiction at all, and that when God is just, He does not cease to be merciful, or when He is wrathful, He does not cease to be loving.

One result of his endeavour to square the attributes assigned to God by Christian faith, instructed by the Scriptures, with his primary postulate of sovereignty is that he uses words descriptive of these attributes in a sense not commonly attached to them. He declares that all the events of life, accepted as being the direct appointment of God, are the expression of His goodness, but it is a goodness which is only really experienced by the limited circle of the elect. What happens to those outside it is not goodness as ordinarily understood. They are only apparently its objects, being made the instruments for the promotion of God's gracious purposes to the elect. It is only through the elect and for the elect's sake that they participate in the divine goodness at all. If it be necessary for the benefit of the elect that they suffer, Providence imposes upon them what is needful. "The goodness of God shines forth the brighter in this that on account of the favour He bears to one of His servants He spared not even whole nations" (Comm. on Ps. ix. 5). Such a saying makes it difficult to understand what exactly Calvin meant by "goodness."[1]

Calvin found refuge from pressing difficulties in another line of defence. He points out that our knowledge of God is only fragmentary and in a manner exterior. We only know such things about Him as He chooses to let us know, out of regard either to our profit or capacity.[2] We are denied for ever a view of the Being Himself in whom these find their reconciling unity. In nature, but chiefly in Christ, He has revealed himself so far as is expedient, but He, the Person Himself, lives in light unsearchable, shrouded in impenetrable mystery.[3] Speculation cannot reach to Him; it is indeed impious to attempt to pierce the veil which God has drawn over His face. It is not given us to know what He is in Himself (*quis sit apud se*), but only what He is towards or in relation to us (*sed qualis erga nos*). We never can get behind the functioning of God to the Person who chooses to reveal Himself after that fashion and in those specific ways.[4] The qualities given us to perceive are no more than rays streaming from

---

[1] Ritschl accuses Calvin of using such a term as justice in a sense incomprehensible to us, inasmuch as he asserts that God does things justly but for a reason which we cannot comprehend. (Doum. iv. 124.)

[2] It is a point on which Calvin frequently insists that God accommodates himself to our capacity. In this way he gets over the difficulties of the O.T., *e.g.* where we should explain by regard to the state of religious knowledge at the time, saying, this is how men then thought about God, Calvin would explain by saying, this is how God made men think about Himself, translating Himself into the language of ideas intelligible to men. *E.g.* commenting on Job. i. 7, he explains that God did not need to ask Satan where he had been, but he inspires the writer to say so out of regard to "our rudeness and the small measure of our understanding," "humbling Himself to us, and, as it were, transforming Himself to the end that we should know that which is good and convenient for us."

[3] Instit. III. ii. § 1.

[4] "We shall never know God as He is, but we shall know Him in such measure as it shall please Him to manifest Himself to us, that is, to wit, according to that which He knoweth to be profitable for our salvation." (Sermon on Job i. 6-8.)

the screened and unapproachable central glory. However it may sometimes appear, they are never really at odds with one another. It is the part of faith to believe that behind the veil mercy and judgment kiss one another. The facts of life, could we but see it, are all of a piece with the highest and best we can think of God, who, though He hide Himself, is yet the Saviour. Calvin's doctrine of God is indeed a compound of very definite assertions and as pronounced agnosticism. Occasionally he leaves one with the impression that the God of revelation might turn out to be something quite different from the God of reality. Ultimate inscrutability characterises both His nature and the purposes and principles of His Providence and government.

II

It is of course a simple axiom of all theology that all things have come into being by the will of God. But the question arises why things are just as they are. Could they have been different? Could the world have been constructed on different lines and principles? Could the laws of nature have been otherwise? Could the moral law have been something else, so that goodness and badness would have been different from what we now reckon them to be? Is there any necessity that things should be just as they are? To that Calvin answered emphatically, No, if there was any such necessity, it would imply Some Other higher than God, a supreme God to whom He was subject, to whom in turn the same conclusion would apply, and so on ad infinitum. The ultimate reason for things being as they are, then, is just the sovereign will of God. Existence in all its forms, phases and activities is derived from His self-determined decree. The attitude Calvin adopted as regards this question evidences that he along with Luther had come under the influence of a philosophy which largely dominated theological thought for a considerable period, whose chief exponents were Duns Scotus and his successor William Occam, who lived in the end of the thirteenth and the beginning of the fourteenth centuries and who both belonged to the British Isles.

Summarily the teaching of these schoolmen amounted to this. God is practically identified with freewill exercising omnipotent power. All is contingent relatively to Him, though in history it is certain. Anything whatever might have been anything else. Not only might the laws of nature [1] have been altogether different but the moral law as well, so that righteousness might have been something other than that which is now regarded as such. Even though God has laid down a moral code to be observed, He Himself is under no necessity to respect it. He could at any time change the principle which forbids murder or theft or adultery so that these things would not have the stamp of sin upon them, just as He has abrogated by the Gospel all the ceremonial part of the O.T. For God there is nothing fixed or immutable about law. It is only the divine decree that established it and the same decree might annul, suspend or reverse it. Its author could dispense men from obedience to it—did He not command Abraham to kill his son and Hosea to marry a prostitute and the patriarchs to violate monogamy? Righteousness is simply what pleases God or what it pleases Him to make so.[2]

The same view is carried into the region of Christian doctrine. The means of grace are entirely arbitrary; God might have chosen others. Christ's satisfaction is necessary only because God wills it. It is sufficient because God accepts it as such, not because it is intrinsically satisfying to justice. So arbitrary is everything that reason could not by any study of things seen or unseen instruct us as to the requirements of the divine law. For the knowledge of God's will we are entirely dependent on Scripture; good and evil receive their definition there. " Nothing is of itself good or evil, the freewill of God being the Sovereign arbiter of what is so." (Occam.) The way of salvation determined upon by God is revealed in the

---

[1] Cf. Prof. J. Y. Simpson's *Spiritual Interpretation of Nature*, p. 133.

[2] " R. Johanan b. Zaccai, a contemporary of Jesus, was once asked what was the reason for performing all the ritual of the sacrifices and the other minutiae of the ceremonial law. He answered : ' A corpse does not defile and waters do not cleanse, but it is a decree of the King of kings. The Holy One, blessed be He ! hath said : I have ordained my statute, I have decreed my decree ; and man is not entitled to transgress my decree ' " (Herford, *Pharisaism*, p. 105).

Scriptures and could not otherwise be known. All Christian doctrines are articles of faith derived solely from the Word for whose authenticity the Church stands sponsor. The dogmas of the oecumenical creeds are the concentrated expression of the doctrine of Scripture with which they are in exact accord. It was assumed that Scripture from beginning to end was self-consistent in its picture of God and in its account of His will, otherwise of course we should be left in irremovable doubt as to both, inasmuch as no other court of appeal was accessible. No progress in the apprehension of truth or increasing fulness of its communication was recognised in Scripture; all parts of it were of equal authority and on the same level of religious value.

These views in a modified form constitute part of the furniture of Calvin's mind. He held that the sovereign will of God was governed by no considerations but its own good pleasure. He found refuge in these principles from difficulties which frequently confronted him in his exposition of Scripture. If it plainly laid the responsibility upon God for acts that were offensive to our moral sense, he fell back upon the postulate that that is good which God wills to be so. He was not himself bound by the law which He had enacted. Just as He could have made a man an ass or a dog [1] and might have given any property to stars, so His good pleasure was limited neither by physical laws nor even on occasion by moral laws. That was not murder which He commanded, any more than is the execution of a criminal ordained by the magistrate. If the Israelites had spoiled the Egyptians on their own initiative it would have been rapine and fraud, but the authorisation of God acquitted them of theft or bad faith.[2] In a different sense than that intended by the hymn, " all is right that seems most wrong, if it be His sweet will."

Calvin applies the same principle freely in the sphere of theology. There is nothing in nature that necessitates the transmission of Adam's sin and guilt to his descendants; these pass over by the fiat of God. It is of His will that the nature of man is such that the state of sin is bequeathed.[3] As it pleased Him to ordain that such and such endowments

---
[1] Instit. III. xxii, § 1.   [2] Comm. on Exodus *in loco*.
[3] Inst. II. i. §§ 7, 8.

should be bestowed upon the first man, so it pleased Him that he should lose them for His posterity as well as for himself. He attributes to "the council of God" the fact that Christ after His resurrection appeared only to a few; "that is best which God hath thought meet." He adds other reasons to prove its wisdom, but concludes that if any one is dissatisfied with these, "let him take away or overthrow, if he can, that inviolable decree of God which Peter commendeth to us in this phrase." (Comm. Acts. x. 41.) Again, it was not necessary that the Mediator should be both God and man ; " that flows from the divine decrees on which the salvation of man depended."[1] By the same decree " that which is Christ's by nature becomes ours by grace."[2]

Calvin however safeguards himself from the accusation, to which Duns Scotus and Occam expose themselves, of attributing pure caprice to the will of God. God does not display caprice but exercises freedom limited only by the restraints of His own nature. In the ultimate analysis the Divine will is the prius of all things : but this will does not reside in a kind of inorganic Being morally formless and void, an unimaginable Something constituting an irresponsible centre of energising power. If God is above law, if His will is determinative of law, He is not without law. There are necessities of His nature which constitute law to Him. He is essentially good, and goodness is not simply what He chooses to be so, but what is in accordance with His own nature. " It is not less necessary for Him to be good than to be God." If the existence of God must be attributed to some mysterious necessity, so must His nature be. As God Himself is eternally immutable, so must that for ever remain goodness which is determined to be so by His nature. The cosmos of the universe is the reflection of the cosmos of His own being. There is no moral caprice in Him, however there may seem to be. That which offends our moral sense must be reconcilable with His holiness. This is a certainty which no happenings can disprove or controvert or render dubious ; this is at once the bedrock and the bulwark of faith's confidence.

[1] *Ib.* 12, § 1. [2] *Ib.* § 2.

III

Calvin conceived of the universe as the result of the continual forthputting of God's power, always however in accordance with certain determinate principles of action from which He never varied and which appeared to us as laws of nature. Every moment of its existence in every one of its parts it was dependent on Him. Every slightest motion had God's power immediately behind it. Miracle was then not really of the nature of a disruptive act of God, involving suspension or violation of natural law, it was part of the unceasing, purposive energising of God, directed by the principles from which He never swerved.[1] Calvin would not allow that nature, once made, was a closed system, closed to its Maker, nor would he allow it to be thought of as a complicated piece of mechanism with which God could do only what was permitted by potencies He had initially imparted. The uniformity of Nature is just the self-consistency of God; therein was provided a guarantee that the cosmos would not lapse into chaos. Miracles are no more miraculous in the sense of being the result of law-regardless action on the part of God than nature is. They are not interventions of a power tearing asunder the fabric of things to accomplish them. They are acts of the Providence which has ordained that water shall fall from the clouds but rise in the waterspout. There is no more self-contradiction in that than there is inconsistency in miracle with God's ordinary acting. All is of Him, and nothing is without Him.

Calvin would refuse to regard the universe as a modern materialist does, as a system in which an adequate intelligence could explain whatever happens by reference to the forces at work in it each operating in a uniform and unvarying way, and in which nothing happens but what these forces so operating can completely account for. Calvin would say that the forces of nature are just the forms in which the energy of God's will manifests itself.[2] There

---

[1] " Pie hoc potest dici; Deum esse Naturam."

[2] " The course of nature which is so wonderful, so beautiful and so fearful, is effected by the ministry of these unseen beings. . . . Nature is not inanimate; its daily toil is intelligent; its works are duties. . . . Every breath of air, and ray of light and heat, every beautiful prospect

is no necessity that anything should happen in a certain way or exist in a certain form. It required only that God should energise in a different way but in perfect consistency with Himself to bring about something else or the same thing in a different way. He could as easily make Christ walk on the water as the disciples sail on it, or make bread multiply from bread as from fields of corn. God is always back of all operations, sometimes using second causes, sometimes moving things directly with the finger of His power, but never so as to contravene the principles by which He resolved to guide Himself from the beginning. It is the purpose of His will that determines all things and occurrences in the exact shape which they take. There is no more and no less mystery in the sun's standing still upon Mount Ajalon than in its rising every morning.

IV

There are questions concerning the ultimates of things before which conjecture stands tongue-tied. When Calvin had no answers to give them, he was wont to take refuge in the phrase, for the glory of God. In the assertion, maintenance or advancement of that glory lay the key to all riddles. Creation, reprobation, heaven and hell, all alike find their explanation in the enhancement of God's glory. To glorify Himself was the supreme purpose and final end of all His activities, as man's chief end was to glorify God. It was a convenient formula whose sense varied with the matter under consideration. All subsequent Protestant doctrine is water-marked with the thought, as it stands in the forefront of practically all Calvinistic Confessions. It may be well to give some consideration as to its significance.

In one respect it may be said to signify the manifestation of God's character. When He does anything for His glory, it is to show forth one or other of His attributes, an exhibition of wrath being as much a display of His glory as the revelation of His love. The universe declares His glory

is, as it were, the skirts of the garments, the waving of the robes of those whose faces see God in heaven " (Newman's *Sermons*, ii. 361-2).

in that it is shot through with the attributes which conspired to the making of it. Do we not see in heaven and earth but little rays of the power, justice, goodness and wisdom, which are infinite in Him? Reprobation is to the glory of God, inasmuch as it throws into relief His justice which condemns the sinner to suffer the due penalty of his sins. If you probe behind such a doctrine and put questions which impeach the justice of God in such an act, Calvin confesses he cannot answer you, but declares his assurance that it is all for the glory of God, so making the phrase almost equivalent to the mystery of the ultimate reason of things. Thus it comes to imply the reverse of the meaning which it is ordinarily given, being used to vindicate providences in which God does not manifest Himself but hides Himself. " It is the glory of God to conceal a thing." It is His glory to do what He pleases and hide His reasons.

The end and purpose of creation and providence may be summed up in the assertion that all things are for the glory of God. The opening questions of Calvin's Second Catechism, that of 1541, sum up in a manner his philosophy of existence and life. " What is the principal end of human life? To know God. Why do you say that? Because He has created us and put us into the world to be glorified in us, and it is right that we should devote our life to His glory since He is the commencement of it." [1] That is the final answer to the enquiry as to the ultimate reason of things being at all and being as they are. These things are needed for the glory of God; but for its demands they would not be. We may not be able to see how it is advanced by the appointments of His providence, but it is not for us to question; we must just accept, submit and believe. "If we cannot comprehend this," he says in reference to a perplexity, "let us recollect how glorious are all the works of God and how secret is His counsel." It should be man's supreme aim to advance this glory in whatever way it pleases God that he should. The godly

---

[1] What Calvin meant by living to the glory of God, he explains in the Second Catechism. It is " to honour Him by putting all our trust in Him, by serving Him in obeying His will, and by recognising that all has proceeded from Him alone."

man will be vigilantly jealous for it; he will consent to anything rather than that it should be in any wise diminished. Nothing is of any account in comparison with its promotion. "Believers would rather choose that the whole world should perish than that the smallest portion of the glory of God should be withdrawn." (Comm. Gal. v. 12.) If God did from the beginning choose some to bliss and others to damnation for no other reason than His own good pleasure, then it was somehow for His glory. It is in this spirit that Calvin answers the objection to eternal punishment based on the ground that it is excessive. "Sins are temporal, they say; I confess it, but the majesty of God which they have offended is eternal. It is then quite right that the memory of their iniquity should not perish. But if it is so, they say, the correction surpasses the measure of their sin. I reply that that is an unutterable blasphemy, when the majesty of God is of so little account with us that we think less of its being despised than of the perdition of a soul."

Man has indeed no rights over against the demands of God's glory. "As long as men advance the smallest claim to anything as their own, God is defrauded of His right." (Comm. Isai. lxiv. 8.) In common with Luther, Calvin refused to allow that man had any claim upon God whatsoever or that there were any ends in humanity itself which God, having created it, must be held responsible for working out. Salvation itself is not for man's sake but for God's glory, not in the sense that the love and the grace of it glorify God, but that it is part of the whole scheme of things whereby God attains the glory He desires. "The principal end of human life is not to be saved," says Luther, "but to honour God"; that is "the sovereign good of man." If he be damned, he ought, if he realised what he is here for, to give glory to God. There is "a thing more worthy and precious (than your salvation)," echoes Calvin in a letter to the King of Navarre, "and that is the glory of God and the advancement of the kingdom of Jesus Christ, wherein consists the salvation of you and all the world." The human personality has no intrinsic value, but only that which is attributed to it by God. Its proper attitude to Him is that of a humility that claims nothing and a dependence that gratefully accepts anything. To the objection that it is possible for a man to abase himself too much, Calvin answers, God might have made of you an ass or a dog. To expostulate with God as if He had been bound to confer a more excellent nature upon man, (such, *e.g.* as would not and could not sin) would be more than unjust, seeing that He had full right to determine how much or how little He would give. (Instit. I. xv. § 8.) " No necessity was laid upon God to give man more than that intermediate and transient will, that out of man's fall He might extract materials for His own glory."[1]

From these instances, it becomes evident that what Calvin understood by the glory of God ultimately was what He attained and achieved by the exercise of His sovereignty, freed from all restraints, guiding itself by purposes incomprehensible in general to any but Himself, winning honour often by means and in ways whose fitness for that purpose was apparent only to Himself. The only becoming attitude of man was that of the humble adoration which gave glory to God in presence of all mysteries though it saw no glory in them.

This was not a view to which human nature would long consent. As the religion of Christ, struggling into freedom from dogmatic statements that smothered it, deepened the sense of the intrinsic value of the individual personality and gave the soul a new setting in the counsels of God and a new " place in the sun," it began increasingly to be felt that this was not a worthy attitude, nor one of which God Himself would approve. There was a native

---

[1] " The fact that God has need of us is ultimate to the religious consciousness," says Moberley in *Foundations*. To which a trenchant critic, R. A. Knox, Fellow and Chaplain of Trinity College, Oxford, in *Some Loose Stones* (p. 205 f.) answers : " I find no difficulty at all in reason in conceiving God as existing in all the self sufficiency of His triune nature, without so much as a solitary angel to chant His praises, without a solitary planet to serve Him on its course. . . . What I seem to have learnt in all the books of devotional theology I have ever read is primarily that God has no need of me. At the background of every act of humility I ever make, I reflect that I have no possible right to exist, whereas God exists in his own right ; that neither I nor any other creature were made because we were necessary to God, but just in order that we might have the privilege of serving Him. To say that we were created for God's glory is a very different thing from saying that He could not have got on without us."

dignity in man corresponding to the place God has manifestly assigned him in the scheme of things and the task God has set him. Even in relation to God man was not without rights. In making him as he was, God assigned him rights, as He laid on him duties. He instilled into his heart, as part of that in him which excites the sense of his proper dignity, the instinct which demands that these rights should be respected, whether by other men or by the God who made him. That God does anything to any man in violation of these elementary rights—for example, that He lays upon any man a doom antecedent to his very existence and that He should appoint that existence to be necessarily of a kind which would justify that doom—such ideas could not long subsist in view of the offence they occasioned to that sense of human worth which the world owes supremely to Christ who revealed God's mind. Let all things be for the glory of God, willingly accords the modern Christian, but let nothing be thought to the glory of God which sets up in the human heart both an instinctive and reasoned feeling of righteous accusation against Him, and which, if it were proved true, would sap the very foundations of our faith in His mercy, grace and love. We give no glory to God when we give it out of a feeling of awe that is mixed with inexpressible horror, but only when it is the tribute of minds and hearts to whom the perception of His glory has brought exceeding joy. Nothing but the heartfelt praises of men can give a halo to His throne.

CHAPTER V

THE HOLY SCRIPTURES

I

CALVIN does not find it necessary to insist at length upon the supreme and final authority of Scripture in the realm of doctrine and morals. Except for the comparative few infected with the virus of rationalism, that was an accepted axiom amongst theologians of whatever Church or school. So little was it one of the matters in dispute that the Augsburg Confession did not contain any article asserting it. The whole teaching of the Church, whether Catholic or Reformed, had its sole source in the Holy Scriptures. Not till the Council of Trent was tradition given a place alongside them as an authoritative contributor to the substance of faith.

Calvin however discussed with considerable care the grounds on which the authority of the Scriptures rested. For the Catholic it was sufficient that it had the imprimatur of the Church. Theologians like Occam required nothing more, whatever other proofs might be offered. They submissively accepted doctrines which they declared to be in their judgment unbelievable on the mere assurance of the Church that the Scriptures in which they were contained was the veritable word of God. Calvin had to substantiate its authority on other grounds. These he found in the proofs of its divineness elaborated by apologists of previous centuries, such as its antiquity, the beautiful harmony of its various parts, its richness in the qualities which give an air of majesty to composition, its assertion of sentiments which men could never of themselves have conceived, and the fulfilment of prophecy. One circumstance sufficient of itself, he declares, to "exalt the apostolic doctrine above the world," is that Matthew, who was formerly fixed down to his money table, Peter and John, who were employed with their little boats, being all rude and illiterate, had never learned in any human school that which they delivered to others. "No human writings," he asserts, "however skilfully composed, are at all capable of affecting us in a similar way. Read Demosthenes or Cicero, read Plato, Aristotle, or any other of that class: you will, I admit, feel wonderfully allured, pleased, moved, enchanted; but turn from them to the reading of the sacred volume, and, whether you will or not, it will so affect you, so pierce your heart, so work its way into your very marrow, that, in comparison with the impression so produced, that of orators and philosophers will almost disappear, making it manifest that in the sacred volume there is a truth divine, a something which makes it immeasurably superior to all the gifts and graces attainable by man." (Instit. I. viii. § 1.) If there be any who disagree, and "feel the words of the prophets insipid," he has no argument for them except that they must be absolutely devoid of taste.

But Calvin clearly perceives that such grounds as these do not in themselves secure conviction. It is not on them that the believer rests his assurance that the Scriptures are from God, and "our faith in doctrine is not established until we have perfect conviction that God is its author."[1] The prophets and apostles all claim indeed to speak from God, but we must be certain that "the name of God is neither rashly nor cunningly pretended." "If we would save our consciences from being driven about in a whirl of uncertainty, our conviction of the truth of Scripture must be derived from a higher source than human conjectures, judgments, or reasons." How then shall we reach absolute conviction?

When the Reformers challenged and overthrew the authority of the Church, religion was left in a perilous position. The average man demands authoritative guidance in regard to unseen things; he asks to be told what

[1] Instit. I. vii. § 4.

THE HOLY SCRIPTURES 61

to believe. The power of the Roman Catholic Church lay partly at least in its claim to meet that need. The destruction of its authority was tantamount to the annihilation of the foundations on which religious belief for most men rested. It amounted to the severing of the moorings that had kept them in a haven of refuge from the miseries of uncertainty about the things which men most want to know. For the Church stood sponsor for the Scriptures, and if its word was worth nothing, what claim had the Scriptures upon their belief and allegiance? It was the task of the Reformers and especially of Calvin to provide them with new and secure moorings. This they did by replacing the authority of the Church by that of Scripture, and establishing it on grounds which dispensed with the authorisation of the Church. There had need to be such an authority not only for the assurance of the soul, but to provide a weapon against Rome. No other arbiter was possible in their quarrel. Rome had to be met on its own ground or not at all. It could not repudiate the supreme authority of Scripture, to which tradition must bow. It was by the aid of an authoritative Word that the battle was won for the Reformation.

Although Calvin repudiated the notion that the authority of the Bible rested upon the affidavit of the Church, he could not help admitting that the Church had a great deal to do with procuring the state of mind which assented to the authority of the Scriptures. If the Church was given existence through the agency of the Scriptures, it was itself a proof of their source and origin; the divine power in the Church witnessed to the divine power of the Word. But apart from that, the Church stood sponsor for the sovereign right of the Word to command the submission of all. It is the herald of its claims. (Instit. I. vii. § 3.) Its authority prepares men to believe the Bible. The Church puts it into their hands with the attestation that, by consent of all Christian ages and all Christian thinkers, it is to be regarded as the sole reservoir of religious truth. Here alone are to be found the wells of salvation. (*Ibid.* I. viii. § 13.)

Calvin was keenly alive to the peril of surrendering the weapon of an authoritative Scripture. Difference of opinion there might be in interpretation—that was to be expected and tolerated—but the claim of Scripture to be the impregnable rock of saving truth must be asserted and defended with the utmost energy. That is why he threw himself with such vehemence into such a contest as that with Castellio. To yield an inch to his strictures was to imperil the ark of God. There was no greater enemy of truth and life than he who laid a sacrilegious finger on the Word. So strongly did he feel on this matter that he regarded the death of Castellio as a divine judgment for what he called his blasphemies.

Castellio was a thorough-going representative of the principles of Humanism and Rationalism. He was no theologian but essentially a philologist. He conceived of Christianity more as a philosophical doctrine proceeding from the ancient world than as a divine revelation of which no portion was to be rejected and on whose unconditional acceptance salvation was dependent. He handled the Bible almost as he would any other book, making frank comparisons between the merits of its individual parts, criticising its contents freely and censuring its statements and sentiments. He asserted the right of the individual to exercise his private judgment upon the contents and doctrine of Scripture, accepting or rejecting, approving or disapproving, according as it satisfied the tests he chose to apply. He was indeed a pioneer of modern higher criticism, bringing to his critical analysis a shrewd brain and an adequate scholarship, if untempered by the sensitive devoutness and jealous reverence of those for whom the Bible was the Word of God.

Unquestionably such an attitude and temper were in the highest degree dangerous at that critical period. With the Roman Church discredited and the Scriptures deposed from their seat of supreme and unchallengeable authority, on what was a reformed Church to build securely? There was nothing left but the shifting sands of opinion. If men were to take what they liked out of Scripture and reject what they disliked, on what stable grounds was a creed to rest? Out of what was it to be constructed? And without a creed no Church could exist or even be constituted. Not only so, but on what food of guaranteed wholesomeness was the religious life to be nourished? How was the moral life to be guided? On what principles was social life to be organised? Depose the Scriptures from their throne, and you consign the world to the outer darkness of an agnosticism from which there is no escape. You invite an anarchism of thought and conduct which would reduce society to a chaos fatal to its life. So it seemed to Calvin and those who thought with him. It was of first importance therefore that the foundations of the Church in Scripture should be preserved in complete integrity; with that was bound up the moral and spiritual health of the world and the future of mankind. Scripture must be established in such a position in the regard of all that personal opinion must bow to its dictum. The truth was here and nowhere else; all controversies and difficulties must be settled by reference to it. This was the bar of God where only unerring judgments and verdicts were passed. Calvin came to every question with the open Bible in his hand; his pages bristled with quotations, references, and proof-texts. He insisted that, whatever we may feel about any matter, the decision of Scripture was final. It is obvious how such an attitude imparted to Calvin's work an irresistible power. The sword of the Spirit, wielded by such a dexterous and tireless arm, won victories on all hands.

But Calvin recognised that only a hearty acceptance of the Scripture as the Word of God could make it sharper than a two-edged sword. A mere passive assent to a dogmatic assertion thereanent brought it into no vital relation with mind and heart. Only the sincere conviction of its source in God would make it a rule of life and the dictator of genuine belief. The Church by its mere fiat cannot procure or ensure that. Men might be admiringly responsive to the peerless excellencies of both its matter and its style without being influenced at all in thought and conduct. They might be touched, as were the exiles of Babylon who heard Ezekiel's passionate addresses and went away as those who had listened to one singing a lovely song. Something more and other than external credentials or literary arguments addressed to the reason was requisite to induce that regard for Scripture which could make it a power for righteousness in the individual soul. The Scriptures were not really the Word of God to any one, whatever his professed belief, unless they did the sanctifying work of God on mind and heart. If they did that, they substantiated their own claim and vindicated themselves. If, however, they were not received as divinely inspired, it simply meant that they had not fulfilled their intention in the individuals concerned. (Instit. II. ii. § 20.) Luther had already taken up the position that " the Church cannot give any more authority or power to Scripture than it has of itself. A Council cannot make that to be Scripture which is not Scripture of its own nature." It must make its own immediate and convincing appeal if it is to be received as from God. In this matter Calvin would have agreed with a modern theologian in the assertion that " nothing may be proved true by external certification."

Prior to the Reformation the school of Occam had laid down the same principle in their scholastic fashion. Before there was readiness to receive the thoughts of the Bible as divine, there must be the "*fides infusa*," faith divinely implanted. Then he who possesses that, on reading the Bible, immediately assents to any and every assertion therein contained, because he feels inwardly compelled thereto. This *fides infusa* is bracketed with the prescription of the Church as co-operative factors in securing an acceptance which is more than formal and passive.[1] But Calvin goes behind both Luther's emphasis on the immediate and self-evidencing appeal of Scripture and the Occamist presupposition of an infused faith to the cause of that state of mind and heart which accepts the Scripture as the very Word of God, authoritatively regulative of life and thought. He rests all upon the working and witness

[1] Occam declared that there were many things asserted to be found in Scripture which he could not believe, were it not for the authority of the Church. The result of such an attitude was, of course, an unbelief which concealed itself behind a mask of submissive assent. The scepticism that was rife in Europe before the Reformation was doubtless due in no small degree to such teaching. Calvin would not echo Occam ; he would say that there was nothing in Scripture which you would not heartily believe provided the Holy Spirit authenticated it to you and disposed your mind to credence.

of the Holy Spirit. Where that is effective, no other proof is required; where it is absent, no proof will suffice, and the Word remains inefficacious. (Instit. II. ii. § 20.) " Let it be considered, then, as an undeniable truth, that they who have been inwardly taught by the Spirit, feel an entire acquiescence in the Scripture, and that it is self-authenticated, carrying with it its own evidence, and ought not to be made the subject of demonstrations and arguments from reason ; but it obtains the credit it deserves with us by the testimony of the Spirit. For though it commands our reverence by its internal majesty, it never seriously affects us till it is confirmed by the Spirit in our hearts." (*Ibid.* I. vii. § 5.) It requires " the enlightening and renewing influences of the Holy Spirit to give to instruction its proper weight and efficacy that we may not be blind to the light of heaven nor deaf to the strains of truth." (Comm. Ephes. iii. 14.)

Calvin was the first to construct, develop, and give dogmatic form to a doctrine of the authority and inspiration of Scripture on these lines, and the Reformed Church followed his lead. The Symbols of Lutheranism contained no such theory, influenced no doubt by the absence of one in Luther himself. The theology of that Church did not formulate a dogma on the subject till the seventeenth century.

II

Calvin had little to say in vindication of his acceptance of the canon as containing the *whole* Word of God. He offers no proof of the presumption that the Bible in our hands is wholly and exclusively the Word of God. A historical account of how it came into our hands, of its wonderful preservation, of the consent of the Church, leaves the point untouched. What he provides in his doctrine of the witness of the Holy Spirit is really an explanation of how conviction is reached as to the divine origin of the Scriptures. It does not necessarily involve that that witness certifies and identifies the whole canon and nothing but the canon as the divine Word. The canon is the bequest of the Church. To complete his doctrine, Calvin would need to show reason for believing that its compilers were in such wise under the guidance of the Holy Spirit that they included nothing which was not divinely inspired and excluded nothing which was. The witness of the Holy Spirit in each believer's heart would then be the testimony to the trustworthiness of His own editorship. Calvin either failed to see or evaded the problem of finding guarantees that the area of Scripture was coterminous with the extent of the revelation of God attested by the inward witness of the Holy Spirit. The weakness of his position appears in the variety of attitudes taken up in the Reformed Church to the Apocrypha, which were accepted by some, merely ignored and left out of the canon by others and expressly rejected by still others as sources of doctrine.

If Luther and Melanchthon made no attempt to establish the authority of Scripture by the formulation of relevant tests and proofs, they were in a position to handle it with a freedom which Calvin was unable to exercise in consistency with his doctrine. They were not bound to accept the canon as coincident with the whole revealed Word of God. They could cut and carve it according as its parts approved or failed to approve themselves as divinely inspired. They were not trammelled by the difficulty of exhibiting the absolute harmony of the parts and their uniform consistency. Luther could and did acknowledge discrepancies and contradictions in Scripture, declaring them to be " of little consequence if the main facts of faith were fully grasped." He could with an easy mind say, " When a contradiction occurs in Scripture and it cannot be reconciled, so let it go."[1] He could challenge any to reconcile the teaching of James and Paul, confidently offering to set his doctor's cap upon the head of any one who could make them accord and submitting to be himself called a fool. He could characterise the Book of Jonah as " more lying and more absurd than any fable of the poets ; if it did not stand in the Bible, I should laugh at it as a lie." He could say such things because his attitude to and his view of Scripture left him free to criticise or reject whatever did not approve itself as consistent with

[1] Beard, *The Reformation*, p. 159.

the form of faith found in the Gospels and Epistles of Paul.[1] It was different with Calvin. He committed himself to the principle that the whole body of Scripture as bequeathed to us by the early Church would certainly approve itself as divinely inspired to every one to whom the witness of the Spirit was given. For such it was authentic and authoritative from beginning to end. We shall see the difficulties into which Calvin was plunged by this view when he came to expound the Bible in conscientious detail.

The problem Calvin evaded or declined to face seems to have been perceived only by certain of the Anabaptists. "We cannot give the godless any certain reason why Scripture is to be accepted and not thrown away," said Münzer,[2] "except that it comes from antiquity and has been received by many men. But this is Jewish and Turkish." He declined to admit that God spoke to men only in Scripture and that outside its oracles there was no word from the Lord. Indeed whether it was the Word of God or a mere dead letter, depended on whether a man first of all heard the voice of the Father speaking within him ; then he distinguished its accents within the Scripture. Anticipating the Quakers, Münzer held that "God still spake to His own to-day, as once He spoke to Abraham, Isaac, and Jacob." To that Calvin, of course, could not agree ; to do so would have deprived him of his infallible criterion and touchstone of truth, and he could then no longer clinch an argument or silence an opponent by the final words, Thus saith the Lord, with his finger on a text. To admit a possible inspiration conferring an equal authority with Scripture was to put into the hands of every visionary, doctrinaire, or self-constituted prophet a weapon against which the sword of the written Word was unavailing. Against the chaos of doctrine which would surely result from an admission so damaging to the irrefutable guarantees of sure belief, there could be no defence but in the unequivocal, unqualified assertion of a closed canon with which inspiration began and ended. Only on such an assumption

---

[1] Luther's attitude to Scripture is perplexing as Otto Ritschl points out. (*Die Dogmen des Protest.*) He frequently expresses himself as though he accepted the whole canon as inspired.

[2] Beard, *op. cit.* p. 190. Cf. 207 f.

could Scripture wield an authority which could neither be challenged nor shared. To allow its throne to be shared was tantamount to deposing it. You invalidate its supreme, indisputable authority by extending it to other claimants. "Since no daily responses are given from heaven, the Scriptures are the only records in which God has been pleased to consign His truth to perpetual remembrance." (Instit. I. vii. § 1.)

III

The logical concomitant of such a view was the assertion of the inerrancy of Scripture.[1] If God's revelation was confined to this volume, if its contents were to be the infallible touchstone of truth, if the perfect harmony of its parts was to be depended upon, it must be that Providence, which preserved the constituent books and secured their compilation into a canon, took care that no error should creep into its pages.[2] For the assurance of faith, it was necessary to be able to trust the accuracy of every word of the record. The inerrancy of the letter was the corollary of its exclusive and inclusive inspiration. "The full authority which the Scriptures ought to possess with the faithful is not recognised unless they are believed to have come from heaven as directly as if God had been heard giving utterance to them." (Instit. I. vii. § 1.) "The word 'Scripture,'" he asserts in one of his sermons, "imports that Moses was not the author of the Law, but that he was simply a kind of amanuensis or secretary who wrote what he received from God and not what he had

---

[1] Calvin had predecessors in this uncompromising view. Wyclif and Wesel had both asserted the inerrancy of Scripture. The scholastic Occam had gone the length of declaring that "the Scripture cannot err, while the Pope may," and that the Pope's dicta were to be tested by Scripture.

[2] Cf. Augustine's *Letters*, i. 319 (Dods's translation). "I confess that I have learnt to yield this respect and honour only to the canonical books of Scripture; of these alone do I most firmly believe that the authors were completely free from error. And if in these writings I am perplexed by anything which appears to me to be opposed to truth, I do not hesitate to suppose that either the MS. is faulty, or the translator has not caught the meaning of what was said, or I myself have failed to understand it."

manufactured in his own brain." And again, "The Holy Spirit so governed the language of Paul that not a superfluous word escaped from him." No words could more emphatically or plainly assert the view that there was nothing in Scripture which was not from God and that its extent was determined by God's sense of what was sufficient. No more was included than was required; no less was given than was needed. Though Calvin might have disclaimed responsibility for the mode of expression, the article in the Formula Consensus Helv. pertaining to the Scripture only carries his views to their conclusion. "The Hebrew O.T. codex which we have received from the tradition of the Jewish Church to which the oracles of God were committed, we receive to-day, both as to consonants and vowels and punctuation, both as to facts and words as θεοπνεύστος (inspired by God)."

Calvin could not help recognising with a certain timidity and reluctance a human element in the composition of Scripture. The various writings betrayed the qualities and temperaments of their respective authors. The differences were too manifest to be denied, but he held that the idiosyncrasies of the writers were always under such control of the real author of all, the Holy Spirit, that they manifested themselves exactly according to His requirements. He restrained or stimulated them so as to secure the precise results He desired. A significant example of his attitude is offered in his Comm. on Phil. iii. 1, where he says: " In this we have an instance tending to show that the Holy Spirit in His organs (Fr. ed. ' in his organs or instruments, that is to say, His servants by whom He has spoken ') has not in every case avoided wit and humour, yet so as at the same time to keep at a distance from such pleasantry as were unworthy of His majesty." So then it is Calvin's mind that nothing spoken by the Holy Spirit's organs proceeds from themselves in such wise as to be the expression of their own mind, that is, of their "natural man." He is at pains to show that in such passages as Isaiah lxiii. 17 the prophet must not be supposed to be expostulating with God. When Renèe, Duchess of Ferrara, alleges that the example of David in hating his enemies is not applicable to those who live under the milder dispensation of the Gospel, Calvin sternly replies that " such a gloss would upset all Scripture," and affirms that the Holy Spirit has in this respect set David before us as a pattern. There is no appeal against the assertion of Scripture that God actually said or prompted the saying of what is reported regarded Him. Calvin refuses to regard the speeches of the friends of Job as " the doctrine of mortal man " ; they are of the Holy Spirit. He justifies God's declared disapprobation of them by explaining that they contain good doctrine, but the friends apply it ill by " wresting all things to the person of Job." [1]

Calvin perceived and appreciated the difficulty offered to his theory by the possibility of mistranslation or various readings, and the absence of unanimity of interpretation. He was quite alive to the inaccuracies of the Vulgate.[2] If the apparatus of criticism was then comparatively meagre, it was sufficient to make scholars like him take account of contending versions of texts. Nevertheless he does not hesitate occasionally, where important texts are under consideration, to make his rendering the vehicle of the mind of the Spirit. He was not abashed by his occasionally having to admit that later knowledge had forced him to recognise the error of that rendering, nor did he scruple on adopting a different version of the words to find in them also the divine truth.

The inerrancy of Scripture with Calvin implied the indisputable accuracy of assertions of a scientific nature. In such a Vade Mecum of truth, there could be nothing which would mislead or misinform ; the truth of its statements regarding things seen must be as reliable as that of those regarding things unseen. Of course, this did not apply to passages recognisably symbolic or parabolic, or to the offspring of poetic licence. But what was soberly affirmed regarding Nature was to be accepted as the truth, and it remained for reason not to scrutinise it critically, much less sceptically, but to build it into its structure of certified knowledge. The science of Scripture was to be regarded as equally trustworthy with its history.

---

[1] Sermons on Job.   [2] v. Against the Council of Trent.

THE HOLY SCRIPTURES

For example, expounding Job xxxviii. 9, Calvin takes " darkness " to mean " mists," and accepts it as a fact that it is " mists " that hold back the sea from overwhelming the earth (" swallowing up all and putting the world in confusion "). God does not use " any violent means " to " restrain so furious a creature " (as the sea) ; " for proof thereof we see that mists are nothing but vapours engendered in the air, and it is a wonder that the same should get the upper hand of the sea, so that as soon as the mist ariseth, by-and-bye the sea becometh calm."

IV

Calvin's exaltation of Scripture is partly traceable to a profound agnosticism of the same type as possessed the minds of men like Duns Scotus and Occam. They held that the truths peculiar to Scripture were of such a kind as were not to be reached by the exercise of pure reason, or by reason working on the data of experience. The contents of faith were given only in Revelation inasmuch as Scripture took us into a region of the hitherto unknown and otherwise unknowable. Nor may its teachings be tested by reason which has no right of scrutiny or judgment within this domain, its function being limited to elucidation and the correct statement of the doctrines revealed. The Bible therefore is the primary subject of faith seeing that it alone presents the positive will of God as He has revealed it to man. This view was a necessary presumption on the part of theologians who asserted the arbitrariness of God's will and the contingency, relative to Himself, of His working. There were no clues for reason where all might have been different from what it actually is. By searching you cannot find out the Almighty, whose ways are not our ways nor His thoughts our thoughts. Within the spiritual realm, everything is an ' If,' until God Himself turns it into an ' Amen,' recording it in the Book which was the mirror of His mind.

Calvin held essentially the same position. The Scripture was absolutely necessary inasmuch as the truths it contained were such as reason could not possibly discover.

"It is impossible for any man to obtain even the minutest portion of right and sound doctrine without being a disciple of Scripture." (Instit. I. vi. § 2.) He did not mean that there were no truths or principles attainable by reason aided by conscience, but that to the knowledge of those which constituted peculiarly the Gospel, the mysteries of the plan of salvation, the truth about God, and the method He resorted to for the saving of men, Scripture alone provided the key and the entrance. This was in full accord with Luther's attitude; witness the assertion in his Comm. on Galatians that "all the articles of our Christian faith which God has revealed to us in His Word are in presence of reason sheerly impossible, absurd, false." He instances the raising of the dead at the last day, the virgin birth, the Trinity, the derivation of all sin from Adam and his eating of an apple (which he calls "a laughable doctrine ").

Calvin's doctrine of Scripture was really a hypothesis necessitated by the exigencies of the situation, a presupposition requisite to the stability of his whole theological system, the Creed, and the Church. He came to Scripture with that doctrine rather than drew it from Scripture, though he discovered therein assertions which substantiated his view to his own satisfaction. The Commentaries afford abundant evidence of the embarrassments into which he was driven by his theory. Its vindication in detail demanded an amazing amount of strenuous ingenuity, of whose disingenuousness he seems to be as conscious at times as of its unconvincingness. One may say that never did the idea of the verbal inspiration of the Scriptures receive such emphatic refutation as at the hands of this vehement champion, whose frequent transparent evasions, jugglings, and violences are in themselves a confession of its futility.

The postulate forbids him to allow that David could speak as a man out of a passing mood; whatever he says must be doctrinally correct. If in Ps. xviii. 21-24 the words seem to contradict the doctrine of total depravity, he is at pains to prove that that is to misunderstand them. If Christ utters a sentiment in John iv. 44 which is only partially true, Calvin finds refuge from any unfavourable inference in the supposition that the words were a proverb

THE HOLY SCRIPTURES 73

and " we know that proverbs are intended to be the graceful expression of what commonly and most frequently happens. In such cases, therefore, it is not necessary that we should rigidly demand uniform accuracy, as if what is stated in the proverb were always true."

He finds himself in more desperate straits when forced to defend Paul for inaccurate quotations of Scripture, as in 1 Cor. ii. 9. If he cannot deny the fact of the inaccuracy, he audaciously declares that the meaning Paul puts into the quotation must be taken as the decisive guide to the exact form of the original! " We ought to place more dependence on Paul's meaning than upon any other consideration. For where shall we find a surer or more faithful interpreter of this authoritative declaration, which the Spirit of God dictated to Isaiah than He Himself in the exposition which He has furnished by the mouth of Paul." Calvin is resourceful in expedients which will enable him to square facts with theory. If the phrase " those who love Him " (cf. 1 Cor. ii. 9) does not appear in the original Hebrew, (though Paul evidently regards the words as belonging to it), the apostle must have been following the Greek interpreters " who have translated it in this way through having been misled by the resemblance between one letter and another." As a matter of fact, the LXX word is quite different from the one Paul uses, and the corresponding Hebrew words could scarcely be mistaken for one another. If there is no doubt that there is something wrong about the words of Scripture as they stand, Calvin suavely reminds you that after all it is not the words but the doctrine that is of prime concern. The apostles were not specially careful to quote the O.T. correctly, being content if they were faithful to the sense. (Cf. Rom. x. 6, 7, 9; Ephes. iv. 8, 9.) That is to import a very far-reaching qualification into the theory of verbal inspiration. When there was no other way out of a difficulty, Calvin proved ready to avail himself of the Higher Criticism of which Luther was an unblushing exponent. If the majesty of the Spirit of Christ was not to be seen in all parts of the Bible and some portions seemed ' out of the picture,' an intrusion upon a harmonious and consistent volume of inspired truth, " I regard it as a matter of religion utterly to reject every phrase which cannot be recognised as the genuine expression of the author." (Pref. to 2 Peter.)

But with all his wealth of expository ingenuity and the best will to use it, Calvin is driven to admit the existence of errors. Before them, he simply holds up his hands in discreet surrender. (Cf. Comm. Acts vi. 1.) If Paul tortures a verse of Isaiah into giving a different meaning from its natural one, he remarks with a subdued air, recollecting other such offences; "In this respect, the apostles were not squeamish; for they paid more attention to the matter than the words." (Comm. Isai. lxiv. 4.) Here Calvin seems to suggest that misquotation in the mouth of an apostle was guaranteed by his inspiration against misrepresentation of the original.

V

Along with the inerrancy of Scripture, Calvin asserted its equal authority and uniform consistency. What was said in Genesis was as much divine truth as what was said in Revelation. Yet Calvin was very conscious that this could not be asserted without qualification. He could not shut his eyes to the unequal value of the various portions, and frequently defends asserted divine utterances as examples of God's accommodating Himself to the capacity of those to whom He spoke or revealed Himself. The idea that the Evangelical law is superior to that of Moses he pronounces to be "in many ways most pernicious," involving "the infliction of great indignity upon the Divine law." Christ, he holds, did not add to the law, thereby infringing the unqualified injunction of Deut. xii. 28; He only restored it to its integrity by purifying it of the obscurities occasioned by the falsehood of the Pharisees. (Instit. II. viii. § 6.) Calvin will not allow that there is any evolution of thought or belief contained in the Bible. The articles of faith stand as sure in the knowledge of Abraham as in that of Paul. A future of immortality was the hope of the patriarchs as much as of the Christian. He has no scruples about importing into the O.T. a content supplied by the N.T., a device which rescues him from many a staggering difficulty. If Ps. xix. 8 acclaims the Law as "restoring the soul," while Paul regards it as "a dead and deadly letter," the seeming contradiction at once disappears in the light of the reflection that David, in praising the Law, "speaks of the whole doctrine of the Law, which includes also the Gospel, and therefore under the law he comprehends also Christ." (Comm. *in loco*). Calvin waxed furious at Castellio for daring to regard the Song of Songs as a poem of a loose and obscene description composed in Solomon's youth which ought to be struck out of the canon. Rather he revelled in it as an evangelical symphony. Nowhere does he show himself engaged in more congenial work than when demonstrating the pertinency and propriety of prophecies used in the N.T. for the establishment of truths or facts therein asserted. (Cf. Comm. Acts ii.)

This view of Scripture was indeed a presupposition necessary to legitimise the construction of a rigid system of Christian doctrine. The Bible was the only source of the materials which went to its making. It must be assumed that, as it constitutes the sole revelation of God, its teaching on all things necessary to be known is complete, sufficient, self-consistent, harmonious, and that from it may be extracted by ordinary processes of reason a system of doctrine capable of logical and luminous statement, any item of which could be substantiated from any pertinent portion of the divine Word. It is obvious how Calvin should assert for a system, claiming to be so extracted, an authority of the same order as that of Scripture itself. The assumption that such a system was to be found therein guaranteed its actual finding, and the finding of it in turn guaranteed the soundness of the assumption.

The Christian faith and hope rested upon such a definite and unassailable creed. Calvin's nervous denunciation of the suspicions which Castellio presumed to cast on the integrity of Scripture doubtless proceeded from his apprehensive recognition of the impossibility of putting limits to such perilous tampering with it. Once concede the justice of any one critical inference and you surrender the right to stay the hand of doubt or scepticism anywhere.

The whole of Scripture becomes exposed to destructive criticism with capitulation at any single point. To allow each one to pick and choose what he liked would be to give faith feet of clay and instil uncertainty of all things into the human soul, whose salvation requires more than a "Grand Peut-être." Let the rock of Scripture cease to be impregnable, and life was driven to build its feeble forts of faith on shifting sands.

Nevertheless Calvin's honesty prevailed so far as to concede enough whereby the hated harpies of criticism might justify their methods. The admission that there was much in Scripture of merely temporary force and validity, that circumstances alter cases and annul teaching, was sufficient to give support to the objection that he himself was countenancing the "diminishing" of Scripture anathematised in Deut. xii. 28. His candid recognition of the unauthenticity of 2 Pet. and his readiness to reject anything therein which did not approve itself as belonging to revelation placed him in the ranks of the higher critics. Such blemishes in his record of fidelity to his general principle might well have invited the retort from such as Castellio, Doth Beelzebub cast out Beelzebub?

VI

Along with its indispensability, Calvin affirms the sufficiency of Scripture. Whatever is requisite for the needs of mind and soul is therein provided. The Author of this Revelation has forgotten nothing that is essential. If much is not revealed which we should like to know, it must be better that we should not know it. No religious practice is legitimate which is not sanctioned by the oracles; if it were of advantage or desirable, God would have expressly enjoined it. Silence is as much a revelation of the divine mind as speech. Whatever it is well for man to know, that is expressly declared. Only impiety pries into the realm of what God has designedly kept mysterious, and conjecture is futile, for it can arrive at no certainty.[1]

[1] *E.g.* He refuses to speculate as to whether animals are immortal. (*Comm. Rom.* viii. 21.)

THE HOLY SCRIPTURES 77

To Calvin, curiosity about things unrevealed that do not touch the all-important and the only important matters of salvation is both obnoxious and irreverent. The limits of the content of the revelation are determined by the necessity of focussing attention upon central things, the things that concern eternity. The ignorance in which we are left regarding Christ's early life, for example, is intended to bridle an idle inquisitiveness. It might have been good to know all about it in order that we might have a complete text-book for the Imitatio Christi from the cradle to the grave. But that was inexpedient to God's mind in view of the special main purposes He desired to effect through His Son, whose example was of far less moment than His Saviourhood. (*v.* Comm. Acts i. 22.)

The Bible is to Calvin a perfect and complete rule of righteousness. It specifies exactly in what goodness consists; no item is left out and none should be added. It is irreligious to "coin and feign" other good works in addition to those enjoined here. "To go a-wandering after good works that are not prescribed by the law of God, is an intolerable violation of true and divine righteousness." (Instit. II. viii. § 5.) This was his fundamental principle of opposition to the impositions of the Roman Church.

Calvin is well aware that many epistles of Paul, both of a public and private nature, have been lost, but that occasions him no regrets. He is not troubled by the possibility of their containing much which would add to our treasures of wisdom and knowledge. That the loss should have been divinely permitted causes him no perplexity, as though mankind had been deprived of knowledge which would have been of incalculable benefit. Inspired no doubt they were, but inspiration does not guarantee preservation. God's purposes require things of transient value and even ephemeral importance; the need that begot them passes away. Their preservation, we may believe, would have been a tactical mistake, providing ground of disputation occasioned by their being treated as of age-long moment. Only that which was pregnant with timeless truth became the special care of Providence. "These Epistles of Paul which the Lord judged to be necessary for His Church have been selected by His providence for everlasting remembrance." " Let us rest assured that what is left is enough for us, and that the smallness of the remaining number is not the result of accident, but that the body of Scripture which is in our possession has been determined by the wonderful counsel of God." (Ephes. iii. 4.)

Calvin occasionally expresses himself in such wise as to give the impression that he regards the limits of all legitimate knowledge as set by the contents of Scripture. To seek to know what cannot be learnt from it is to overstep bounds divinely appointed and to presumptuously defy the divine desire. Nothing of real value or reliable worth is to be ascertained by the exercise of unaided reason. " Almost all men are infected with the disease of desiring to obtain useless knowledge," he says. " But he who is in possession of it (the knowledge of the love of Christ) alone has enough. Beyond it, there is nothing solid, nothing useful,—nothing in short that is proper or sound. Though you survey heaven and earth and sea, you will never go beyond this (the revelation) without overstepping the lawful boundary of wisdom." (Comm. Ephes. iii. 19.) That might seem to lay an embargo on all secular study and enquiry, and indeed it had that effect upon the mind of the Reformed Church in which study was concentrated upon and almost limited to the Bible. There was little literature of a ' profane ' kind produced within that body as the outcome of an effort to advance human knowledge. History as then written was just the story of the Church. Very few books of edification, comparable with those in which Roman Catholic saints were prolific, proceeded from the Reformers, but of these there was no felt need ; rather such productions intruded upon the sphere which was completely filled by the text-book of God. 'One book is enough in the Holy Spirit.' Nevertheless for this attitude Calvin must not be held responsible. It is true that apart from his earliest work on Seneca, he produced nothing which did not immediately deal with matters arising out of Scripture ; but he did not burn his classics ; nor did he cease to peruse them. Even his marvellous memory, unaided by frequent consultation with the originals, can scarcely be credited with the illustrations and references with which his pages are sprinkled. He must not be held as disapproving of the application of the mind to anything but Scripture. What he means is that all other studies must be correlated with and subordinated to that of Biblical theology.[1] In whatever directions men may look for light and knowledge, all that they gather should be brought into relation with the subject matter of the Gospel. Where you pass beyond that with which Scripture deals (as in astrology), or wander into paths along which it does not lead, you transgress the appointed boundaries of legitimate knowledge. " It is of great importance," he says, " that we should be told what it is necessary for us to know, and what the Lord desires us to contemplate." (Comm. Eph. iii. 19.)

There was another side to the sufficiency of Scripture in Calvin's view. If there was nothing needful to be known outside its pages, everything within its pages must be needful to be known ; that is indeed the reason for its being there. God has not inserted superfluities or allowed his amanuenses to indulge in gratuitous comments or asides. The exact content of Scripture is a considered thing ; the Bible is no haphazard compilation ; it is exactly what it requires to be for the accomplishment of the divine purposes. The inference is that as, on the one hand, it would be presumptuous to add to it, on the other hand, to ignore or neglect, much less reject any doctrine plainly taught, is to slight or insult God. " If these truths were not useful to be known, God never would have ordained His prophets and apostles to teach them."[2] (Instit. II. i. § 4.) We shall see how this principle forced Calvin to become champion of a doctrine which has brought upon himself and his system cataracts of horrified abuse.

[1] In this Calvin was at one with the mediaeval theologians. Even such a pioneer as Roger Bacon accepted " the universally prevailing view that the end of all the sciences is to serve their queen, theology," and in her service their study found its justification. *E.g.* in his *Optics* he discusses the spiritual significations of refracted rays. (Taylor, *The Mediaeval Mind*, ii. p. 480 ff.)

[2] " The Scripture is the school of the Holy Spirit, in which, as nothing is passed over that is necessary and useful, so nothing is taught but what it is good to know."

Moreover, there must be no questioning of these doctrines which can neither be proved nor disproved by external evidence. Transcending the sphere in which reason legitimately operates, they claim the immediate assent of faith, their sole authority being the *ipse dixit* of God. Disputation has no right of entry upon the realm of these truths which are known to us solely through revelation. If it pleased God to transmit them, not only must they be necessary to the requisite completeness of revelation, but they must be accepted as in the highest degree reasonable, that is, consonant with the principles of the divine mind. It is the part of faith humbly and solely to consider wherein they may contribute to its edification.

An example of Calvin's employment of Scripture as the final test from which there can be no appeal appeared in his rebuke of Bucer for his " pious shuffling " in asserting that the invocation of saints is not entirely to be condemned, because "we owe deference to the authority of the holy fathers who recommend it," although it is not sanctioned in the Word of God. Again, in his Comm. on Acts xii. 12, he calls the common notion of two angels attending every man 'a vain surmise and profane,' as Scripture gives no countenance to it, but only to the fact that " the whole host of heaven doth watch for the safety of the Church, and that as the necessity of time requireth assistance, sometimes one angel, sometimes more, do defend us with their aid." The Scriptures testify that "sometimes there is one angel given to a great people, and to one man only, a great host." (Ex. xiv. 10; 2 Kings vi. 17; Dan. x. 5, 12.)[1] He regarded many current astrological beliefs as sound because of their agreement with the statements of Scripture, for example, that the stars exercise certain influences assigned to them by God. That the earth is fresh in springtime is due to the Pleiades reigning then. (Sermon on Job xxxvii. 31.) Again, on the ground of the silence of Scripture he repudiated the anointing with oil at baptism and *in extremis*, also prayers for the dead at communion. He permitted political alliances with those outside the pale

---

[1] In the *Institutes* he remarks with sterling commonsense that he does not see what a man is to gain by knowing that he has one angel as a special guardian, when all the angels are watching for his safety.

of true faith on the ground of Biblical precedents. It was on the same principle that the Reformed Church disapproved of any pictorial representation of either God or Christ,[1] finding their authority in Exodus xx. 4. Similarly they condemned organs, church bells, and gravestones. It may be remembered that Calvin forbade any tombstone to be erected above himself.

VII

The Scripture being regarded as not merely containing but being the very Word of God, it was a matter of the utmost moment that its interpretation by expositors should be such as to provoke confidence in their readers that they are actually learning what the Lord would say to them. Luther and Calvin were both guilty of somewhat reckless assertions regarding the simplicity of Scripture and its accommodation to the capacity of " little ones and lowly." " God showeth us how his meaning is, not only to instruct the great clerkes, and such as are very subtle and well exercised in schools, but also to apply Himself unto us that are of the rudest and unskilfullest sort that can be." (Sermon on Job i. 6-8.) He lays great stress on seeking " the natural and obvious meaning " which any passage yields. His own voluminous and elaborate expositions scarcely prove that the meaning is always obvious, however natural it may appear when once it is seen. It is true that we wonder why we did not at once perceive that which becomes plain to us only after much thinking, as so often happens with resemblances seen in the outlines of rocks or the contour of mountains. But the obviousness that is not immediate is a misnomer. Calvin was really claiming for his exposition the merit of eliciting and setting down that which promptly approves itself to sanctified common sense, when once it has been put at the right point of view.

If this is the meaning to be assigned to the phrase " the

[1] The Helvetic Confession represented that Christ had promised to be present with the Church spiritually, denying His bodily presence. How then could a likeness be of any utility to the pious ?

F

natural and obvious meaning " of Scripture, Calvin certainly made it his fundamental principle of interpretation. He believed that Scripture meant what it said, and said what it meant. The meaning apprehended by the plain intelligent man, reading with unbiassed mind, earnest to know the truth, must be the true one, and no other was to be looked for. The artificial and disingenuous method practised and popularised by Origen which discovered layers of meaning under the outer skin of the letter, deep mysteries lurking under the deceptive surface " only to be extracted by beating out allegories," he denounced as " torturing Scripture away from its true sense." He was well aware of the attractions of this method, giving ample scope, as it did, to fascinating speculation. (Comm. Gal. iv. 22.) Erasmus had fallen a victim to it, holding that you must penetrate below the literal meaning of Scripture to get at its true significance. " Choose these interpreters," said he, " who depart as far as possible from the letter." He scornfully disparages those who uphold the grammatical sense. The story of Adam was not better worth reading than that of Prometheus, he averred, if you take it only in the literal sense.[1] Calvin had no sympathy with such a view, so far as it implied that Scripture concealed, rather than revealed, the truth God purposed to teach. If he might not agree with Luther in asserting that " the Holy Spirit is the simplest writer and speaker that is in heaven and earth," he was entirely at one with him in holding that " His words can have no more than one simplest sense, which we call the scriptural or literal meaning." He perceived how the habit of allegorising reduced the Scripture to " a nose of wax," as he aptly puts it.[2] The wildest interpretations were made possible; the most fantastic views might be and had been supported by its aid.[3] Truth was at the mercy of personal idiosyncrasy.

The first business of the interpreter, then, was to get at the literal meaning. Biblical history was not an involved and

---

[1] Beard, *op. cit.* 119 f. [2] *Sermon on Job*, xli. 1-25.

[3] To treat the Scriptures this way was " to wanton with them as with a play-thing." (Preface to *Romans*. Cf. *Comm. Gal.* iv. 22-26.)

THE HOLY SCRIPTURES

imaginative allegory requiring exegetical ingenuity and penetration to resolve. The divine instruction contained was to be reached through the appreciative understanding of the principles animating the characters appearing in it or determining the situation presented. The Scripture narrative was meant to be a transparency, not a screen. Calvin insisted that the Bible should be studied in its historical setting and its words taken at their face value. Common sense with adequate knowledge was more serviceable for its interpretation than scholarly equipment with a scent for mysteries. He had no patience with those to whom the far-fetched was more probable and acceptable than that which struck the normal eye.

Of course neither he nor Luther denied that there might be much more in any passage than appeared on the surface. It was legitimate and proper to extract all the teaching possible and give it the widest application; but that was a different matter from finding various layers of meaning. Their aim and effort was to let the primary teaching of Scripture illuminate all that was cognate to the original situation as well as all the areas of life to which its search light penetrated. For example, to find in a certain text a rebuke of the Papacy as well as a condemnation of any common swindler was not to infringe the guiding principle. But no application was of any value which did not flow directly from the truth or teaching immediately imparted by the text. Calvin's loyalty to this canon of interpretation saved him from committing not a few of the absurdities perpetrated by the scholastic theologians, who with amazingly perverted ingenuity discovered proof passages of specifically Christian doctrines in O.T. utterances or statements that conveyed no hint of them to any who dealt frankly and sincerely with the text. To one of Calvin's dogmatic propensities and temperament, it must have been difficult to resist the temptation of buttressing fundamental dogmas, especially if admittedly inferential, with the texts commonly adduced by their classical apologists. It says much for his honesty that he refused, for example, to regard such standard references as Gen. i. 1; Ps. vi. 3; xviii. 2; xxxiii. 6, as legitimate supports for the doctrine of the Trinity.

This honesty of purpose is all the more evident in view of the way in which he gave free play to his dogmatic bias when opportunity was offered by symbolical expressions or picturesque or poetical figures. From words thrown off in some descriptive or elegiac ecstasy of a Hebrew prophet's imagination he will draw tremendous conclusions convincingly corroborative of favourite dogmas. In the phrase, "trees of righteousness" in Isai. lxi. 3, he finds witness of a "universal doctrine," namely that "there is no other way in which we are restored to life than when we are planted by the Lord." Occasionally his dogmatic prepossessions will deprive him of the scholarly poise of judgment he generally exhibits. Translating "Hephzibah" (Is. lxii. 4) "my good pleasure in her," he makes the name teach that "this proceeds from the good pleasure of God, that is, from His undeserved favour, that nothing may be ascribed to the merits or excellence of men." From Is. lxiii. 16, "thou art my Father," he infers that Christ, as the first-born or rather the only-begotten Son of God, always governed the Church, for "in no other way than through Him can God be called Father," a conclusion only to be justified by the intrusion of premises supplied by a Christian Creed. Again, in calling His mother "woman" (John iii. 4), he infers that Jesus intended to "lay down a perpetual and general instruction for all ages that His divine glory must not be obscured by excessive honour paid to His mother." It is unlikely that Calvin would have thought of the alleged intention but for his hostility to the worship of the Virgin.

But such blemishes on the general straightforwardness of his interpretations are comparatively rare. Some of them are excusable or at least explicable by the lack of such critical apparatus, linguistic and historical knowledge, as now affords protection to expositors. In the absence of such restraints, it was inevitable that the heated controversial atmosphere of the times along with the necessity of finding every possible support for Protestant doctrine and every possible refutation of Roman Catholic, would warp on occasion even the most self-controlled exegete's mind. The passion of battle was never out of Calvin's heart, and it is scarcely to be wondered at if it

sometimes prejudiced his judgment. One has often the
feeling that he had an eye on some opponent " behind the
scenes " whom he seized the chance of discomfiting by means
of some Scripture passage offering itself in the course of
his exposition.

The perfect consistency and harmony attributed to
Scripture provided the principal rule of its interpretation.
It was held that its various parts were mutually explanatory
and illuminative, what was obscure receiving light from
what was plain, and ambiguities being resolved by reference to what was certain. Self-contradictions in Scripture
were out of the question ; if two passages seemed to clash
then the meaning of one of them must be other than what
it seemed. *E.g.*, in enjoining that the wheat and tares
should be allowed to grow together till the harvest, Christ
could not have meant His words to be taken literally,
otherwise the force of the sanctions, elsewhere found,
for the suppression of misdemeanants and troublers of the
peace would be annulled. So too, in view of other injunc-
tions, Christ's command to Peter to put up his sword must
not be regarded as warrant for the disarmament of those
entrusted with the defence of righteousness or for the
policy of non-resistance to evil. The final arbiter in all
perplexities was Scripture itself ; it was both self-sufficient
and self-interpreting. " Scriptura sacra . . . ipsa per se
sui ipsius interpres," said Luther, echoed by Calvin, a
principle they constantly applied, marshalling defensive
or illustrative texts indiscriminately from all its parts
to the support of their exposition of some disputed passage.

But such acute minds as theirs did not fail to perceive
that there must be a form of doctrine in Scripture to act
as a base from which to attack passages of dubious import
and as a touchstone of the truth of interpretation. Where
there were disconcerting differences of teaching or embarrass-
ing appearance of inner contradiction, irreconcilable
without the assistance of some unifying thought, where
was the authoritative truth to be found which would
dissolve all such difficulties ? Luther found it in the
Pauline conception of justification by faith, specially as
it is given in the Epistles to the Romans and Galatians,
and this he made the basis of his operations upon Scripture.

All its teaching elsewhere must be qualified by that and must be read in its light. Also, the doctrine provided a test of what should belong to Scripture; what did not satisfy it, at once fell under suspicion as having no divine right there. The Epistle of James, with its emphasis on works, only had value when supplemented and corrected by the master-truth of justification by faith. But no one was competent to apply this test unless he had this faith himself. Possessed of it, he could not err; Scripture at once became clear and plain without the aid of Fathers or teachers. With this Calvin would on the whole agree, though he would not expect to find anything in Scripture which could not be brought into harmony with the master-truth. He too regarded the Ep. to the Romans as containing the key to the whole Word of God, and with it he started on that prodigious work of exposition which he did not cease to pursue throughout his career.[1]

It must be clearly understood, however, in what sense the doctrine of justification by faith was taken as the master-key. Put otherwise, it meant that Scripture was to be read in the light of the Cross of Christ and all that it signified. You must survey its expanse from the crest of the hill Calvary, if you would discern in it all that was to be rightly seen. The background and presupposition of all its teachings was "Christ crucified." "All Scripture teaches nothing but the Cross," said Luther, and Calvin was in thorough sympathy. He industriously read the N.T. into the O.T. It was because of Christ being in the O.T. that it became a living word instead of a dead letter. With Christ shining through, its darkest pages became illuminated transparencies,[2] and he saw Christ everywhere. There was scarcely an outstanding character of Hebrew

[1] "It is quite clear that the Reformers operated with a particular content of Scripture as regulative, if not of the meaning, at least of the value of the rest of the biblical material. It was so with Luther, who frankly refers us to the Pauline epistles, the Fourth Gospel, and 1 Peter for the form of revelation. The actual procedure of Calvin did not differ in principle from that of Luther, since he operated with a scheme of thought in which he combined the doctrines of grace and of predestination which he found in St. Paul, while he merely utilised as much of the remaining material as could be usefully worked into this doctrinal framework." (W. P. Paterson, *The Rule of Faith*, p. 75 f.)

[2] "Vetus Testamentum in Novo patet." (Augustine.)

history in whom he did not descry in some wise " a type or figure of Christ." The viewless voices that spake from heaven were His. In the angel of the burning bush Christ appeared to Moses. (Comm. Acts vii. 30.) All prophecy shone with the reflected radiance of the Light of the world that was to come. With Christ as the Sun of his life, Calvin always had the sun in his eyes. He could echo Luther's saying that " Scripture teaches nothing through and through but who this Christ is, what He is to you, and what you may hope from Him." " In our reading of Scripture," he said speaking from his heart, " we shall hold simply to that which speaks clearly and definitely to our conscience and makes us feel that it leads us to Christ."

It was the presence of Christ in every didactic part of Scripture that made it holy and divine. The oracles and stories of the O.T. were providentially preserved because they contained " mysteries " which only the coming of Christ could unlock and display to the eye of faith anointed with the salve of the Spirit. It needed the Incarnation to fructify the fields of truth that lay fallow, to open up the hidden treasures of wisdom and knowledge deposited in story and psalm and prophecy. To the Jew, the ancient Scriptures were as fields lying in the baffling twilight of a day that had not yet dawned. But there stood One among their holy books whom they knew not, and it needed His coming in the flesh to open their eyes to see in them Him who had always been there in the spirit. The Word had dwelt in Israel since the beginning; to this and that one He had imparted hints of the likeness of the Son of Man that was to be; by this and that experience of His saints and heroes of faith He had sought to prepare the minds of His people for His coming in order that He might be recognisable when He came unto His own.[1]

---

[1] Seeing that Christ gave its meaning to the O.T. even as He formed its constant theme, it followed that it had much to say of the Church which was His body. It might be said that to Calvin the Church was its coordinate theme. What its functions were, its experience, its dimensions, its features, and marks, these were all foreshadowed in wealth of detail by type and symbol, prophecy and psalm.

CHAPTER VI

PREDESTINATION

In the first and second editions of the Institutes, the subjects of Predestination and Providence are treated in the same chapter. The former, according to Calvin's definition of it, included the latter. But in the more detailed and elaborate treatment of the last editions he assigned them to different chapters as relating to operations of the divine will which could at least be differentiated in thought. The doctrine of Predestination deals with God's relation to the ultimate destinies of individual men, that of Providence with His treatment of men here and now. Providence is concerned with this world and this life, though of course its issues pass beyond into the next: it is the experiential side of the divine decrees. Predestination in its limited sense is concerned solely with the fate of men hereafter, though it in turn takes this life into its purview as providing material for justifying the ways of God with man. It constitutes the metaphysical side of the divine decrees. It will be well then to follow Calvin and give separate treatment to these two interrelated though distinguishable themes.

I

There has been considerable discussion as to the place occupied in Calvin's system by the doctrine of predestination. It is generally understood to be its distinguishing feature; that it was at least of front-rank importance will be perceived on even a cursory acquaintance with his writings. Whether it is central and determinative of the character of the whole, or organic to it while not absolutely essential, is a question about which doctors differ. Doumergue decides that it is not the foundation stone of Calvin's theology but the keystone which sustains the edifice. Victor Monod is of opinion that it is for Calvin a point of arrival not of departure, a necessary hypothesis not a principle of explanation. Seeberg holds that it occupied a secondary place in his teaching, and Scheibe also refuses to regard it as central, though gradually approaching that position. The truth seems to be that Calvin would have found it difficult to answer for himself, or that his answers would have varied. A survey of his pronouncements makes it apparent that his views on its relative importance and its claim to be regarded as a primary and indispensable element in any Christian creed underwent considerable change and even display some vacillation. It might be said that from occupying a subordinate position in his system as an article of faith it came to be one on which he laid increasing stress and for which he battled more fiercely than for any other.

Reliable evidence as to his sense of its importance is offered by the degree of emphasis he gave it or the place he assigned it in the various summaries of Christian doctrine which he composed from time to time. In his first Catechism (1537) there is a paragraph in which the doctrine is stated as a fact of observation, while he strongly deprecates looking into the mystery lying behind it as likely to lead to pain and madness. There is no mention of it, however, in the Confession of Faith drawn up in the same year, nor does any explicit statement of it appear in the Second Catechism (1541) although it is incidentally and allusively referred to in three places. Four Confessions are attributed to Calvin, and of these three allude only in passing to predestination and then only in the sense of election,[1] namely the Confession for the French king 1557, the Confession for the scholars in Geneva 1559, and that for the Emperor and the States 1562. That drawn up for the Synod of Paris mentions it specifically, but still only

[1] *I.e.*, as opposed to reprobation.

in the sense of election. In the Creed which had to be subscribed by teachers and pupils of the Academy it does not appear. It receives no notice in his earlier theological writings, in the historic address prepared by him for Michael Cop in 1533, or in his preface to Olivetan's translation of the Bible (1535). The earliest treatment is given in the first edition of the Institutes and even there it gets no special prominence. He had the *Loci* of Melanchthon translated and published with a preface by himself strongly recommending the work as " a brief summary of the things which a Christian ought to know to guide him in the way of salvation." He speaks of Melanchthon as " leaving in suspense or omitting that of which ignorance or doubt is by no means perilous," and as " passing lightly or leaving behind that of which he does not hope such profit." Now it was the second edition of this work which was so translated and introduced, and therein Melanchthon resiled from the pronounced predestinarian views of the first edition, teaching instead the synergism which allows that much depends upon man himself as to whether he accepts God's grace or not, and also admitting contingency. Calvin's approbation was due to no oversight of what the *Loci* did not contain; in a letter in which he disputes certain of Melanchthon's views and expresses the opinion that they could not be really so far apart, he declares it absurd to suppose that the doctrine of predestination was really rejected by any theologian. It is on record that he did not refuse to receive a converted Anabaptist into the Church even though he could not see his way to accept the doctrine.

Over against all this, however, must be placed such facts as that he broke off one of his most intimate and valued friendships, that with de Falais, because of his taking sides with an opponent on this question.[1] In that controversy he declared that " the honour of God and the salvation of the world depended on this doctrine and that they who opposed it assailed God, and that unity on this subject must be established, cost what it might." At another time he declared that " the reception of this simple doctrine

[1] He had dedicated his Comm. on 1 Cor. to de Falais, but after his defection he wrathfully substituted another dedication to the Marquis Carracioli in a new edition.

is and ever will continue to be to me the only rule of wisdom." The dispute between Berne and Geneva turned largely upon predestination, Berne wishing to make no categorical pronouncement regarding it as one of the deep secrets of God, while Calvin and his colleagues demanded that it should be held and taught. There can be little doubt that latterly he attempted to force it upon the whole Reformed Church as an inherent part of the substance of its faith.

From a review of Calvin's relation to this doctrine throughout his career it may be concluded that his position was of this nature. He regarded it as part of the substance of the faith but would not force it at the bayonet's point upon any one reluctant to accept it. If any one however made a deliberate subversive attack on it, he considered him as menacing a truth or principle which could not be surrendered or jeopardised without endangering all the rest, and he therefore set himself to combat the aggressor with all the strength of which he was capable. Indeed, had it not been for the exigencies of controversy, Calvin might never have given the doctrine the prominence it came to assume in his teaching. It was the physician Bolsec's shrewd and vigorous assault that made Calvin magnify its importance as never before in his zeal to provide what he regarded as needed safeguards for the evangelical principle of grace. When Albert Pighius, "the prince of contemporary sophists," as Beza calls him, entered the lists intent on its overthrow, publishing a damaging attack in which he marshals with skill most of the objections which have ever been taken to the doctrine, Calvin was in such haste to repel the onslaught that he replied with a treatise in which he did not take time to deal with more than a portion of the objections. Before he could follow it up with a complete vindication, Pighius died, and Calvin stopped proceedings, spilling a drop of harmless venom on his opponent's grave as he disclaimed the desire of "insulting a dead dog."

II

The doctrine of predestination has become so identified with Calvin in popular thought as to make it appear that he was its originator. That, of course, is far from the truth. It had been agitated in a more or less vigorous way almost from the beginning of theological controversy, and had stimulated the same hot feeling which its reiterated prominence invariably stirred. In a writing of c. 180 A.D., a sceptic, Caecilius, in a dialogue with a believer, Octavius, attacks it vigorously and puts in a nutshell the argument which has never failed to play a leading part in all subsequent discussion. " They tell us that only those chosen by their god become believers, and thus they represent him as an unjust judge, punishing men not for their will but for the lot he assigns to them." How far away Calvin's line of assertion and defence was from that of this early apologist is evident from the reply of Octavius : " a man's lot may be due to fortune, but his will is free ; and thus a foreseeing God assigns each man's destiny in accordance with his merits." It is perhaps worth noticing how Celsus, that arch-enemy of Christianity whom Origen needed all his skill to counter effectually, blames God for the fault of Adam because it was foreseen, for " liberty cannot subsist unimpaired in presence of the divine foreknowledge,"—an utterance which indicates that the perplexities surrounding the matter had by then been fully ventilated. In the ninth century a monk, Gottschalk, asserted Calvin's views almost exactly and with the same uncompromising pertinacity. He set ablaze a controversy which raged fiercely for some time and necessitated three Synods whose differing pronouncements prove the current division of opinion, two of these, Mayence (848) and Cliersy (849) condemning Gottschalk, that of Lyons (854) approving him. In this dispute all the arguments for and against with which Reformed times became so familiar were advanced, and the lines of all subsequent controversy were marked out. It may be said, too, of later controversy, as Neander said of this one, that it was not really a dispute of ideas but only of harsher or milder forms of expression.

PREDESTINATION

Ratramnus, Gottschalk's chief opponent, contended that Christ died for all and that God would have all men to be saved, but taught that these only could be actually saved upon whom God bestowed the grace necessary to enable them to secure salvation, and this was done only in the case of the elect. Why God did this, he referred to His secret incomprehensible decree.

During subsequent centuries the doctrine forces itself from time to time to the front in Christian thought and discussion. In the systems of such Reformers before the Reformation as Wyclif, it was strenuously asserted and indeed may be said to have held a central place, though here again assuming a different shape from that given by Calvin. In some form or other it was practically universally held by both Protestants and Catholics. Where wide and acute difference did arise was in regard to its statement. Its emphatic and uncompromising assertion by Calvin in a form which was neither nebulous nor hazy brought it into the arena of controversy in an unprecedented way. In the height of the disputation, almost every sermon rang with the distinctive cries of the combatants, reverend opponents hurling unmeasured abuse upon one another, as was the habit of these rough-and-tumble times. Barbers' shops and taverns were cockpits of windy conflict. If Calvin did not make the elements of the storm, at least he let it loose.

III

Calvin then was no pioneer in the assertion of this doctrine of predestination; it came into his hands already hammered into rough dogmatic shape in previous centuries. What he did was to give precision of outline to all its sides, not leaving anything timorously indeterminate. He demanded the bold and plain assertion of that which men shrink from saying, choosing rather to respect the elemental sensibilities of human hearts than to make themselves reluctant trumpeters of a doctrine of Scripture which might inspire dread repulsion.

Calvin of course found in Scripture his ultimate and decisive authority for the doctrine on both its sides of election and reprobation. Nevertheless his mind had received a strong bias towards certain views on the subject from men whose early influence upon him had been very great. It is noteworthy that his first published writing, the Commentary on the Stoic Seneca's De Clementia, disclosed an intellectual sympathy with a philosopher whose fatalistic doctrine, though radically different from that of predestination, appealed to the same mental disposition. It was undoubtedly Augustine, however, who made the profoundest impression upon Calvin, not only in this particular but in many others. A rapid comparison with that Father's Anti-Pelagian writings is enough to show that Calvin reproduces in large measure his argumentation on the doctrine, the only considerable difference being that the later champion lays greater stress on the reprobation side of it. The influence of Luther could not but strongly reinforce the impression made upon him by Augustine. Calvin echoes the older Reformer in deprecating the attempt to explore the secrets of the divine will and in asserting the Christian duty of limiting ourselves to what is revealed in Scripture and through Christ. It may be that he was more indebted for the exact form of his views to Le Fèvre whose teaching was transmitted through his pupil Roussel, one of Calvin's instructors. In Le Fèvre's Commentary on Paul's Epp. the same attitude is assumed to the matter as Calvin subsequently adopted, especially in his insistence that all things, however mysterious, contribute to enhance the glory of God, the interest of His creatures being of only secondary moment. According to Calvin's own witness, however, it was Bucer who was most of all the informing mind and guiding spirit. "Principally," said he, "I have wished to follow Bucer, man of holy memory." But here again Calvin's independent mind would allow him to call no man master. Bucer, touched by the common repugnance, kept reprobation in the background, while Calvin kept it in the foreground in line with its better half, election. Calvin's convictions were not the result of his respect for the *ipse dixit* of any man, whatever his regard for him. Doubtless others disposed his mind to a more zealous and unhesitating adoption of views in harmony with theirs, but nothing save proof, based on grounds that approved themselves to him as incontrovertible, would produce the absolute certainty with which he held them. He was no parrot; he was one of those who, like Paul, can say, I believed, therefore do I speak. Nor was his acceptance of the doctrine due to the compulsion of mere logical syllogisms with the sovereignty of God as major premiss, any more than it was held by him with the jealous assertion of the professional theologian who wishes the children of his brain to command the homage of all. His convictions were of the heart as well as of the mind and rested on a variety of grounds.

Ultimately, of course, the doctrine was rooted and grounded in Scripture; of that Calvin had no manner of doubt, and he could never understand why any intelligent person could fail to see a thing so plain. Always his final appeal was to the Word of God; there he took refuge from all perplexities and objections against which he could find no other defence. Thither he retreated and therein he made his last stand, defying all and sundry to compel his surrender. Not only did he himself accept the doctrine as being found there, but he regarded it as a mere matter of loyalty to the Scripture that it should be embodied in the articles of faith to be plainly and unequivocally taught. He constantly resorted to this position, especially when assailed by protests based on the inadvisability or inexpediency of its frank assertion, insisting that, as it was taught in Scripture, it must form part of the staple doctrine of the Church. The Holy Spirit does not impart anything gratuitous or without purpose and value. "If one is determined to throw aside this doctrine," he argued in his remonstrance with the Bernese Council, "such a proceeding amounts to an attempt to improve upon the Holy Spirit, and consequently we should strike out of Scripture what is revealed to us on the subject." In his Commentary on John vi. 40 he declares that those who refuse to assent to the simple teaching of the Holy Spirit on this matter "offer Him aggravated insult." He charges those who repudiate the doctrine because of the fear of inspiring antagonism to the whole body of Christian truth with accusing God of "foolish inadvisedness" in revealing it, "as though He foresaw not the danger against which they imagine they prudently provide," and as though "something had unadvisedly slipped from Him which is hurtful to the Church." (Instit. III. xxi. § 4.) Let us hold fast to Scripture, he cries; there is nothing taught in it which is not useful and necessary for salvation. "If such truths were not useful to be known, God would never have ordered His prophets and apostles to teach them." (Instit. II. i. § 4.)

But he finds ample corroboration of the doctrine on all sides, in history, in observed facts, and in personal experience. However it may seem to violate or outrage the sense of justice or mercy, it provides the only satisfactory explanation of things seen and recorded which in themselves might well stagger faith. If the doctrine in its ultimate rationale runs back into mystery, it provides the key to mysteries of life before which reason, unaided by revelation, stands utterly baffled. How are we to explain the fact that the fall of Adam should have involved so many nations with their infant children in eternal death? (Instit. III. xxiii. § 7.) He challenges Castellio to explain how God allows innocent infants to be torn and devoured by tigers or bears or lions or wolves. How comes it, he asks, that many peoples are deprived of that light of the Gospel which we enjoy? How comes it that the pure knowledge of the doctrine of godliness has never reached some and others have scarcely tasted some obscure rudiments of it? (Instit. III. xxiv. § 16.) Again and again he asks how otherwise the obvious differences in the attitude of men to Christ and God are to be explained. There is no reason in men themselves why one should follow Christ and another refuse to do so. Paul might just as well have completed the work of Judas, crucifying those who clung to the Cross. In the first Genevan Catechism, 1537, the treatment of the doctrine arises out of the observed fact that most men, blinded and hardened in unbelief, despise the extraordinary grace of God in Christ, although the word of the Gospel calls all to share it.

He appealed also to the personal experience of those who had been brought into the Kingdom. Can you account for that by anything in yourself? he asks. Would you of yourself have chosen the better part? Must you not acknowledge that for reasons known only to God and for no merit of your own you have been called into the light?[1] Why you rather than your next-door neighbour who remains in the bondage of sin? Must you not ascribe all to the calling and election of God? Calvin's own conversion remained an abiding wonder to him, a miracle of divine grace at which he could only worship and adore.

Behind this ground of belief lay the deep sense of the total corruption of man and his utter inability to choose and take of himself the way of salvation. There was not enough strength or good left in him to stop and turn. It was not in him even to say, I will arise and go unto my Father, till the Holy Spirit put it into his heart. There was no reason why one Prodigal should say that more than another except that God chose this and that particular one of His own sovereign and inscrutable will to be a vessel of grace.

Probably nothing made Calvin cling so fiercely to the doctrine more than the religious assurance it provided.[2] His quarrel with the Roman Catholic Church had been in no small degree due to the uncertainty in which its teaching left the individual regarding personal salvation. To a man of his spiritual temperament and mental complexion, such uncertainty was intolerable. A merely problematic salvation could not bestow upon any one the stable joy and peace of Christ. Assurance was required to release one from the dispiriting and burdensome doubts and fears to which fluctuating feeling rendered one liable, and assurance was the gift of this doctrine to those who satisfied the plain tests provided for determining whether

---

[1] "The ineradicable sense which every converted man has that if God had not chosen him, he would not have chosen God, and that if God by his Holy Spirit had not exerted a decisive and determining influence in the matter, he would never have been turned from darkness to light and been led to embrace Christ as his Saviour, that is really the sum and substance of Calvinism." (Cunningham, *Theology of the Reformation*, p. 209.)

[2] In the discourse Calvin prepared for Cop at the beginning of his career, the main point held in view is that we must have certainty of salvation. At the end of his life, preaching from the Epistle to the Ephesians, he said there were two principal things we must hold and which summed up all that God teaches us in Scripture, (1) that God be glorified as He deserves, (2) that we be certified of our salvation so that we may invoke our Father in perfect liberty. "If we do not have these two things, we have neither faith nor religion."

they belonged to the number of the elect or not. Assured of one's election, one was assured of everything else, of the unfailing favour of God and all that it brought of lovingkindness and tender mercy. For the elect there was no falling out of God's hand. Destiny fixed in eternity was settled for good and all; nothing could or would change it. That which God had eternally willed would surely be. On these convictions Calvin rested in quietness and in confidence.

In this he differed somewhat from Luther. Luther did not draw his assurance from this doctrine and value it accordingly. He drew his confidence from the revelation of God through Jesus Christ. God, being such as He had been revealed, could not refuse to save one who committed himself in well-doing trustfully into His hands. If a man could do that, he had immediate assurance of being possessed of the faith that saves. Luther found his assurance in the Gospel which offered God's forgiving love and grace to all. It was in the character of God that he found confidence, not in any certainty, however reached, that he was one of the elect. The doctrine was thus less to him than to Calvin and he often exhibited a "genial inconsequence" in his treatment of it. It could not but be otherwise with Calvin who found his unshakable assurance in the certainty of his election mediated by the conscious possession of saving faith. This practical value of the doctrine he was never tired of impressing upon his hearers and readers, making it one of its chief recommendations.

IV

To appreciate adequately and estimate fairly the doctrine of predestination, it is necessary to start with the presuppositions of its advocates. To ignore these is to take a very partial view of it and perhaps to do it serious injustice. In this matter the fruit is in the root.

The starting point of the doctrine is to be found in the assumption, based on alleged assertions of Scripture, that the whole human race, untouched by grace, is without exception in a state of total moral corruption. No exaggeration of statement is possible as regards this dogma. All the leading Reformers alike assented without qualification or reserve to this verdict upon human life. They applied literally and universally Isaiah's assertion that "there was no soundness in (man)." Luther and Melanchthon declared that all man's powers were impure and that he could only sin. The so-called virtues of such heathen as Socrates and Zeno were only "carnales affectus" void of all pure spiritual quality. Calvin was equally uncompromising in his refusal to admit anything in even the best of the pagans which could be pronounced true goodness. This view was justified on the ground that the quality of an act in the eyes of God is determined by its inspiring motive and informing spirit. No judgment could be passed upon isolated acts without taking into account the state of heart from which they proceeded. Always, said these Reformers, the best in pagan life was vitiated by something self-regarding, and whatever was done from anything but the purest God-honouring motives and for any other but God-glorifying ends must be labelled as sinful.[1] It was perfectly true that the heathen did many virtuous acts— Calvin was not sparing in his admiration of them—but these he attributed to the internal restraints or constraints of divine grace working upon their minds and wills without purifying their natures. God exercises this restraint to prevent the diseases of the soul breaking forth to a degree incompatible with the preservation of the established order of things. But these restraints act through shame or such a consideration as fear of loss. Some practise honesty as most conducive to their interest; others behave well that "by the dignity of their station they may keep inferiors to their duty." In no instance is there anything intrinsically good in the considerations which move "the natural man." Calvin appeals for confirmation to the evidence of personal experience according to which we must all admit that, were it not for divine grace, any one

---

[1] The good works of unbelievers are still punishable because "they are kept from acting ill, not by sincere love of goodness, but merely by ambition or self-love, or some other crooked affection." (Inst. III. xiv, § 1.)

of us would be capable of committing all possible crimes. (Instit. II. iii. § 3.) Corruption extends to all parts of the being and so everything that proceeds from unregenerate man is tainted with sin.[1]

This condition results from the moral downfall of the first man, who was betrayed by pride into disobedience. In regarding pride as occasioning the first sin, Calvin departed from Augustine and the Catholic tradition which held that concupiscence was to blame. But that, he argued, produces only an accidental and incidental fault which does not change the nature of man nor reduce him to a sinful state. Pride of self-hood, on the other hand, affects the whole man, inspiring him with the desire to become God. It is the sin of sins. This first sin was committed not by a mere individual but by the only existing individual, that is to say, by the whole of living humanity. Thus it is that a moral and spiritual revolution has been worked in humanity as a whole. It became from that moment separated from God and was precipitated into a state of sin. This original sin is transmitted to all subsequent members of the race. Why and how it is transmitted, Calvin refuses to discuss, while recognising that there is no reason in the nature of things for its being so. It is by the will of God that the nature of man should be such that the state of sin is passed on. It is a fact of experience behind which we cannot go, that every infant inherits the original sin which vitiates its whole nature.

Now the crucial point appears in the assertion that this state of sin is in itself penal, a condition to which blame and guilt attach. It is not of the nature of a mere possibility or potency which has no moral quality until it fructifies in act, until the may-be has become a has-been. Every infant from the moment it draws its first breath is under condemnation. It does not need that the corruption,

[1] " We must strongly insist upon these two things, that no believer ever performed one work which, if tested by the strict judgment of God, could escape condemnation ; and moreover that were this granted to be possible (though it is not), yet, the act being vitiated and polluted by the sins of which it is certain the author of it is guilty, it is deprived of its merit." (Inst. III. xiv, § 1.) This was the point on which Calvin joined issue with the schoolmen, and that went to the root of the Protestant and Roman Catholic differences regarding human merit before God. As he himself said, This is the chief point in dispute.

resident and inherent, should materialize in actual sin. Infants "suffer for their own defect," to use Calvin's own words. That there may be no mistake as to his meaning, he takes pains to make plain that it is not for Adam's fault that all his descendants are punished but for the moral condition, the pollution of nature, inherited from him. His warrant for this fundamental view is taken from Scripture, where it is declared that all men are born under condemnation. If that be so, it follows that God must attach guilt to the mere sinful condition, the corrupt nature in itself, irrespective of any evil actually done. (Instit. II. i. §§ 7, 8.) Calvin's teaching is accurately reflected in the Helvetic Confession which holds that before a man admits any actual sin into his nature, he is "obnoxius irae et maledictioni divinae" in virtue of his inherited corruption. Before God deals with it, says Calvin in his Comm. on Acts x. 43, the whole human race "is hostile and hateful to God."

Now God had created man to be immortal, and sin has not deprived him of this immortality; it has only condemned him to an immortality of retribution, in other words, to eternal death. For the whole race in its natural state there is nothing but a certain fearful looking for of judgment. There is no possible way of escape by human effort; the stream of life, left to itself, flows helplessly towards and into the pit.

But God will not have it to be so. By allowing the whole race He had created to go to perdition He would lose in glory. As the inspiration of all His acts is the advancement of His glory, He attains this by intervening to save. Creation had shown forth the glory of His wisdom and power; redemption would show forth the glory of His mercy and grace. But in displaying His mercy He must not violate His righteousness, else would He stultify Himself. Therefore to do justice to all the attributes of His nature, detracting from none but simultaneously enhancing all, His resolve to save must be limited by the necessity of safeguarding the righteousness on which His throne is founded. He must let mercy have its desire but also let justice have its course. He will save some, the rest He will leave to their merited doom, the doom of sin.

Who then shall be saved? That is what His sovereign will decides and nothing else. It is not because of anything whatever in the individuals elected that they are chosen. There is nothing to choose between men in respect of merit from God's standpoint. Nor is His choice controlled or directed by what He foresees they will turn out to be. Election is not because of life, but life because of election. Simon and Saul were not elect because God foresaw that they would become Peter and Paul, but in order that they might become Peter and Paul. The divine selection is in no wise guided by individual deserts or possibilities.[1] It is purely a matter of the divine sovereign will which, doubtless for good reasons known to God Himself but none of them relative to anything distinguishing one man morally from another, chooses some and rejects the rest. This is a cardinal point in Calvin's teaching on which he insistently harps and which must be kept in view if it is to be properly estimated.[2] God's election has nothing to do with His foreknowledge [3] except in so far as He foreknows who are to be members of the human race. It does not turn upon His prevision of any individual's character and life. It is as if, with His eyes shut to all that, He separated out this one and that, always acting in each of His choices, it must be remembered, not without a reason, inscrutable perhaps to us but sufficient for Himself. Whether Calvin, had he been pressed, would have made a distinction between God's not being influenced by what He foresaw that a person was to be in nature and character and His effecting that the individual should be such as to justify His choice, does not appear. He would more probably have said that the power of the Almighty was equal to making what He pleased out of any stuff of human nature whatever, that He could have turned a Pilate into a John just as He turned a Jacob into an Israel. In any case he distinctly says (Comm. Gal. i. 15) "God is said to separate us, not because He bestows any peculiar disposition of mind which distinguishes us from others, but because He appoints us by His own

---

[1] "The grace of God does not find, but makes persons fit to be chosen." (Instit. III. xxii. § 8, following Augustine.)
[2] Cf. Instit. III. xxiii. § 10.   [3] Cf. West. Conf. ch. iii. § 2.

purpose." He illustrates by asking, What had Paul, before he was born, to entitle him to so high an honour? Paul is the apostle not because of any peculiar fitness or capacity, but solely because he was destined so to be in the counsels of eternity.[1]

It is along the same lines that he develops the other side of predestination, that of reprobation. No man is reprobate because of what he is in contradistinction to those who are saved. Certainly his doom is strictly in accordance with his deservings, as a like doom would be in the case of the elect but for God's grace; but there is nothing in him as a person which determines God to leave him to that doom as though he were one, say, of a class upon whom God's grace would be thrown away or whose demerit was such as to make them peculiarly deserving of rejection. The reprobate like the elect are appointed to be so by the secret counsel of God's will and by nothing else. (Instit. II. xxii. § 11.) Though their life justifies that will, their rejection is not determined originally because of their life. Rather the life is the outcome of the decree, the decree necessitating that the life should be such as justified it. We shall see how this led Calvin to wade deeper into enigmas and to raise a problem which resulted in contending schools of Calvinistic thought. Here, in his resolute denial that character and life had anything to do with determining the decrees of God, Calvin went farther than his master Augustine, who in his

[1] It may help to define his position if his distinction between God's foreknowledge and His predestination is quoted. By the former " we mean that all things always and ever continue under God's eye, that to His knowledge there is no past or future, but all things are present, indeed so present that it is not merely the idea of them that is before Him (as these objects are which we retain in our memory) but He truly sees and contemplates them as actually under His immediate inspection.... By predestination we mean the eternal decree of God by which He determined with Himself whatever He wished to happen with regard to every man." (Instit. III. xxi, § 5.)

Cf. West. Conf. iii. § 5 : "Those of mankind that are predestinated unto life, God, before the foundation of the world was laid, according to his eternal and immutable purpose, and the secret counsel and good pleasure of his will, hath chosen in Christ unto everlasting glory, out of his mere free grace and love, without any foresight of faith or good works, or perseverance in either of them, or any other thing in the creature, as conditions, or causes moving him thereunto, and all to the praise of his glorious grace."

anti-Pelagian treatise suggests his inclination to a contrary opinion, conjecturing that in the case of those whom God gives over to evil " some ill-deserts of their own must have first occurred, so that they are justly requited with delinquency and obduracy."[1]

It is Calvin's distinction that he laid equal stress on both sides of predestination. He would not gloss over reprobation or keep it discreetly in the background lest it become a stone of stumbling. The one side involved the other, and no one loyal to Scripture must flinch from declaring the whole counsel of God. Reprobation, he held, is a necessary conclusion from the fact of the patent rejection of the Gospel by so many, which cannot imply the failure or thwarting of God's plan in their case, but must be in accordance with His will. "You are much deceived," he writes to Christopher Libertet, " if you think that the eternal decrees of God can be so mutilated as that he shall have chosen some to salvation but destined none to destruction. . . . There must be a mutual relation between the elect and the reprobate." In this attitude he differed from most of his contemporaries. Bucer, whom he so largely followed, made reprobation a secondary matter. Predestination proper was to him confined to the *electio sanctorum*, whilst reprobation fell within the scope of the general world-rule of God; that is, whilst God deliberately chose the elect, He dealt with the rest on the lines of strict justice, allowing them to reap as they had sown according to the laws appointed by Himself which associated penalty with sin. It was only indirectly therefore that He assigned the reprobate their doom, that being necessitated by His laws.[2] Calvin, on the other hand,

---

[1] Cf. The *Confession of Faith* of Cyril, patriarch of Constantinople (1621), who attempted to infuse Calvinism into the Greek Church :—
" We believe . . . that before the foundation of the world God reprobated whom he would reprobate ; of which reprobation, if a man will regard the absolute right and sovereignty of God, he will without doubt find the cause to be the will of God ; but if again he regards the laws and rules of good order which the Divine will employs for the government of the world, he will find it to be justice, for God is long-suffering, but yet just." (Adeney, *The Greek and Eastern Churches*, p. 317.)

[2] Bucer accepted reprobation too in the sense that the evil also have a definite place in God's world-plan ; He knows for what He will use

held that their fate was the direct immediate appointment of God, justified indeed by their life but not its necessary consequence. He might have saved them from their doom as He did in the case of the elect who were no more worthy in themselves to be saved ; but that doom was fixed from all eternity and nothing in them could transfer them to the contrary class any more than anything in the elect could result in their becoming reprobate.[1]

Bullinger, while he commended Calvin's zeal in asserting the purity of the divine grace in every way, declared that he certainly would not dare to speak as Calvin did about reprobation, affirming that such a doctrine was not recognised by the Fathers. Melanchthon also shrank from such extreme views. Luther assented to the eternal rejection of some while asserting God's universal purpose of grace, but he made no attempt to reconcile the two assertions, holding that we cannot do so and must simply accept them both. But to that Calvin would not agree, on his part declaring that reprobation as much glorified God as election. If " the wicked were purposely created that they might be destroyed " (in accordance with Prov. xvi. 4, Rom. ix. 13 f.), it followed that they must "glorify God by their destruction." (Instit. II. xxii. § 6.) He acknowledges the awfulness of the doctrine ; *decretum quidem horribile fateor*, he says,—the Latin adjective " horribile," as we are industriously cautioned, being equivalent not to " horrible " but to " awe-inspiring."[2] He was not singular however in his attitude to the doctrine. Long before, Gottschalk had insisted on laying emphasis upon

them. He has destined them for that before creating them. He does all things "by a predetermined and certain counsel." (Seeberg, *Dogmengeschichte*, ii. 382, orig. ed.)

[1] Cf. West. Conf. iii. 4 : " These angels and men, thus predestinated and foreordained, are particularly and unchangeably designed ; and their number is so certain and definite, that it cannot be either increased or diminished."

[2] These words do not appear in the 1st or 2nd ed. of the Instit. In the French translation he speaks of " ce decrét qui nous doit epouvanter " (this decree which ought to put us in awe or dread). The sentiment is much more creditable to him than that which he expressed in earlier years in the *Psychopannychia*, " Quibus (*i.e.* to the reprobate) quid accidit non magnae curae nobis esse debet " (What happens to the reprobate, ought not to be of much concern to us).

reprobation on substantially the very same ground as that of Calvin, namely that to deny that God predestinated the wicked to everlasting punishment was to make Him a mutable being. Calvin was jealous more for God's glory, Gottschalk for His character.[1]

V

It might seem that in such a scheme there was no necessity for any Christ. The will of God, acting in such a sovereign fashion, was in itself sufficient to effect what He purposed for His glory. His fiat was enough for redemption. God had need to justify Himself to no one. Where then was there place for Christ the Crucified in the "plan of salvation"? What essential part, too, did faith play in the matter?

It must be admitted that in Calvin's reasoning all these factors, predestination, the work of Christ, and faith, are somewhat loosely correlated. Their intimate and necessary connection is constantly asserted, but their relative priority in importance and in time and their mutual consistency are not clearly stated. Election was not irrespective of Christ. The divine decrees must be regarded as assuming the work of Christ and as being vindicated thereby. Whether redemption could have been effected without it or some equivalent, Calvin would have refused to consider, in consistency with his whole attitude to ultimate mysteries. Certainly as God could suspend even moral law according to His pleasure, He was not bound by some high necessity to justify the dictates of His will. Whatever He commanded or determined was right by virtue of His mere command or decree. It was enough for Calvin that God chose the "way of salvation" through Christ. It might not be intrinsically necessary, but that there was in it some inherent reasonableness might be taken for granted.

---

[1] Gottschalk vindicates reprobation after the same fashion as Calvin, namely that it is "propter ipsorum mala merita" (because of their own evil merits), and therefore they are consigned "per justum judicium Dei ad mortem merito sempiternam" (by the just judgment of God deservedly to eternal death). Seeberg, iii. 61 f.

When Christ was given the central place in the divine scheme of redemption, the doctrine of election received notable qualification. A tacit admission was implied that, after all, God's eternal decrees were not absolutely inscrutable in the sense that they proceeded from a will operating out of impenetrable mystery. God had to take into account certain considerations which, as it appears to us looking back from the consummation to the origination of the divine purposes, were acknowledged by Him as laying a certain necessity on His will. Election after all was not purely arbitrary, the result of an autocratic decree which by its mere fiat effected what was determined upon. God could not merely by a stroke of the pen cancel the doom written in the Book of Life by the hand of justice opposite the name of every sinner. He must somehow secure that the merited penalty be at least compounded for, else His law would be stultified and righteousness be affronted. Election was morally impossible without atonement, if all interests involved were to be safe-guarded. At least we must argue to this position from revealed and recorded facts, for Calvin allows himself no license in *a priori* reasoning. It is possible that God might have done otherwise; in fact it is difficult to see how Calvin could refuse to admit that He could have done otherwise in view of His general conception of God and His sovereign will. But what practically concerns us, and that is all we need care about, is that for good reasons known to Himself, though only within the scope of our surmise, God took the way described in Scripture. If we cannot say that a price had to be paid, we may at least say that a price was paid. The atonement of Christ must therefore have been an essential part of the divine plan of salvation. The divine election neither preceded it as a primary resolve on the part of God, the way of the Cross being subsequently decided upon, nor followed it as an afterthought, but formed in the mind of God, along with the foreordained work of Christ, which it at once necessitated and rested upon, the sum of the will of God regarding the salvation of man.

Calvin strongly and unequivocally holds the substitutionary view of the atonement. If Christ did not bear the exact penalty due to us, (he believes that He suffered the torment of the damned in descending into hell), He suffered that in our stead which was its equivalent. But again it must be recalled that there was no arithmetical equivalence between the penalty borne by Christ and the penalty corresponding to our deserts. The satisfaction made upon the Cross was determined to be and accepted as equivalent by God, exercising His supreme right to declare what was righteous. Forgiveness follows on the ground of Christ's merits divinely determined as sufficient and made available to the elect.

VI

On the human side, Calvin had to find a place for faith which in some' wise is a condition of salvation according to Scripture. If election is necessary on the divine side and faith on the human, how are the two to be brought into relation ? The divine choice is always effectual and cannot be frustrated. In what way then can our salvation be regarded as conditioned by the exercise of faith ?

Calvin had no difficulty in answering the question in entire consistency with his fundamental and ruling conception of the sovereignty of God, which always effects what it purposes, and also of man's state. Saving faith, he taught, is dependent upon election and it results from election.[1] It is not a condition of soul gained by any exercise of human will such that a man might say, Go to, let me have faith that I may be saved. Man's corrupt condition renders that impossible. In his natural state not only can he not acquire faith, but he does not even desire it. It can only become his as a gift of God. Grace is the beginning of the whole saving process and is given only to the elect, its first operation being to produce that condition of heart which is receptive of the blessings of salvation. It never is given in vain ; even as man cannot desire or gain it, he cannot resist or reject it. It is not that God merely prepares men's hearts so that they may embrace

[1] Cf. Zwingli, " Electio Dei libera non sequitur fidem, sed fides electionem sequitur " (The free election of God does not follow faith, but faith follows election).

faith ; He instils faith so that man finds himself at once in possession of it without any effort on his part. Calvin refers for Scripture proof of this (as the true view to be taken of the matter) to Jeremiah xxxii. 39 f., Ezek. xi. 19, which he expounds as declarations on the part of God that, in order to our conversion to righteousness, what is ours must be taken away while that which is substituted in its place is of Himself alone.

It is characteristic of Calvin that he points to facts of experience for additional proof that faith depends upon God's election. Consider the case of two, he says, "who hear the same doctrine together; the one shows himself apt to be taught, the other continues in his obstinacy. It is not therefore because they differ by nature, but because God illumines the former while He does not vouchsafe to the latter the like grace. He does not begin to choose us after that we believe, but He seals His adoption, which was hidden in our hearts, by the gift of faith that it may be manifest and sure." (Comm. Acts x. 43.)

This is a point upon which he is insistent, that it must not be thought that God's choice follows on the appearance of faith, as though He waited to be gracious in that sense, but that His eternal decree effectuates salvation by imparting faith to the heart of the elect. When John (i. 12) speaks of God giving "power to become sons of God," he does not mean that men obtain nothing more than that they may become sons of God if they choose, which would be "to put instead of a present effect, a power which is held in uncertainty and suspense." The word "power," Calvin argues, really means "fitness" ($\iota\kappa\alpha\nu\acute{o}\tau\eta\varsigma$) after the analogy of Col. i. 12, and power in this sense comes only to those who already have faith. The privilege in question is already theirs, not merely the liberty of choice regarding it. God gives faith, and faith brings with it all the blessings that are contained in Christ.

To penetrate a little further into the matter, this God-given faith mediates God-given righteousness, that is, the status of justification. Justification to Calvin consists solely in forgiveness of sins.[1] The condition of being

---

[1] As against Osiander, who held that forgiveness was an essential pre-condition of justification.

forgiven is the state of righteousness of which Paul speaks as the gift of God. It is not to be regarded as a reward bestowed upon faith, but as an immediate experience of faith. Faith indeed is not the precondition of forgiveness; it is that God-worked experience itself. The birth of faith and the assurance of forgiveness coincide.

This faith is the sole, as it is the sufficient, attestation of the eternal predestination of God, while it is also the medium by which it receives realisation. To eliminate it on the ground that the choice of God is in itself determinative and final and has no relation to anything in man, is sheer madness and overturns the force and effect of predestination. If we cannot penetrate to the reason of the divine decrees, we have in the presence or absence of faith a sure test of the distinction between the elect and the rejected.

While Calvin reiterated that men were chosen for nothing in themselves, either in the way of merit or capacity, he as vehemently insisted that the favour of God did not just mean the bestowal of favours. If election was not conditioned by holiness, it eventuated in a holiness that was at least recognisable and appreciable. No man dare presume on the assurance of election to continue in sin. To do so would be in itself a convincing disproof of the correctness of his assurance. If election was the root in eternity, holiness was the fruit in time. Election is unto eternal life, and eternal life means holy life from the moment it is bestowed. If it is not immediately realised holiness, at least the seeds of it are there and prove themselves by the indefatigable endeavour after holiness which results from the operation of the Holy Spirit in the heart. In working out our own salvation, it is God that is working to fulfil His ultimate eternal purpose. The truly elect have ever God within them and His holiness is the constantly impelling dynamic of their life. For the elect to do what they like, is to do what God likes. The Decalogue is not rescinded; with all its implications it is kept in the forefront of Calvin's teaching. In his Catechisms it follows immediately after the Creed " because good works have faith for their principle." It was a Calvinist who formulated the paradox, " one should live as though there had

PREDESTINATION

been no Gospel and die as though there had been no law." It is not to a life of safe and easy comfort that the elect are called, but to one which involves unceasing struggle with much fear and trembling and a continual sharing in the sufferings of Christ. It may be said that Calvin was nothing less than passionately concerned to make this plain, and the urgency with which he pushed the doctrine of election into the foreground or his indisposition to let it retire into the background may be partly explained by his anxiety lest it should become a stumbling-block or a snare to those who misread it, wilfully or otherwise, either rejecting it as an incitement to evil living in others or embracing it as making their own evil living a matter of no concern, so rendering the election of God compatible with the service of the devil.[1]

VII

No one was more keenly aware than Calvin of the insoluble perplexities surrounding this doctrine. Any one who seeks to satisfy his curiosity, he warns us, will find himself in a labyrinth, out of which he can find no way.[2] Nevertheless he faced all objections and offered such answers or solutions as he could. The consideration of these will help to clarify and illuminate his teaching and give sharper definition to his views.

The objection was inevitable that if God exercised choice irrespective altogether of what men were or solely because He willed so to choose, He stood convicted of an irrational partiality and a capricious arbitrariness unworthy of Him. Not so, replied Calvin; to assert that is to misjudge the whole situation and prove that the relation between God and man has not been properly grasped. Consider the

[1] "I know that we must distinguish between the person and the abominable and cursed see (the papal chair). But it seems to me that they who pray by name for him who bears such a mark of reprobation must have a great deal of leisure." (Quoted by Henry, ii. 332 note.)

[2] Calvin strongly deprecated looking into the mystery; it can only bring pain and madness, he said. We should be content with the evidences by which God confirms certainty; the believer should not concern himself about anything else; the reprobate will not concern himself about the matter at all. Cf *Comm. Rom.* ix. 14, also on *Ephes.* i. 4.

state of things. On the one side, a race of men every one of whom is the willing servant of sin. On the other side, a holy God who has appointed laws to be observed on pain of penalties, temporal and eternal. What is demanded of God in dealing with the race of men? Would it be consistent with Himself, would it accord with His position, to treat sinful men as though His laws were non-existent? Would that not rather convict Him of caprice or of changeableness unworthy of Him? Would that not be to disestablish His authority, to render insecure the foundations of His throne of righteousness? All men were rightly under sentence of doom; to absolve or reprieve some on the ground of Christ's merits was not to exhibit partiality, but mercy. That is the salient characteristic which is stamped upon God's sovereign act. The reprieve of some gave an opportunity for the display of that side of the divine nature, that facet of it, which along with all the others combines to make up the glory of God whose showing forth was the final end of all things. The thing to be astonished at to Calvin's mind, lay not in reprobation but in election. In view of all the circumstances, it was a matter for amazed adoration that God should have saved any at all.

But, granted that in this God's mercy was wonderfully displayed, why did He not save all? Would that not have enhanced His glory still more? And if it be true that the saved are in no wise morally different from or of more spiritual merit than the rest, would not the choice of some and the rejection of the rest argue irrational caprice in the divine nature? When pressed, Calvin is ready to admit that appearances give ground for such a charge. But he simply denies that God can do anything irrational, however it may seem so to us. Good reasons there must be, sufficient for Himself, to justify the determinations of His will in each particular case. He affirms the justice of Augustine's contention that "it is acting a most perverse part to set up the measure of human justice as the standard by which to measure the justice of God." As to the larger question, he again resorts to the idea of the only necessity (if it can be called such) laid upon God, that of making all His counsels in their totality exhibit the glory of His nature. Without reprobation in addition to election, how would the greatness of His mercy appear? It is rejection which throws into relief the fact that God acted according to the good pleasure of His will, which proved to demonstration that He was *sui juris* a law unto Himself. To have adopted all as sons would have made it seem as if God owed this to men, as if He felt somehow bound to do this. But He owes nothing to any one,—that is the primary consideration to be kept in view. He owes it only to Himself to do whatever He does. Calvin reiterates that God must assert and vindicate His righteousness, must protect it from risks of wanton violation. He must to this end "make an example." Law is honoured not more by the observance than by the penalty. The convict in the cells pays his tribute to it as does the irreproachable citizen in the streets. The claims of righteousness would lose their force if He, whose will determined its laws, set all offenders free.

If you ask why God created the reprobate at all, Calvin refers you again to the necessities of the exhibition of His glory. He commits himself at least once to the view that even for them life was a good thing. To have created Judas, he says, was good of God, life being "an invaluable gift of God." (Harmony of Gospels, III. on Mark xiv. 21.)

To the question, Why preach the Gospel at all if all destinies are settled from all eternity? he answers that God works always by means, and He has chosen that men should be saved by the Gospel. As for the reprobate, the Word preached to them has another use. Though it effects no amendment, it impinges upon their consciences and renders them more inexcusable in the day of judgment. Sometimes they do receive a measure of enlightenment, but as they refuse to walk in the light, God, in just punishment for their ingratitude, "abandons and smites them with great blindness." (Instit. III. xxiv. § 8.) The preaching of the Gospel to them brings into relief their hardheartedness and wilful stubbornness against God and so renders them the more inexcusable.[1] So by the appeals, precepts and promises of the Gospel, God "takes the ungodly to witness how unworthy they are of His kindness," for they can impute "the hardness of heart to none but themselves." (Instit. II. v. § 5.)

---

[1] Sermon on Job xxxvi. 15-19.

VIII

But a more perplexing difficulty emerges. Calvin consistently assigns reprobation to two causes, the will of God and the sin of man. The sin of a man however was not the ultimate reason of his rejection, but its justification. Rejection preceded actual sin; it was an eternal decree of God. Sin was the consequence of that decree, being itself decreed to provide justification for the divine rejection.[1] Now the sinful and guilty condition in which every soul was born into the world was inherited by the express appointment of God. So the state of all men was traced back to the Fall of the first man. Calvin was compelled to attribute this Fall also to the divine decree. It had to take place if the eternal divine counsels were to be realised by which the Divine glory was to be manifested in all its fulness.[2] That could not depend on a 'perhaps'; the Fall must have been a definite moment in the development of the divine plans. It was not merely foreseen but deliberately foreordained. In a sense Adam might have kept his innocence; that had been a possibility. If he fell, it was by his own fault; nevertheless it was written in the book of Providence that he should fall; he could not escape that moral disaster; his Fall was at once a penalty and a doom. "I am free to confess," Calvin said in a letter, "that I have stated that God not only has foreseen but also foreordained the Fall of Adam, which I maintain to be true, not without good grounds and evidences from holy writ." He refused to shelter this stark assertion behind some distinction between God's permission and His volition. God cannot permit what He does not will. So he sums up the matter in a sentence, Cadit igitur homo Dei providentia sui ordinante, sed suo vitio cadit.[3]

---

[1] Letter, Oct. 6, 1552.

[2] "It is certain that (the decree of the Fall) was just because He saw that His own glory would thereby be displayed." (Instit. III. x i i. §8,)

[3] Cf. West. Conf. chap. v. § 4 : "The almighty power, unsearchable wisdom, and infinite goodness of God, so far manifest themselves in his providence, that it extendeth itself even to the first fall, and all other sins of angels and men, and that not by a bare permission, but such as hath joined with it a most wise and powerful bounding, and otherwise ordering and governing of them, in a manifold dispensation

(Man therefore falls by the providential ordinance of God Himself, yet he falls by his own fault.) (Instit. III. xxiii. § 8.)

But wherein is the justice of punishing men for what they cannot help? If every link in the chain of things which leads from the eternal purpose through the Fall and inherited sin to damnation is forged by the hand of God so that it may not be broken, how can the righteousness which dooms sin to penalty be squared with the decree which ordained that man should be such that he could not be otherwise than what he is? A man cannot help being born, and being born he cannot help being what he is. Then can he be said in any sense to deserve anything which can be properly called punishment?

Here we come upon one of the most elusive elements in Calvin's system, resulting from his attempt to escape from the apparent irreconcilability of the two positions he takes up,—that man could not help being what he is and inevitably incurs the penalty attached to inevitable sin, while yet he must be regarded as in some wise responsible for his sin and therefore as meriting his condemnation. Fate masters him and yet he is master of his fate.

The solution, so far as it can be considered a solution, Calvin found in his view of the condition of the human will. Of free-will he held that there was no trace. The only time when it might be reasonably asserted to have existed was in Adam before the Fall. His unsmirched nature was then such that alternatives of good and evil were open to him. He was as much at liberty to choose the one as the other, for he exercised the power of free self-determination. That is involved in such a conclusion as that " Adam could have stood if he would, since he fell merely by his own will."[1] "God furnished the soul of man with a mind capable of discerning good and evil, and of discovering by the light of reason, what ought to be pursued or avoided.

to his own holy ends; yet so as the sinfulness thereof proceedeth only from the creature, and not from God; who, being most holy and righteous, neither is nor can be the author or approver of sin."

The Cumberland Presbyterian Confession adopts the position that God has decreed " to bring to pass what shall be for his own glory," and adds, " sin not being for God's glory, therefore He hath not decreed it." (v. Schaff's *Hist. Creeds*, i. 816.)

[1] Instit. I. xv. § 8.

... To this He annexed the will, on which depends the choice. The primitive condition of man was ennobled by these eminent faculties; he possessed reason, understanding, prudence and judgment, not only for the government of his life on earth, but to enable him to ascend even to God and eternal felicity. To these were added choice, to direct the appetites, so that the will was entirely conformed to the government of reason. In this integrity man was endowed with freewill, by which, if he had chosen, he might have obtained eternal life." (Instit. I. xv. § 8.) Nevertheless there is no reality in the freewill thus attributed to man, inasmuch as God had decreed the Fall, and therefore must have in some wise already biased Adam's will. It was not left in neutral equilibrium, nor was his future ever in suspense or uncertainty. It was certain that sooner or later Adam would fall into evil, and with that inevitable Fall there disappeared every trace of the freewill which man may have had. From that time the will became corrupt along with the whole of the nature. Man no longer possessed the capacity to choose between good and evil.[1] His choice was predetermined by the condition of his nature which was wholly "sold under sin." He could not choose good because he would not. Calvin descried a grave peril in the very use of the term 'freewill' as suggesting an idea corresponding to some supposititious actuality, and so confusing the issues while making it appear that man could if he would, and that he could will good if he liked. That was to threaten the foundation of the whole doctrine of the grace of God as the only cause and agent of salvation and so indirectly and implicitly to impugn the sovereignty of God. To assert as Bolsec did, that "all men are endowed with freewill so that the power of obtaining salvation is placed at their disposal" is " to tear predestination up by the roots."[2] Therefore Calvin was strongly of the opinion that the abolition of the term 'freewill'

[1] "If man possesses both of these (free power of judging and of willing), then Attilius Regulus, shut up in a barrel studded with nails, will have a will no less free than Augustus Caesar ruling with imperial sway over a large part of the globe." (Instit. II. iv, § 8.)

[2] In the Confession of Faith adopted by the English congregation at Geneva and received and approved by the Church of Scotland, it is declared to be the duty of the magistrate to "roote owt all doctrine

would be of great advantage to the Church. " I am unwilling to use it myself," he says, " and others, if they take my advice, will do well to abstain from it."

The will, then, being in this condition of inability to move in any direction but towards evil, what was the inevitable conclusion? That man of necessity sinned, it might be said. With this Calvin would be in hearty agreement so long as the word ' necessity ' is carefully defined. No suggestion of compulsion must be imported into it.[1] The ' necessity ' flows from the fact of man's nature being what it is: he sins necessarily, but at the same time voluntarily.[2] He cannot help sinning because he is not disposed to do anything else. His sin is therefore spontaneous, being the result of the exercise of a will invariably following its native disposition towards evil.[3] He acts spontaneously because he wills what he does, but never freely because his will is the bond-servant of sin.

It may make Calvin's position clearer if we quote the distinction drawn in his treatise *contra* Pighius between the four sets of terms, (1) a constrained will, which he pronounces a contradiction in terms, (2) a freewill, which has the power to choose between good and evil, (3) a voluntary will, which inclines of itself one way or another and is not forced or drawn against its nature, (4) an enslaved will, which is held captive by evil desires so that it can only choose evil, not being forced to do so, but exercising its own choice. This last is what must be attributed to man. By way of illustrating how necessity can be the same time spontaneity, he instances God Himself who is necessarily good but whose will is not hindered thereby from being free to do good.

of devils and men," and amongst other items of that doctrine is mentioned " freewyll."

[1] " If force be opposed to freedom, I acknowledge and shall always affirm that there is a freewill, a will determining itself. Let the will be called free in this sense, that is, because it is not constrained or impelled irresistibly from without but determines itself by itself, and I will no longer dispute." (*Contra* Pighius.) " A thing may be done voluntarily, though not subject to free choice." (Instit. II. v, § 1.)

[2] Cf. " Video meliora proboque, Deteriora sequor " (Ovid's *Metamor.* vii. 20).

[3] " It is not always in man's power to be good, and then he is willingly evil." (Aristotle, quoted by Calvin in *contra* Pighius.)

On the other hand, the devil acts under no compulsion but because it is his nature so to act. (Instit. II. iii. § 5.)

In all this Calvin largely followed the lead of Augustine, his teacher and master in so many things. As he himself pointed out, "this distinction between necessity and compulsion was no new thing. It was as old as Augustine, but was shut up in cloisters of monks for almost a thousand years." He accuses Peter the Lombard of having overlooked the distinction and given rise to a pernicious error,— the French edition of the Institutes adding, "namely that man could avoid sin because he sins freely." (Instit. II. iii. § 5.) If Calvin echoes Augustine, he anticipates such a modern psychologist as Wundt, who defines liberty (in its psychological aspect) as "the absence of constraint but not of causes." Provided constraint is limited to that which is external, and excludes that which arises from the essential nature, Calvin would accept that as a satisfactory summing up of his view.

On such a view of the spontaneous nature of sin, man cannot be acquitted of guilt. He must be held responsible for the evil he commits inasmuch as he does it by his own will, not under any outward compulsion but because of the disposition of his nature to which he has willingly yielded. He sins by choice not by constraint. This is Calvin's answer to the theoretic objection that there can be no responsibility for that which comes to pass by the divine decree. He appeals to experience, offering a psychological analysis of the springs of action and showing that "alongside the divine decrees and in spite of them we have the means and the possibility of acting ourselves."[1] He does not succeed in proving that this measure of self-determination is anything but the appearance of real liberty. Howsoever it may seem that man does what he chooses, the hand of God is on him all the time. If he is not a mere automaton, at least in the last analysis he only moves at the bidding of God's will. Nor does Calvin carry the question further back to the decree that issues in birth. Man had no choice at least as regards his entrance into this world nor as regards the nature with which he entered it.

[1] Bohatec, Calvin's *Vorsehungslehre*, p. 363.

On Calvin's own showing that nature cannot do other than sin from the very first. Man cannot even try to be good, because neither the will nor the desire is in him, so totally corrupt is he. Can responsibility in any proper sense be attached to acts which cannot but be of a certain moral quality because of the nature being what it is by no fault of the sinful party, a nature which inevitably works out in a certain way? Can you blame a child for being an imbecile, for being born with a defective brain, or for limping when one foot is shorter than the other? If Calvin does not evade that difficulty, he seeks to escape it by again appealing to experience backed by Scripture. He invokes the witness of conscience which plainly pronounces us to be answerable for our conduct. Can any one deny, he asks, that his sin is the outcome of his own evil will? There he leaves the matter. The reprobate are doomed by the eternal decree which inevitably takes effect, but at the same time they cannot deny that they justly suffer for what they have chosen to do.

If Calvin denies freewill in the natural man, he denies it also as emphatically in the man who is under grace. In this he differs from Augustine, who held that the Holy Spirit restored to man the power of willing good. He does good then of himself, his regenerate nature now disposing him thereto, and his freed will enabling him. Calvin, ever jealous for the glory of the divine grace, took a different view. The difference between the old man and the new consists in this, that the old man in every thought and act was moved by sin, the new man by God. Are not all good works declared in Scripture to be the gifts of the spirit of God? It is not as if we were assisted to do them by God. Nor is it as if the will were prepared by God and then left to run by its own strength, or that the power of choosing aright, "some indescribable kind of preparation or assistance," were bestowed upon us and we were afterwards left to make our choice. Paul affirms that we are God's workmanship and that everything good in us is His creation. In the regenerate, every single good work is God's as necessarily (in the same sense of the word) as in the natural man every act is sinful. God supplies the right will for the good He desires to be done in each particular instance.

Man may think he freely chooses good, but he really does so under the impulsion, if not the compulsion, of God. His will is no more free now than it ever was. What he has is what Calvin calls a right will, which would seem to be of the nature of a directive impulse communicated by God according to what He would have a man do, or withheld according to His good pleasure. This will is not resident in a man, not really part of his being, but a spiritual dynamic intermittently energising him according to God's will and according as His purposes demand the man's activity or passivity.

Calvin of course cannot maintain such a view consistently throughout all his writing. He is constantly betrayed into expressing himself in apparent, if not real, contradiction to it; but that is the position logically necessitated by all his teaching regarding predestination. Nothing in man accounts for his election or reprobation. Everything in man and his life is there by God's appointment. He can claim no merits, if he must admit demerits. What is good in him is wholly of God, as what is evil in him is his own. Man as he is born cannot help being bad; as redeemed, he can as little help seeking good. Grace bestowed gives both impulse and power. The glory is all God's.

IX

It is scarcely to be wondered at (as Beza says) that " the report went everywhere that Calvin made God the author of sin and persecuted to blood whoever contradicted such an impiety." That belief was indeed shared by many leaders of the Reform party and occasioned coolness and even estrangement on the part of many friends, amongst them Bullinger and de Falais. The feeling of mistrust which simmered in a more or less considerable section of the French congregation at Geneva was accentuated by the publication of volumes of extracts from his writings wrested from their context and so made to convey the desired unfavourable impression. No one who has struggled to grasp the intricacies and subtleties of his elusive doctrine will deny that there was good ground for the general failure to understand it. Objectors must have felt that Calvin constantly evaded them. They seldom seemed to find him at the point of their attack but somewhere else setting up defences against objections which were at least not theirs. They would have said that he was a master in the art of confusing or dodging the adversary. Even Melanchthon wishes that "what concerns necessity according to the perpetual decree of the divine will" had not been written, objecting that it was imprudent to say that the crime of Nero had been necessarily committed. At another time he writes, "in Geneva will they revive Stoic fatalism, and whoever does not agree with Zeno is thrown into prison." This last accusation Calvin indignantly repudiated, pointing out that the Stoics subjected even God to necessity, while "we make Him Lord and Master in full liberty," and insisting upon his fundamental position that back of all happenings were the holiness, justice, and love of God. (Instit. I. xvi. § 8.) But however he sought to clear himself of the suspicion, so damning to his whole system if true, that he made God the author of sin, he resolutely stood by the doctrine summarily asserted in Prov. xvi. 4, The Lord hath made everything for its own end, yea, even the wicked for the day of evil. (Comm. Rom. ix. 18.)

After Calvin's day, the doctrine, which had been handled by him as one primarily of indispensable usefulness for the religious life, came into the arena of pure theological discussion. Protestant scholasticism sought to give it a rigid dogmatic framework, and in the process of giving it precision, many subtle differences emerged which accentuated its inner perplexities. Controversy arose over the question as to the order of the divine decrees. Those who came to be known as the supralapsarians held that God, as a means to His own glory, conceived of a human race of certain definite dimensions out of which He would save some while dooming the rest. Then He decreed to create those who ideally existed in His mind as already elect or reprobate. Following upon this creation, there was to be a Fall. That is to say the elect were chosen from a number of men whose actual existence was as yet only projected. Those who took the so-called infra- or sublapsarian view held that the decree of predestination was subsequent to the decree permitting man to fall. In that case it is man as actually created and fallen who is the object of election. The order of the decrees was then (1) to create man, (2) to permit him to fall, (3) to elect certain men out of the mass of the fallen and justly condemned race to eternal life and to reject others, leaving them to the righteous consequence of their sins.

Calvin himself, ever imbued with practical religious aims and dogmatic only when authorised by Scripture, seems to have given the question little definite thought.[1] His position is certainly sufficiently undefined to allow of both parties claiming him as sponsor for their view. He professed to have a hearty dislike for subtleties, as he once told Beza, and this was essentially the kind of matter over which he would be indisposed to waste time. Logical he was, but logic became an irrelevancy and irreverence when it attempted to penetrate audaciously into the realm of ultimate divine mysteries. So little importance did he appear to attach to the question that he subscribed to and indeed inspired two Confessions whose terms might bear a contrary significance in regard to this point. The Consensus Genevensis (1552) assumes the supralapsarian view, while the French Confession, of which Calvin was practically the author, is infralapsarian in affirming that God chose out of the universal corruption and damnation in which all men were submerged some to eternal life. Cunningham stoutly asserts that the latter more truly represents the Reformer's real opinion, yet it is significant that Beza, who so largely echoed Calvin, was a supralapsarian. Schaff suggests that the English A.V. shows signs of Beza's

---

[1] All that Calvin was concerned to establish was that the observed division between men into believing and unbelieving was to be traced back through the Fall to the decree of God which brought about the Fall, without which His eternal decree of election would have had no point. Perhaps he comes as near to a pronouncement on the matter in the following statement as anywhere : " Before the creation of the first man, God had resolved by an eternal counsel what He wished to happen concerning the whole human race. By this secret counsel of God it came about that Adam lapsed from the state of integrity of his nature, and by his lapse drew upon all his posterity the sentence of eternal death." (Quoted by Scheibe, *Calvin's Prädestinationslehre* p. 89.)

PREDESTINATION

influence in its adoption of his rendering of texts bearing on the matter, such as Acts ii. 47, where it follows his Greek version, translating "the Lord added to the Church such as should be saved," (as though it were τοὺς σωθησομένους instead of τοὺς σωζομένους). In the same way it betrays its bias in adopting Beza's Latin version of Heb. x. 38, translating, "if any man draw back," instead of "if he draw back," so avoiding an argument against the doctrine of the final perseverance of the saints which is involved in that of election.

The Westminster Confession attempts a compromise in this as on so many other points, assigning the Fall of Adam to a permissive decree, but nevertheless including it in the eternal purpose of God who ordered it for His own glory. It is highly probable that Calvin himself would have objected to such phraseology. He declined to accept the distinction between the permission of God and His volition, on the ground that God cannot permit what He does not will; to permit is for Him synonymous with willing.

Later scholastic Calvinists sought to allay the repulsion engendered by their master's stark and uncompromising assertion of reprobation as resulting from the express divine and eternal decree. They tried to eliminate from the doctrine what was repulsive by stating it in a negative way, characterising God's act as of the nature of a "praeteritio" (passing over) or an "indebitae gratiae negatio" (the denial of unmerited grace) in contradistinction from "praedamnatio" or "debitae poenae destinatio" (appointment to merited punishment). That is, God did not expressly decree the doom of the unsaved but simply passed them over. This is the term adopted by the Westminster Confession.[1] The Gallic and the Belgian Confessions find a still milder term with a more inoffensive significance in "laisser," "relinqui," that is, to leave in the natural state of condemnation. Calvin would again have declined to see any real distinction. To pass by the

---

[1] v. chap. iii. § 7 : "The rest of mankind, God was pleased, according to the unsearchable counsel of his own will, whereby he extendeth or withholdeth mercy as he pleased, for the glory of his sovereign power over his creatures, to pass by, and to ordain them to dishonour and wrath for their sin, to the praise of his glorious justice."

reprobate was equivalent to permitting them to suffer the merited penalty of their sins, and with God permission amounts to volition. The only thing the distinction had to say for itself was that praeterition consigned the fact to the realm of mystery, while praedamnatio was vindicated by the sin that justified it. As Shedd puts it, "the reason of praeterition is unknown; the reason of damnation is sin."

X

From Calvin's own day onwards, as might be expected, the doctrine of predestination as taught by him made widely different impressions. In its completeness, it was simply submitted to by many out of loyalty to the authority of Scripture and under the compulsion of Calvin's logic. Others, while unable to deny or refute the accuracy and legitimacy of his conclusions, deprecated the obtrusion of the reprobation side of the doctrine, urging that it should be numbered amongst things better left to the secret counsel of God. But Calvin's own insistence upon the whole truth, as he regarded it, concentrated the attention of unfriendly eyes upon the "decretum horribile," and drew upon the whole doctrine hearty denunciation and upon himself, as its sponsor, vehement execration. Charles Wesley in a later day gives expression to the sentiment rife ever since the rage of controversy broke out.

> " Increase (if that can be)
> The perfect hate I feel
> To Satan's HORRIBLE DECREE,
> That genuine child of hell;
> Which feigns Thee to pass by
> The most of Adam's race,
> And leave them in their blood to die,
> Shut out from saving grace."

> "O Horrible Decree,
> Worthy of whence it came!
> Forgive their hellish blasphemy,
> Who charge it on the Lamb."

John Wesley entered the lists as the uncompromising

antagonist of the doctrine in any shape.[1] He called it " a doctrine full of blasphemy," because "it represents our blessed Lord as a hypocrite, a deceiver of the people, a man void of common sincerity, as mocking his helpless creatures by offering what he never intends to give, by saying one thing and meaning another." He was accustomed to put his objections in this compendious form : " the sum of all this is then ; one in twenty, suppose, of mankind are elected ; nineteen in twenty are reprobated. The elect shall be saved, do what they will ; the reprobate shall be damned, do what they can." Doubtless this is how the matter appears to most of those who abhor the doctrine, and there are utterances of Calvin which might seem to justify such a statement of it. But Wesley unfairly created prejudice by repeatedly attributing a notion to Calvinists of which they may well claim innocence. There is nothing in what Calvin at least ever said to give rise to the idea that the proportion of the saved to the reprobate according to his mind would be one to nineteen (to use Wesley's figures). No assertion as to the possible proportion was ever made, and it is open to the Calvinist to believe that the majority of the human race may be saved. There is nothing in Calvinism to hinder any one who embraces it from holding that all dying in infancy may be given a place amongst the blest. As for the rest of Wesley's indictment, it must be observed that he did not do justice to Calvin's position, that instead of the elect being saved, do what they will, God had foreordained means to the end He purposed regarding them, namely, faith in Christ, true repentance, holiness, and perseverance. Wesley's suggestion that the elect might deliberately continue in a state of ungodliness and unbelief to the last implies an impossible supposition. As for the reprobate being doomed, do what they can, Calvin would deny that they ever make any effort after such a life as might conceivably deserve the reward of their being transferred to the class of the elect. As a matter of fact, they establish no claim to a revision of their sentence by successful

---

[1] " I reject," said Wesley, " the assertion that God might justly have passed by me and all men as an evil, precarious assertion, utterly unsupported by Scripture." To which Calvin would answer that in that case the Gospel was of debt and not of grace.

endeavour to live a sober, godly, and righteous life. Of course, Wesley might find justification for his description in the admission of Calvinists that the reprobate fail to live as they ought because they are not granted the divine grace which would enable them to do so.[1] But Calvin refused to go behind the plain fact that the life of the reprobate, voluntarily so spent, justified their doom.

A common charge was that Calvin had reintroduced under a Christian mask the fatalistic teaching of Stoicism. Even Melanchthon, as has been seen, gave countenance to that idea. Calvin repudiated it, pointing out the fundamental difference that, while Stoic fatalism was based on the assumption of a mechanical, irrational, impersonal necessity operating to bring about inevitably all that happens, his doctrine rested on the belief in a personal God, presiding over the world and all destinies, ruling the hearts and wills of men and directing them according to His good pleasure, so that in whatsoever they undertake, they effect what He has appointed. Behind the necessity of fatalism, there is an iron chain of cause and effect which cannot be broken, traceable to no ultimate responsible Person. Behind the apparent necessity of predestination there was the will of a Being, perfect in wisdom, goodness, holiness, justice, and love.

XI

In spite of all that was said against it, the doctrine of predestination entered into the bone and marrow of the Calvinistic Church, and exercised a profound influence upon its progress. It was peculiarly fitted to the needs of the age, when perils on all hands threatened the life of loyalty to the truth. It needed courage of no mean order to join the meagre fighting-line of those arrayed against the unscrupulous and pitiless hosts of Rome. The duty of testimony was felt to be a primary one, as in all such epochs of insurgent evangelicalism. Calvin's strenuous assertion of the doctrine was due in some degree at

[1] To the objection that "the reprobate lose their labour if they try to make themselves acceptable," Calvin answers, How can they try, when such endeavour comes only by election? (Instit. III. xxiii. § 12.)

least to his perception of the part it was fitted to play in making the kind of men that were needed. It inspired them with the unflinching courage displayed by Gottschalk of old, martyr for his belief, of whom it has been said that he " bore his fate with that fortitude and resignation which have at all times characterised these individuals or bodies of men who have adopted the doctrine of predestination."[1] It was on this doctrine that Calvin's wife stayed her heart when she had to leave her young children in a world so rife with perils to body and soul. There is much to be said for Michelet's opinion that the doctrine proved in practice "a machine for making martyrs." It was the inspiration, as it was the comfort, of Calvin's own soul, steeling his will and reassuring his heart with the conviction that he was only an instrument in God's almighty hand to do with as He pleased. The task was his, but the purpose was God's. No man ever had a more settled consciousness of mission than Calvin; like another John, he reckoned himself " a man sent from God." His place and function in the scheme of things was no matter of chance or contingency; it was assigned him in the counsels of eternity. He was necessary to God and no man could snatch him out of God's hand before his work was done. That consciousness and that assurance imbued him with a courage which lifted him above his natural timidity and with a masterfulness which was almost imperial, as it was often imperious. With this elated, confident spirit he infected thousands in all countries. Neither spiritual nor civil tribunals could daunt them or quench their invincible ardour. There was nothing of the braggart in them; if they boasted, it was in God. Nor did they wage the conflict as automata without mind or will of their own. Calvin never ceased to make the divine pity and mercy shine through the doctrine in such wise as to draw forth the spirit of grateful love and glad, self-sacrificing consecration in those who felt the vitalising touch of God upon their souls.[2]

[1] Hagenbach, *Hist. of Doctrine*, ii. 48.

[2] Motley, a Unitarian, bears this witness: "The doctrine of predestination, the consciousness of being chosen soldiers of Christ, inspired those Puritans who founded the commonwealths of England, of Holland, and of America with a contempt of toil, danger, and death which

Therefore it was that Calvin urged that the doctrine be insistently preached. He never failed to seize every opportunity that offered in the course of exposition to declare and extol it. Yet he uttered many cautions against injudicious, partial, and reckless modes of presenting it. He denounced any who would declare from the pulpit that those who do not believe are doomed to destruction. That, he perceived, is simply to encourage wickedness; "it is imprecation rather than doctrine."[1] He protested against assumptions being made as regards the destiny of any one in particular. "It is strictly forbidden us," he said, "to exclude any one from the number of the elect or to despair of him, as if he were already lost, unless it be a matter of certainty that he is condemned by the Word of God." But such certainty could seldom if ever be substantiated. Never in a calm moment would Calvin subscribe to the certain doom of any. His prayer for the Duke of Guise is worth many declarations as showing how little the thought of reprobation entered into his practical attitude towards others. He would definitely pronounce none castaway; that would be to anticipate presumptuously the final judgment of God, and his profound reverence would not let him even appear to do that. It is for ministers to press the claims of God with equal urgency upon all alike. Not the sinister, dark side of the doctrine, but the inspiring side should be presented. He would have heartily endorsed that counsel of the Westminster Confession: "The doctrine of this high mystery of predestination is to be handled with especial prudence and care, that men, attending to the will of God revealed in His Word, and yielding obedience thereto,

---

enabled them to accomplish things almost supernatural. No uncouthness of phraseology, no unlovely austerity of deportment, could, except to vulgar minds, make that sublime enthusiasm ridiculous, which on either side the ocean ever confronted tyranny with dauntless front, and welcomed death on battlefield, scaffold, or rack with perfect composure. The early Puritan at least believed. The very intensity of his belief made him, all unconsciously to himself and narrowed as was his view of his position, the great instrument by which the widest human liberty was to be gained for all mankind." (*Hist. of the United Netherlands*, iv. 548.)

[1] Instit. III. xxviii, § 14.

may, from the certainty of their effectual vocation, be assured of their eternal election. So shall this doctrine afford matter of praise, reverence, and admiration of God, and of humility, diligence, and abundant consolation to all that sincerely obey the Gospel." (Ch. iii. § 8.) No one more than Calvin himself justified the saying that "pious Calvinists preach like Arminians, as pious Arminians pray like Calvinists." To work as if all depended upon our efforts, is Arminian theory but equally Calvinistic practice. That we should pray as if all depended upon God, is the faith and teaching of Calvinism; but, whatever men say, it is also the ultimate conviction which brings Calvinist, Arminian, and the whole world of earnest souls humbly to the throne of grace.

CHAPTER VII

PROVIDENCE

It is a great deal easier to trust in Providence, hard as that sometimes is, than to arrive at a satisfactory theory of it. To establish a self-consistent doctrine, doing full justice to all the elements in the problems it involves and avoiding concealed inner contradictions, has been the endeavour of many but the achievement of none. Calvin's theory stands the tests of logic, given the acceptance of his premisses; but in the course of his writings he constantly gives expression to thoughts and views which are in flat opposition to his dogmatic assertions. Holding that whatever is, had to be, that it is impossible to escape from the iron chain of necessity imposed by the sovereign will of God, he nevertheless speaks as though man were yet a free agent, the occasion of contingencies, responsible for happenings which antagonise the divine will. The Christian theist is constantly confronted with this insoluble antinomy that all depends upon God and yet that much seems to depend on man.

I

Calvin's doctrine of Providence was an immediate corollary of his doctrine of Predestination. In the first edition of the Institutes they were included in one chapter, but in the later elaborate expansions of the work they were given separate treatment. Predestination defines the relation of God to the world; Providence is the working out in detail of that relation. Predestination fixes the gaze upon the eternal destinies; Providence deals with the links, minute as well as vast, in the chain of events which join up the pre-temporal decree with the execution of the final judgment. From eternity, to God's mind, there is no smallest link in that chain amissing. All happens as He appoints, so that His ultimate purposes cannot fail of accomplishment. The activity of His Providence ensures the fulfilment of His Predestination.

While Calvin uses the word Providence to signify that activity of God by which He works out His predestinating decrees, the term itself is not truly descriptive of his view. It suggests that God foresaw all that was to happen and provided that these happenings should be so utilised and guided as to work out His purposes. On that interpretation of the word, the events of time were in some wise independent of Him, being occasioned by causes and in ways not immediately attributable to Him. Had they been according to His will, they might have been different. He permits them, allows for them, and adapts Himself to them. With such a view of Providence Calvin was entirely at variance. He held that God did not merely foresee all that would happen but definitely decreed it. He foreknew it because He had appointed it to be.[1] This did not apply only to the general course of things but to its every detail. In particular, all the activities of spiritual beings are exactly what He has appointed. Not only every act but every thought, feeling, and emotion, is directly attributable to the divine will. "Men do nothing save at the secret instigation of God. They do not discuss and deliberate upon anything but what He has previously decreed with Himself and brings to pass by His secret direction." (Instit. I, xviii. § 1.) It is not that He merely empowers every action; He communicates the initial impulse and ensures that what He wills is done. "The devil and the whole train of the ungodly," he declares, "are, in all directions, held in by the hand of God as by a bridle, so that they can neither conceive any mischief, nor plan what they have conceived, nor, how much soever

---

[1] Cf. Westminster Confession, ch. iii. § 2, "Although God knows whatsoever may or can come to pass upon all supposed conditions, yet hath he not decreed anything because he foresaw it as future, or as that which would come to pass upon such conditions."

they may have planned, move a single finger to perpetrate it, unless in so far as He permits, nay, unless in so far as He commands." (*Ib.* § 11.) Behind the appearance of things, therefore, there is no real initiative or self-direction in man. In a sense true enough to Calvin's mind, all that is done, God does. History in its widest and largest sense exactly mirrors the mind and will of God. The Shorter Catechism accurately reflects Calvin's view in its assertion that " God's works of Providence are His most holy, wise, and powerful preserving and governing all His creatures, *and all their actions.*"

It is obvious that contingency of any description is absolutely excluded from a system based on this fundamental idea of God's relation to the world. There is no possible place for anything to which can be applied the terms accident or chance. There are no mere contingencies or possibilities relative to God; all is certainty. "Single acts are so regulated by God, and all events so proceed from His determinate counsel that nothing happens fortuitously." (Instit. I. xvi. § 4.) Calvin finds the conclusive witness in Prov. xvi. 33, which proves that the only thing which could be attributed to chance (the decision of the lot) is from God. "If all success is blessing from God," he argues in another place, "and calamity and adversity are His curse, there is no place left in human affairs for Fortune and Chance." (*Ib.* § 8.) Absolute inevitability is written upon all things.

II

While Calvin attributes all that happens to the immediate will of God, he recognises the place occupied by " second causes " in the execution of His will ; He operates through agents and instruments. It is not to be supposed that man is nourished by the grace of God alone and not by his own labour and industry, or that it is the pure grace of God which makes the earth fruitful, and not the heat or influence of the sun, or that " it is not bread that sustains and nourishes man, but the strength which God of His goodness puts into us." (Letter of Oct. 6, 1552.) It is because the " proximate causes " strike the eye, however, that men fail to see behind to the directive and determinative divine will. God employs the forces of nature as ministers of His Providence, but these do nothing of themselves. Even natural events do not happen mechanically or by a kind of mechanical necessity through the interaction of forces acting according to their respective laws. Every change is expressly ordained of God. The sun does not daily rise and set by " a blind instinct of nature," but is governed by God in its course. He argues from the great and unequal variations in successive seasons that " every single year, month and day is regulated by a new and special providence of God." (Instit. I. xvi. § 2.) The incalculable variations in the weather, too, do not occur because of the operation of natural law, but because God is adapting them to the working out of His purposes. He declares that it is to defraud God of His glory to suppose that He " allows of things being borne along freely according to the perpetual law of nature." As there is no chance, neither is there any natural necessity. The inevitability of the course of things is not due to the operation of a chain of causes necessarily producing certain effects assigned to them, but to the incessant operation of God's will working out His eternal decrees. " Thunder and lightning can do nothing simply of themselves, but God directeth them where He pleases." (Sermon on Job xxxvii. 1-6.) He adds, " if we once know this, we shall not be afraid of the thunder." So he says in another place, "Although the stars have their natural courses and properties, yet notwithstanding they be not driven by their own power, neither do they give influence to the world otherwise than as God commandeth them, so that they obey His sovereign dominion which He hath over His creatures." They have no " power of themselves to do either good or harm." (Sermon on Job xxxviii. 28 ff.)

The implication of all this was, that, if God's purposes always had reference to man, all happenings in nature were in relation to man, having immediate and intimate connection with man's state. Calvin's philosophy of Providence receives striking expression in a passage of his sermons on Job. " Whensoever a man hath any adversity, God knocketh at his door and provoketh him to think upon his sins. But the man makes none account of it, yea rather (which is worse) he sleepeth soundly in his adversity and fathereth it either upon this thing or upon that, and he will find some casual chance or other which he goeth a great way to seek, and never entereth into the examination of his own life. Therefore whereas we are subject to so many miseries and wants, let us learn to take the whole burden and blame upon ourselves and not charge either heaven or earth with it. As for example, when we see the weather distempered so that there cometh frost or thunder or hail, let us assure ourselves it is not the air that is so disposed of itself; or if there come a drought, it is not heaven that is so hardened of its own nature; or if the earth be barren, it proceedeth not of its own kind, but we ourselves are the cause of all."[1] It might seem from these words that man is directly responsible for natural occurrences and conditions,—an illustration of the difficulty Calvin found in avoiding utterances which seemed to be in contradiction to his basal doctrine. But such a passage must be read in the light of his comprehensive attribution of all the moral state of every man at any time to God, so that the sum-total of the things of man and nature was just the divinely pre-arranged correlation of nature and man. Man is as he is at any time because of the determining will of God. Nature is as it is at any time because of the moral state of man; but to ensure that this is so, its course is constantly shaped by the controlling will of God.

It was in entire consistency with this view that Calvin accepted the transient phenomena of nature as having immediate significance for man. These must have such a meaning otherwise they are meaningless; but they cannot be meaningless, seeing that they occur by the express will of God always with a bearing upon human affairs, present or future. The stars exerted influence upon mankind; comets had their message or their meaning. (Instit. I. xvi. § 2 f.) Intemperate rain and excessive drought were pregnant with heavenly warning or rebuke. So by way of his philosophy, Calvin arrived at the position of the ancient Hebrew prophets whose views on the relation of nature and man he most heartily embraced and endorsed.

[1] Sermon on Job v. 8-10.

Nevertheless, while holding these views, he did not commit himself like the astrologers to a tabulated scheme of the exact nature of the correspondences between natural phenomena and human affairs. He refused to assign a precise significance to particular celestial occurrences. This attitude rescued him from the superstitious notions rife in his age and shared even by such men as Melanchthon. He passed behind the portent to the holy, wise, and loving will which ordereth all things, and on it he rested without fear of evil.

According to this view, prayer and miracle must be regarded as preordained links in the chain of causation which effectuates the divine will. Prayer does not in any wise change the will of God or affect His purpose, but is itself instigated by God, as its answer or consequence has been eternally predetermined. If Scripture speaks of the 'repentance' of God consequent upon the penitent appeal of men, Calvin explains the word as an accommodation to our understanding, intended to indicate that there was a change in the divine procedure. From the first God intended what ultimately happened, only He used means to bring that about which gave to His attitude the appearance of repentance. For example, Nineveh was not to be destroyed; God only employed Jonah to bring about a repentance on the part of its people which would justify Him in sparing it in spite of His proclamation of doom, the reversal of the sentence, described as repentance on God's part, being in His plan. By the agency of Jonah, "he paves the way for His eternal decree, instead of varying it one whit either in will or in language." (Instit. I. xvii. § 13.) He finds proof in Isaiah xiv. 27 that the prayer of penitence occasions no alteration in the divine will.

As for miracle, in the common sense of the word, there is no such thing.[1] There is no rupture of the organic tissue of things by God to bring about whatever was

---

[1] Cf., however, West. Conf. ch. v. § 3, "God in his ordinary providence maketh use of means, yet is free to work without, above, and against them, at his pleasure." 'Means' here evidently includes 'laws of nature,' inasmuch as the instances quoted as illustrative of the phrase 'against them' are the incident of the iron swimming (2 Kings vi. 6) and that of the companions of Daniel passing unscathed through the fire (Dan. iii. 27).

demanded by needs or conditions for which no allowance had been made. No such conditions can ever arise. As there is no real freewill such as could occasion them or create contingency in any sense, all that does or will happen in the course of events is provided for in the divine plan. God may meet the demands of a given situation created by the moral state of man through what appear to be special interventions, but these are really only instances of His constantly acting providence, calculated and designed to strike the eye. To multiply loaves and fishes may be reckoned an extraordinary exercise of the divine power, but it is not a different species of divine act, irreducible to terms of common providence. The provision of the daily bread may rightly be reckoned as much a miracle as the raising of the dead to life. All is immediately of God.

III

It was inevitable that Calvin's view of Providence should at once draw forth the charge that he made God the author of all moral evil. If no single thing happens, except by His will, then all the sin with which the world is rife must be laid at His door. He is responsible for it as being its real cause. No proper guilt can attach to those who necessarily execute His will; that must be attributed not to the perpetrator who cannot do aught else, but to the prime instigator who calls the tune to which men cannot but dance. It must be admitted that this was the charge which Calvin found it hardest to meet.[1] He himself seems to be quite convinced while he is arguing, yet here and there he gives the impression of recognising that his defences are weak and even pierced, and that there is nothing for

---

[1] The Westminster Confession secures itself against the conclusions seemingly contained in the doctrine of predestination and providence which it asserts, by declaring that these are not true. God unchangeably ordained whatsoever comes to pass " yet so, as thereby neither is God the author of sin, nor is violence offered to the will of the creature, nor is the liberty or contingency of second causes taken away, but rather established." That is, the doctrine is what you *must* say of God; the inferences, however inevitable they may seem to be, are what you *cannot* say of God, and therefore they cannot be true.

it but to retire within the impregnable citadel of inerrant Scripture. Again and again he meets and rebukes dangerous attacks with passionate charges of blasphemous arrogancy and with earnest demands for humble and adoring acceptance of divine truth. His logic has carried him to a position from which he cannot resile or which he cannot evacuate without endangering his whole base of fundamental doctrine.

It may be well, first of all, to see how far Calvin admits the truth of the accusation that he makes God responsible for moral evil. He is compelled to confess that that is a necessary conclusion from his doctrine, and he frankly accepts it. He refuses to take refuge in the view that God simply allows sin,[1] after the manner of Melanchthon, who held that God does not wish sin but only permits it,— as in the case of Pharaoh, in regard to whom he views the words " I will harden his heart " as being a Hebrew way of designating a permission, not an efficacious resolve of God. Calvin practically echoed Zwingli, who taught an absolute Determinism, not hesitating to assert that thefts, murders, and all crimes must be attributed to God and are therefore divinely appointed. In the *Consensus Pastorum* compiled by Calvin, he insists that " God does not merely allow sin ; it happens actually by His will." He dubs the contrary notion " a frivolous excuse, a subterfuge, a dream." He dispels all doubt as to his meaning by instancing the case of a merchant straying from his companions in passing through a forest, falling amongst robbers, and being murdered. " His death," he says, " was not only foreseen by the eye of God, but had been fixed by His decree," though " these things appear to us fortuitous."[1]

Boldly accepting these as just conclusions from his doctrine, how does he evade or meet the charge of so making God the true culprit and indeed the only culprit ? How does he vindicate God's holiness in view of such a damaging admission ?[2]

He puts forward various considerations calculated to

[1] Instit. I. xvi. § 9.
[2] *v.* Summary treatment in Letter to the Seigneurs of Geneva regarding the case of Troillet.

provide qualifications which, while leaving God with the ultimate responsibility, yet absolve Him from being chargeable with anything like guilt. The most frequently reiterated of these is the reminder that the moral evil which He brings about is used by Him in the execution of holy and righteous purposes. The idea is not for a moment to be entertained that " God did to make himself pastime toss (human affairs) like tennis balls." It is always by God's righteous impulse that men do even what they ought not to do.[1] Thieves and murderers and other evildoers are instruments of divine Providence, being employed by the Lord Himself " to execute the judgments which He has resolved to inflict."[2] The treachery of Judas was divinely instigated for the furtherance of the plan of salvation. Sarah's quarrel with and casting out of Hagar was directed by a heavenly providence. " That Abraham should have been commanded to humour his wife entirely in this matter is no doubt extraordinary, but proves that God employed the services of Sarah for confirming His own promises. Although it was the revenging of a woman's quarrel, yet God did not the less make known His doctrine by her mouth as a type of the Church." (*Comm. Gal.* iv. 30.) In all such instances Calvin seeks to make it plain that the providences of God are always justified by the fact that He uses the wickedness He decrees for the accomplishment of ends that are perfectly righteous. Wickedness is determined by the intention, and that is what differentiates the evil man from God. The man is actuated by wrong motives, God always by pure and holy ones. An act of man, therefore, which in him is wicked, when conceived of as actuated by God, becomes for Him righteous. An act has no moral quality in itself; that is given relatively to the agent by the governing purpose and spirit. If more than one are responsible, it is quite possible that one person implicated may be thereby constituted a criminal, while another incurs no proper culpability; it may be right for one, wrong for the other. God works in, with, and through wicked men and wicked deeds, but they do not reflect wickedness upon Him, inasmuch

---

[1] Instit. I. xviii. § 4.   [2] *Ib.* I. xvii. § 5.

as the end they assist in achieving, purposed by Him, is holy.[1]

Some concrete examples given by Calvin will help to make his position plain. As illustrative of the simple principle that an act is good or bad according to the intention, he points out that a man may be blamed for killing an inoffensive and useful animal in an access of malice, but not for executing a murderer in accordance with the forms of justice. That however does not go to the root of the matter or touch the core of the difficulty. He succeeds better with another example. A son kills his father to gain an inheritance. God wishes the father to die, whether as a punishment or to save him dire suffering or from some such righteous or merciful motive. The two wills coincide. It is by the will of God that the father dies, but it is not by the will of God that the son *assassinates* the father. It is obvious, however, that this absolves God from complicity only on the assumption that He did not impel the son to the deed but simply foresaw its commission and took advantage of the crime to have His will concerning the father fulfilled (which implies that He *might have had* to employ other means). But if Calvin is not to contradict his emphatic assertion that God does not merely foresee or permit but ordains and appoints, then He must so act upon the son that he commits the deed wilfully, but none the less under the secret compulsion of God. That is to leave the matter exactly where it was, setting God in the relation to sin which demands vindication, if He is not to be judged responsible for it in such wise as to be culpable. Moreover, by his use of the word 'coincidence,' Calvin blurs the real problem. Why this coincidence? Why did it happen that the son's desire to do away with his father and God's will that he should die, coincide so that the commission of the crime fulfilled God's will exactly

---

[1] Cf. *My Lady of the Chimney Corner* (Alexander Irvine), p. 157. After a scrimmage which results in the starving Irish family having a good meal, Anna, the pious mother, speaks of " God bringing relief." Boyle, the cause of the disturbance, and the donor of the meal, says, " Anna, if aanybody brought us here th' night, it was th' ould divil in hell." " 'Deed yer mistaken," she answered sweetly, " When God sends a maan aanywhere, he always gets there, even if he has to be taken there by th' divil."

when God desired this thing to take place? Why might not God have had to wait for the fulfilment of His will? Calvin can only explain the coincidence on the ground that God brought about the crime by inspiring the son to the act which resulted in what He desired at that exact juncture. At another time he tries to find refuge from the inevitable conclusion by instancing a king whose soldiers in war commit acts of brutality, but who cannot be regarded as responsible for them. Calvin fails to notice that the analogy does not hold because of this, that in the one case no king can be held as controlling the acts of every soldier in his army, while in the other case, God (according to his doctrine) controls and appoints every act of every person.

Another example is provided by his treatment of the incident in the book of Job in which the patriarch's sons and daughters are murdered by robbers. Calvin seeks to reconcile the crime with the saying of Job which practically attributes it to the will of God. He points out that there are three parties to the deed, (1) God, who wishes to exercise His servant in patience, (2) Satan, who wishes to cast him into despair, (3) the robbers, who wish to enrich themselves. The evil intentions of the last two are transformed by the good intention of God into means for reaching a good end. "God," he says, "does not cause the evil wills, but He makes use of them as He wishes." Again it is apparent that Calvin fails to make his example square with his theory, inasmuch as he implicitly denies that God *occasions* the crime, and so he evades the very problem his doctrine raised, which was to reconcile with God's holiness an evil act instigated and willed by Him to take place.

Calvin was not unaware of this failure. To cover it up, he had recourse to a desperate piece of verbal juggling, worthy of a scholastic in extremity. He declares that God, simultaneously in diverse manners, wills and does not will that a thing should happen. Because he wills after one manner and does not will after another, the contradiction must be only apparent. If we cannot comprehend how that can be, it is due to our want of sense. What the murderer does is against God's will and yet not without His will. In spite of appearances, it is not to be thought that " God must have two contrary wills, decreeing by a secret counsel what He has openly forbidden in His law." (Instit. I. xviii. § 3.) God, he asserts, makes no pretence of not willing what He wills, but " while in Himself the will is one and undivided, to us it appears manifold, because, from the feebleness of our intellect, we cannot comprehend how, though in a different manner, He wills and does not will the very same thing." " Let us call to mind our imbecility," he exhorts, " and remember that the light in which He dwells is not without cause termed inaccessible, because shrouded in darkness."

Calvin indeed never faces up squarely to the crucial difficulty created by his doctrine. He quotes in his defence a saying of Augustine to the effect that " He who is good would not permit evil to be done, were He not omnipotent to bring good out of evil." (Instit. I. xviii. § 3.) That is a defensible position, but it is so by reason of the use of the word 'permit.' The problem arises for Calvin just because he refuses to allow that God merely permits; He always appoints, ordains, wills, causes. Doubtless it could be said that He who is good would not will evil to be done unless He were omnipotent to bring purposed good out of evil. But does that justify the evil means? Are we to suppose that God could not work out good ends without the deliberate use of moral evil, and that He could both cause and use that to which He Himself attaches guilt, while Himself remaining innocent? Is the law, which He has ordained to be observed by man on pain of penalties, not binding on Himself? It would seem that at the back of Calvin's mind lurked the idea of Zwingli, who said that God stood under no law; for Him there was no sin, but simply action. (He compares how a magistrate may take a man's life without committing a murder; he administers the law while practically violating it.) But a man stands under law and therefore incurs sin. " So far as it is of God to be author, mover, and impeller (of evil), there is no guilt; so far as it is of man, there is guilt. For He is not restrained by law, but the man is condemned by law. For what God does, He does freely, untouched by all evil affection, therefore also by sin."

IV

Another objection to Calvin's doctrine was based on the ground that it made all precautions useless. If all happenings are determined, then nothing that man could do would prevent them. Such an objection, of course, is pertinent to any theory of Providence. Every religious man believes in a Providence by which the will of God is done on earth as it is in Heaven. But if he relies upon God for his daily bread, none the less he works for it; if he trusts God for to-morrow, he does not condemn Savings Banks. A belief in a Providence to which every occurrence is attributed, might, logically applied, put an arrest on all purposive human activities. But the average man, however religious, does not allow himself to be reduced to helpless impotence by the dilemma. *Solvitur ambulando*. Calvin too met the difficulty by an appeal to the facts of experience and self-knowledge. "God," he says, "has furnished men with the faculties of deliberation and caution that they may employ them in subservience to His providence in the preservation of life"; and he drives the matter home by pointing out that "on the contrary, by neglect and sloth men bring upon themselves the evils which He has annexed to them." (Instit. I. xvii. § 4.) That is to say, the capacities and powers with which man is endowed are the agents by which God effects His purposes. Prudence and folly, he argues, are alike the instruments of the divine economy. In practice (*e.g.* in averting the dangers) it is "not our business to enquire what God has determined respecting us in His decree, but what He commands and enjoins on us, what our duty requires and demands, and what is the proper method of regulating our life." We must live as though all depended upon ourselves. He points out that Christ remained in Galilee to escape the murderous intentions of the Jews in Jerusalem. Logic must give place to commonsense. Calvin himself was ever ready with suggestions of the proper precautions which might be taken against danger, as in the letter to the church in Poitou. (Sept. 3. 1554.) By exercising our judgment and following the dictates of reason, we are doing the will of God, and in so doing His will, we are furthering His purposes. " The heart of a man deviseth his way, but the Lord directeth his steps " ; in these words of Wisdom Calvin found summed up a rule of life consonant with his deepest faith. It is in accordance with this working principle that he so far departs from his strict view as to content himself with the assertion that nothing can *finally* happen but what God has before ordained. Whatever we may think about the means or steps, the end at least is predetermined exactly as it comes to pass.

V

The objection taken to the general doctrine of predestination, that it divests evil men of responsibility, seeing that they cannot help being what they are, hits still more forcibly at a doctrine of Providence which holds that every single act and happening is decreed. If God willed that a man should do evil for the furtherance of His purposes, how can any blame attach to him? In reply, Calvin falls back upon the distinction between a thing being done of necessity and by compulsion. The evil a man does, he is not forced to do. He does it spontaneously, the necessity arising from his nature being what it is. He cannot do other because he will not do other. You might as well expect him to will one thing and do something else. Calvin therefore refuses to allow the fact that evildoers are instruments of Providence to form any excuse for their misdeeds. He also draws a subtle distinction, whose reality it is difficult to apprehend, when he asserts that evil happens according to God's will (else it would not happen), but not by His command. He warns against confusing ' will ' with ' precept ' or ' command,' and seems to argue that if a man acts according to God's will while violating His precept in so doing, he is inexcusable. (Instit. I. xviii. § 4.) The man knows he is breaking God's law, yet he does it, thereby incurring guilt. But in saying this, Calvin again puts out of sight his contention that an evil man would not do that unless at the impulse and instigation of God Himself who needs the man's act, wicked though it be, to secure His aims. It is one thing to say that God takes advantage of an evil act freely done, quite another to say that He prompts it to ensure the fulfilment of His purposes, decreeing it to be a link in the chain of events which lead to this issue.

It is to be noted that Calvin did not go the length of saying that the natural man never does anything which can be properly characterised as good, or that he never obeys God's will in the sense of obeying His precepts to the letter. What he held was that, if unregenerate men do obey God, their obedience is not of a kind which springs from " a voluntary affection " ; God's statutes are not their songs. (Cf. *Comm. Acts* ii. 23.) But further, he admitted the truth and reality of a distinction to which Luther latterly attached much importance, namely, between a man's freedom in things external, civil and moral, and his freedom in things properly spiritual, a distinction which was embodied in the Augsburg Confession. The outward appearance of an unregenerate person might be all that could be desired, but it was with him as it was with seemingly clear water flowing from a poisoned spring. In a sense different from what the poet intended, " the heart's aye, the part aye, that maks us richt or wrang." At other times Calvin regarded the good works of the wicked in a different light, reckoning that in things indifferent pertaining to this life, they are under the control of grace. They do good at the impulse of God, not at the impulse of their own nature ; it is really against the grain ; their heart is not in it.

Calvin found proof of Providence in the arbitrariness of the nature and amount of chastisement inflicted upon the good. It was not strictly proportioned to the fault or sin ; it was determined by a man's need of correction. There was no arithmetical or mechanical equivalence between sin and penalty. God administers just that punishment which He sees to be required in order to humble and purify. Calvin says of Job that God might have punished him much more sharply, and again that He often handles good men much more roughly than " such as are altogether unruly and make an utter scorn of God," not because of their sins, but to try them and make them to know whether they are wholly His or no. " For as long as things go on as we would have them, what know we whether we are forward to serve God or no?"[1] "If we will not bow to the corrections He sends us, we do nothing but continually double His strokes."[2]

VI

The practical worth of the doctrine in its absolute form appears from the conduct of those who held it, such as Luther and Calvin, compared with that of Melanchthon and others who allowed a large element of contingency in life. Luther once had to administer a vigorous rebuke to Melanchthon who was tormenting himself with continual cares at the time when the fate of Protestantism seemed to be hanging in the balance after the Diet of Augsburg. "I pray for thee," he wrote, "and am troubled at it that thou by troubling thyself with unceasing cares, makest my prayers of none effect for thee. . . . Thou thinkest to rule these things according to thy philosophy by reason, and killest thyself with immoderate cares about them, not considering that the cause is Christ's who, as he needs not thy counsels, so he will bring about his own ends without thy carefulness, thy vexing thoughts, and heart-eating fears, whereby thou disquietest thyself above measure."

His view of Providence was a spring of profound and inexhaustible comfort to Calvin. (Cf. Pref. to Pss.) It undoubtedly exercised a very practical influence on his own life, confirming his resolution and making his consecration wholehearted. Where duty plainly called, he followed with unfaltering step, believing that in that path nothing could happen to him but what was needed to further God's purposes. Ignorance of Providence he pronounced to be the greatest of miseries, and the knowledge of it the highest happiness. (Instit. I. xvii. § 11.) He speaks of the inestimable felicity of the pious mind amidst the perils and innumerable ills of life. "As (the believer) justly shudders at the idea of chance, so he can confidently commit himself to God. This, I say, is his comfort, that his heavenly Father so embraces all things

---

[1] Sermon on Job xxxiii. 8-14.   [2] Job xxxvi. 1-14.

under His power and so governs them at will by His nod, so regulates them by His wisdom, that nothing takes place save according to His appointment; that, received into His favour, and intrusted to the care of His angels, neither fire nor water nor sword can do him any harm, except in so far as God their master is pleased to permit." (Instit. I. xvii. § 11.) The godly man will draw confidence and strength from his faith in the divine appointments. "His confidence in external aid will not be such that the presence of it will make him feel secure nor its absence fill him with dismay as if he were destitute. His mind will always be fixed on the Providence of God." (*Ib.* § 9.) "Thunder and lightning can do nothing of themselves, but God directeth them where He pleases. If we once know this, we shall not be afraid of the thunder." (Sermon on Job xxxvi. 15 ff.) Such a belief gives assurance that all the mysteries of life must have a satisfying explanation, and that the ultimate triumph of good is as certain as that God is good.[1]

Calvin is keenly conscious of the utter mystery that enshrouds the working of Providence. Of this alone he is sure and on this certainty he constantly falls back, that God's will is invariably conjoined with wisdom, right, and love, that always He must have just and good reasons though we cannot see them now. On that firm faith he rests, and in eager hope he waits for the dawning of the day when the shadows shall flee away and all earth's hidden things be clear.

---

[1] Cf. Carlyle's story of David Hope, a small farmer on the Solway Firth. One year the harvest was very late, but at last it was ready for the leading in. After breakfast came family worship. David took the Book and was putting on his spectacles when some one came running in. "Such a raging wind has risen as will drive the stooks into the sea if they're let alone," he cried. "Wind!" answered David "wind canna get ae straw that has been appointed mine! Sit doon an' let us worship God."

CHAPTER VIII

THE CHURCH

I

IT has already been pointed out that Calvin insistently claimed to be in the true succession from the Pre-papal Church, the Church of the accredited Fathers and of the authoritative Creeds. He protested with the utmost vehemence against the idea that he and other seceders from the Roman communion had unchurched themselves.[1] He retorted the charge upon his opponents, holding as the chief justification for the Reformers' apparently schismatic action that the Papal body had ceased to be a true Church of Christ, though there might be and were within it many who belonged to that Church. It failed to satisfy the tests which every body claiming to be a Christian Church must pass. There was nothing indeed which Calvin was more eagerly concerned to do than to resuscitate the true idea of the Church and to restore a communion conforming thereto. He, no less than his adversaries, did obeisance to the grandeur and authority of the Catholic idea of it so impressively proclaimed throughout the Christian ages.[2] It may be said that the aim of his life's work was to give this idea form and substance corresponding to the pure pattern and exemplar set forth in Scripture. With such a deadweight of established privilege against him, with an

---

[1] Cf. Letter to du Tillet, Oct. 30, 1538.
[2] Said Beza to the King of Navarre, " Sire, it belongs to the Church of God, in whose name I speak, to endure blows rather than inflict them. But it will please your majesty to remember that she is an anvil that has worn out many hammers."

existing religious institution whose life was bound up with its theory and claims, in a world in which that which is, is always a compromise with that which should be, it is not surprising that he should have failed. But he succeeded in creating a Church which, if it was far from satisfying his own mind in constitution or practice, had yet within it the soul of the future.

Calvin was deeply imbued with a conception of the Church as rigid as that of his Catholic opponents. He would have cordially subscribed to the mediaeval dictum, *Extra ecclesiam, nulla salus*, 'Outside the Church, no salvation.' The Church was to him no amorphous, vaguely defined body, a haphazard collocation of individuals accidentally, temporarily, and loosely associated by reason of common beliefs or sympathies. It was not an institution towards which one might adopt an attitude of indifference, or with which a professing Christian might decline to enter into relations. To stand outside it was to cut oneself off from God's storehouse of the bread of life, for the Church was the sphere within which the grace of God exclusively operated. It was the sole reservoir and distributor of the blessings of the Gospel otherwise unattainable. Only by the forgiveness of sins was entrance into it to be gained,[1] for without pardon we can have no union with God. But "that benefit is so peculiar to the Church that we cannot enjoy it unless we continue in communion with the Church."[2] It is dispensed by the ministers or pastors either in the preaching of the Gospel or the administration of the Sacraments. This indeed is "the power of the keys which the Lord has bestowed upon the company of the faithful."

Calvin arrived at this view from the Pauline conception of the Church as the body of Christ, of which He is at once the head, the soul, and the life. It is the creation of His Holy Spirit, growing with the number of those whom He calls into its fellowship. To be in Christ, you must be within that body. Just as that which is not part of the body cannot claim to share its life, so no one outside the Church can receive life from Christ. He unites Himself with the individual only as he becomes a member of His

---

[1] Instit. IV. i. § 20.   [2] *Ib.* § 22. Cf. § 4 and *Comm. Rom.* xiii. 8.

Church, for it is only with the Church as such, and not with the individual, that Christ has promised to unite Himself. Luther was emphatically of the same opinion, holding that outside of the Church no man could come to the Lord Christ, and (going farther than Calvin, as we shall see) that outside of Christendom there could be and was no forgiveness of sin and no possible true holiness. In the view of these Reformers then, Christendom was coterminous with the Church. Where there was no Church there could be no Christians, for there the Holy Spirit was not present to teach, enlighten and convert. Standing on this ground, Calvin rebutted the claims of the 'fanatics,' aliens from the Church, who boasted of secret revelations imparted immediately to them by the Holy Spirit. The Spirit, he said, does not teach any but those who submit to the ministry of the Church, and consequently these others who reject the order which He has appointed are the disciples of the devil and not of God ; for " we see those two things, 'children of the Church' and 'taught of God' are united in such a manner that they cannot be God's disciples who refuse to be taught in the Church." (Comm. Isai. liv. 13.)

The Church is not only the creation of the Holy Spirit of Christ, brought into existence by the association of the elect, who are called and united with Christ ; it is the channel of His redemptive power. He does not work in a purely mystical, intangible way, but through this visible agency. Häring correctly interprets Calvin when he describes the Church as an association of believers through which, as God's instrument, He produces faith in men, and as such, it is really necessary to salvation. It is at once His product and His sole instrument. He brings it into being to realise His eternal election, making it the depositary and distributor of His gifts.

This view, however, Calvin found it impossible to maintain in its rigidity. It had to be regarded as no more than a general rule to which there might be exceptions. To admit any exception, of course, rendered nugatory all uncompromising assertions in the line of the saying, *Extra ecclesiam, nulla salus*. One exception was sufficient to explode the maxim, and the possibility of such was forced upon him by the doctrine of election. He could not withhold the admission that there might be many chosen and called of Christ who yet did not belong to His visible fold. He agreed with Augustine that "there are many sheep without the pale of the Church as there are many wolves within it." His doctrine found itself confronted by express and final declarations of Christ and His apostles and by instances in Scripture of the contrary. His real position is that expressed in the Westminster Confession, according to which out of the visible Church " there is no *ordinary* possibility of salvation."

His doctrine of baptism also logically made a breach in his doctrine of the Church. God's saving grace, according to the R.C. doctrine and that of Luther also, was mediated through baptism, by which the elect were initiated into the kingdom. Apart from it there was no salvation. But Calvin denied the absolute necessity of baptism to salvation, though regarding the rite as the appointed door into the Church, and thereby implicitly conceded that divine grace might savingly be in operation without the Church. While admitting this in a general way, he never seems to have explicitly applied it after the frank fashion of Zwingli, who boldly declared his conviction that such pious heathen as Socrates, Pindar, Zeno, Plato, Cato, Seneca, were within the kingdom, an opinion publicly asserted long before by the early Father, Justin Martyr. Bullinger, who succeeded Zwingli in his leadership, followed him in his belief in " extraordinary modes of salvation."

These exceptions, along with another possibility amounting to a practical certainty, compelled Calvin to adopt a distinction, first drawn by Zwingli, between the visible and invisible Church. The tests of a genuine Christian made it obvious that many within the visible Church, that is, numbered among those participating in its sacraments, could not by any stretch of charity be regarded as amongst the elect who were called to be saints. There were undoubtedly many wolves within the Church, "hypocrites who have nothing of Christ but the name and appearance, many persons, ambitious, avaricious, envious, slanderers, and dissolute in their lives, who are tolerated for a time, either because they cannot be convicted by a legitimate process or because discipline is not always maintained with sufficient rigour." (Instit. IV. i. §7.) Who exactly belong to this admixture of the reprobate was known, however, only to God. The remainder, along with the elect outside any organised body of Christians, constituted the invisible Church, which was therefore made up of the truly chosen, called, and sanctified. Invisible it was in the sense that its precise boundaries were indistinguishable to human eyes.

But the notion was extended to include not merely the mass of true Christians alive in this world, but all those who in any time or place belonged to the fellowship of Christ on earth or now to the communion of saints in heaven. It embraced all the elect who had lived from the beginning of the world, even those who had no historical knowledge of Christ and many who did not even know the true God but who were nevertheless nominated to life everlasting by the secret divine predestination. (Instit. IV. i. § 10.) The Westminster Confession again gives to the idea implied a precision that is wanting in Calvin when it includes amongst the saved " all elect persons who are incapable of being outwardly called by the ministry of the Word." This would apply to imbeciles and others incapacitated by reason of physical or mental infirmity from receiving, understanding, or responding to the Gospel.

II

In view of the place held by the visible Church in the redemptive scheme of God, it was essential that it should be distinguishable by definite marks from other bodies falsely assuming the name. The peremptoriness of this need was the more apparent from the Protestant repudiation of the claims of the Papal communion to be a true Church of Christ. In the Institutes Calvin supplied two brief criteria or tests for a sure judgment ;—(1) the faithful preaching of the pure Word, (2) the right administration of the Sacraments. But along with these he was accustomed to add a third, namely, the exercise of a vigilant discipline. All bodies of worshippers that satisfied these tests, by whatever name they might be called, were provinces of Christ's true Church. But to insert within its creed doctrines unauthorised by Scripture or incompatible with it, to countenance, encourage, or command practices which ran athwart the express will of Christ or were alien to His mind, to fail in the administration of the discipline necessary to foster and secure the holiness that should be characteristic of all members of the body of Christ,—to be guilty of any of these things was to forfeit the right to be called a Christian Church. It was on all these grounds that Calvin challenged the claims of the Papal body to that name. It presumed to exact for the inventions of men the authority which rightfully belongs only to the revealed Word of God. It desecrated and corrupted the purity of the Sacraments as instituted by our Lord Himself, besides claiming for other rites the same gracious efficacy. It permitted to remain within its borders, unrebuked and even smiled upon, many whose lives were patently ungodly. On all these counts, it was as a body no Church of Christ, though Calvin heartily acknowledged that within it were doubtless many who belonged to the invisible Church, inasmuch as here and there its ' notes ' were recognisably present.

It was in consistency with these principles that Calvin vehemently deprecated and denounced the abandonment of a Church which satisfied these tests, though it " teemed with numerous faults." [1] The divisive action of the Cathari and the Donatists in ancient days and of the Anabaptists in his own day was abhorrent to him. He points to the example of Paul in relation to the Corinthian Church of which almost the whole body had become tainted with error and sin, but which was yet called by the Apostle a Church of Christ and a society of saints because the ministration of the Word and of the sacraments was still not rejected. You will look in vain for a Church altogether free from blemish, he argues. Where then are you to draw the line? In respect to doctrines, distinction must be drawn between the essential and the non-essential, the primary and the secondary. " Some are so necessary to be known, that all must hold them to be fixed and undoubted as the proper essentials of religion : for instance,

---

[1] " Revolt from the Church is denial of God and Christ." (Instit. IV. i. § 10.)

that God is one, that Christ is God and the Son of God, that our salvation depends on the mercy of God, and the like. Others, again, which are the subject of controversy amongst the Churches, do not destroy the unity of the faith; for why should it be regarded as a ground of dissension between Churches, if one, without any spirit of contention or perverseness in dogmatism, holds that the soul, on quitting the body, flies to heaven, and another, not daring to speak positively as to the abode, holds it for certain that it lives with the Lord? ... What I say is, that we are not on account of every minute difference to abandon a Church, provided it retains sound and unimpaired that doctrine in which the safety of piety consists and keeps the use of the sacraments instituted by the Lord." (Instit. IV. i. § 12.) Later he adds a reminder which does credit to his own charity, forbearance, and pity, " As God has been pleased that the communion of His Church shall be maintained in this external society, any one who, from hatred of the ungodly, violates the bond of this society, enters on a downward course, in which he incurs great danger of cutting himself off from the communion of the saints. Let them reflect, that in a numerous body there are several truly righteous and innocent in the eye of the Lord who may escape their notice. Let them reflect that, of those who seem diseased, there are many who are far from taking pleasure or flattering themselves in their faults, and who, ever and anon aroused by a serious fear of the Lord, aspire to greater integrity. Let them reflect that they have no right to pass judgment on a man for one act, since the holiest sometimes make the most grievous fall. Let them reflect that it is more important that a Church should be gathered both for the ministry of the Word and the participation of the sacraments, than that all its power should be dissipated by the fault of some ungodly men." (*Ib.* § 16.)

III

It may be that the 'larger hope' which Calvin countenanced was to some extent responsible for his attitude of indifference to heathen peoples. He left them to the tender mercy of God and His extraordinary means of salvation. Certainly he displayed no trace of missionary enthusiasm.[1] Allowance, of course, must be made for his preoccupation with multifarious interests embracing Europe in their scope, and also for the practical impossibility, in that age, of instituting the necessary organisation for the prosecution of missionary enterprise. But there is little in his writings to indicate that he felt the pressure of the foreign mission problem. That his eager evangelical passion did not inspire him to cast at least an eye of concern upon dark continents across the seas is all the more surprising in view of the contrasted attitude of such a man as Erasmus, who, though reputed to be by no means strongly evangelical, first raised a Protestant voice in favour of foreign missions in his book, "*Ecclesiastes sive Concionator Evangelicus*," of which, as Reyburn says, large sections read like a modern missionary address.

It cannot be pled for Calvin that his attention was not drawn to the possibilities and opportunities of evangelising heathen lands. An occasion for showing his sympathy and readiness to co-operate arose in connection with an expedition despatched by Admiral Coligny to Brazil in July 1555. It was a colonizing experiment, inspired by the hope that Protestants might there find a new and happier home. The leader of it was Nicolas Durant of Villegagnon, a sailor of tried skill. After the settlement of his company on an island off Rio de Janeiro, he asked that more colonists be sent out, and along with them two ministers. The request was passed on to Calvin who promptly met the demand by appointing Pierre Richer and Guillaume Chartier, whose names are worthy of remembrance as the first Protestant foreign missionaries. After some experience of the country and the natives Richer wrote to Calvin what may be regarded as the first Protestant foreign missionary report. He describes the land as wild and desolate, the people as barbarous and savage in the extreme, though he will not say that they are cannibals. In any case they are hard and unfeeling as stone and their understanding completely

---

[1] "Love ought to extend itself to all mankind : but those ought to be preferred whom God hath joined to us more closely and with a more holy tie." (*Comm. Acts*, xi. 29.)

THE CHURCH

dead and dark. Of moral sense they show not a trace, being incapable of distinguishing between good and evil. Vices which nature itself condemns and punishes they regard as virtues. In fine they scarcely differ from senseless beasts. The worst is that they know absolutely nothing of a God. How then was Christ to be preached to them? They cannot see how it is to be done. One thought alone comforts them, that the native mind is so much the more a *tabula rasa*, and so it contains nothing to prevent their nature receiving the most beautiful colours. The language too constituted a formidable hindrance. So they must possess their souls in patience until the young people who were being given instruction in French, had learnt what was necessary. He has high hopes that "this Idumea" will yet be a possession of Christ.

Villegagnon had at first introduced the Genevan régime, but as the result of Romanist machinations in France, he turned back at the bidding of self-interest to the Catholicism from which he had never been really emancipated and reversed his whole policy. All that savoured of the Reform was suppressed and the Calvinists had to flee for their lives into the wilds. After a time, the pastors with twenty others succeeded in being taken on board a Breton ship. Two days afterwards it sprang a leak, and five of them took to a boat, thinking there was greater chance of safety in returning to land and giving themselves up to the governor. But his tender mercies proved cruel, and they were pitilessly hurled over a cliff, so becoming the first Protestant martyrs of the New World. The names of three remain, Pierre du Bardel, Matthieu Vermeil, and Pierre Bourdon. So ended Calvin's only association with foreign missionary enterprise.

IV

Calvin's abhorrence of schism and division had its counterpart in his zeal for the promotion of unity. He was mastered by the vision of a world-wide Church one in Christ, and he regarded it as one of the great ends of his earthly mission to promote its realisation. "We strive for nothing else than the restoration of the Church to its primitive condition," he wrote in his letter to Sadolet. He denounced it as one of the greatest evils of the times that the Churches were so widely separated from one another that there was no kind of co-operation between them. The bickerings, mutual recriminations, and divisions amongst Protestants distressed him acutely and filled him with deep shame. "O God of grace," he cries, "what pleasant sport and pastime do we afford to the Papists, as if we had hired ourselves to do their work!"[1] He vowed that he was ready to "sacrifice his neck a hundred times to produce peace." In spite of all discouragements he never ceased strenuously to strive after the unity which more than once seemed on the point of being realised. Always he was buoyed up by the assurance that the ideal was God's purpose and that He would not be for ever baulked. In one of his letters he sets forth his unbroken hope. "One thing there is, however, which enables me to bear up and revives my courage; it is when I reflect in my own mind that God would never have permitted this marvellous restoration of the Church to proceed so far merely to have inspired a fallacious hope destined to vanish immediately away, but that He has undertaken work which not only in spite of Satan but also notwithstanding all the malicious opposition of men, he will defend and establish."[2]

Calvin was the Protestant champion of an idea and ideal which dominated the mediaeval Christian world and enabled the Papacy to maintain its hold even when there was a widespread ferment of rebellion against its exactions and its encroachments upon the civil power. Even the tendency towards the establishment of autonomous national Churches which manifested itself so strongly in the fourteenth century was modified by the acknowledgment of the Pope as the central authority in spiritual affairs round which the whole Church revolved. The Reformers carried over this commanding sense of Christian unity. It had found one of its earliest and most influential exponents in John Sturm, the leader of the Strasburg Reformers, and the

---

[1] Letter to Melanchthon, Jan. 21, 1545. [2] Letter, Nov. 5, 1548.

tireless apostle of the ideal. His clear sense saw that what kept many in the Roman Church was the chaos that reigned in Protestantism. "There are in the Church of the Pope," he said, "many learned and virtuous men; we cannot condemn them; for what keeps them in that communion is not only their respect for their forefathers, but also the spectacle of our defects, our manners, our disunion." He had his dreams of establishing an academic Alma Mater for Protestantism which, while remaining free from dogmatic assertiveness, would devote itself to scientific research, unite and embrace all the friends of religious and spiritual liberty, not only in Germany but in the whole of Europe, and by its mildness, its breadth, its conciliatoriness, would gain and draw to itself the best-intentioned and moderate elements of even the old Church. He found kindred spirits in such as Matthäus Zoll, who, in answer to a question of Melanchthon in 1536 as to what he personally held regarding the Lord's Supper, said that "therein is offered to all who received and enjoyed it the true body and the true blood of Christ, my Saviour. Substantialiter, essentialiter, realiter, naturaliter, praesentialiter, localiter, corporealiter, quantitative, qualitative, ubiqualiter, carnaliter,—the devil brought them out of hell!" Melanchthon responded, "Thou hast rightly spoken." It was from the atmosphere impregnated by the spirit and ideals of such men that Calvin breathed in his ambitions for and hopes of a unification of Protestantism.

The efforts he put forth to bring about this longed for consummation took various forms and directions. The dedication of his various works to reigning heads and religious leaders undoubtedly aimed at promoting friendly relations amongst the Protestant nations and parties. The prolonged negotiations and controversies with representatives of other Swiss and German Churches were engaged in with a view to arriving at a common agreement on a doctrinal basis of union. Calvin's language might frequently make it seem as if that basis must be what he himself dictated; it was for others to agree with him, not he with them. But that may be explained by the fact that he consciously held a mediating position, which afforded ground for the reconciliation of the extremes of Lutheranism and Zwinglianism,

That he did really hold such a position is evidenced from the fact that he subscribed both to the symbol of the Lutherans, the Augsburg Confession, and to that of the Zwinglians, the Consensus Helvetica. It was in no spirit of mere accommodating compromise that he did so ; he was not the man to sacrifice conscientious conviction even in order to promote a sacred ideal. He found it possible to accept the views of both sides as stated in these symbols. Did not that point to the fact that the views of all parties could be given sufficient expression in terms satisfactory to all ? He was convinced that the differences between them were largely a matter of words. He would instance Luther's appreciation and approval of his own published work which dealt with the points in debate. He was sure that, if only they understood one another, they would find themselves in fundamental agreement on all essential matters, and surely it was not beyond the wit of man to devise a statement which would adequately express that agreement. He was prepared to allow a large measure of liberty on other matters such as ceremonial usages, proposing no other tests but that they should not be inconsistent with Scripture and that they should be for edification.[1] *E.g.* he approved of toleration in respect of the use of waxtapers and candles at the altar, as in the Lutheran Church, though he frankly characterised all that as folly. He did not think it worth while to dispute about the ringing of church bells, a practice of which his party did not approve. Nor would he disallow the pronouncing of a discourse at a burial, though that was not their habit. It was otherwise with such matters as the baptism of infants by midwives, which he stigmatised as an impious profanation and sacrilege, an intolerable superstition, to be resisted "*usque ad sanguinem.*" But on the other hand as regards such points as the locality of heaven, there should be no dogmatising by any one.

So convinced was Calvin of the practicability of reaching a doctrinal basis of union that he proposed to summon an international conference composed of representatives from Germany, Switzerland, England, and France, under the presidency of the King of France, to settle matters in

[1] Letter, Oct. 24, 1538.

dispute. He heartily reciprocated the sentiments expressed by Archbishop Cranmer in a letter inviting him with Melanchthon, Bullinger and other leaders to a meeting in Lambeth Palace for the purpose of devising a creed acceptable to all the Reformed Churches. " I wish indeed," he wrote in reply,[1] " it could be brought about that men of learning and authority from the different Churches might meet somewhere and, after thoroughly discussing the different articles of faith, should, by a unanimous decision, hand down to posterity some certain rule of faith. . . . As to myself, if I should be thought of any use, I would not, if need be, object to cross ten seas for such a purpose. If the assisting of England were alone concerned, that would be motive enough for me. Much more, therefore, am I of opinion that I ought to grudge no labour or trouble, seeing that the object in view is an agreement among the learned, to be drawn up by the weight of their authority according to Scripture, in order to unite widely severed Churches." This noble project unfortunately was frustrated by the death of Edward VI. and the martyrdom of Cranmer.

It may be remarked in passing that Calvin aimed higher than a reunion of Protestantism. He desiderated a reunion of Christendom, and to this end advocated a council of representatives of Protestants and Roman Catholics.[2] He forwarded a memorandum to the Reformed Churches of France suggesting in detail the conditions which such "a free and universal" council must observe if it were to be effective. But this large scheme he gradually came to recognise as impracticable and so abandoned its advocacy, deprecating any efforts in that direction as futile in view of the double-dealing and treachery practised by the Papacy and its representatives.

If it be asked what exactly was the ideal of union at which Calvin aimed, it would be easier to say what it was not than what it was. He was fully alive to the difficulties besetting the endeavour. He was no unpractical visionary, expecting humanity to conform itself to theory. He recognised that anything of the nature of a compulsory

---

[1] Letter, April 1552. Also Zürich Letters, i. 21-26.
[2] Letter to Reformed Churches of France, Dec. 1560.

uniformity was unrealisable, and any attempt to procure it would only accentuate differences, inflame antagonisms, and widen such breaches as existed. Nothing more was practicable amidst the inevitably divergent views of Scripture truth and teaching and in face of inherited prepossessions and sympathies than a union of bodies of Christians professing the same fundamental doctrines. It would be characterised not by complete confessional identity in detail, but by a common centrality of faith and a spiritual unity. It would leave room for denominational variety, arising from ecclesiastical predilections or temperamental preferences for allowable ritual. If a form of episcopacy was germane to the Polish or English cast of mind, Presbyterianism should not be imposed. If a liturgy was desired by a body of worshipping Christians, let them be provided with a suitable and reliable one. He recognised that it would be fatal to demand a change in the German character of the Lutheran Reformation, or to exact that it should don Swiss garments. To aim at a strict conformity to a settled standard of creed, organisation, or practice, was to postpone union to the Greek Kalends. In fine, Calvin's ideal may be described as a Protestant Federation such as would constitute a defensive and aggressive force against all the foes of true and pure religion. Something like it is presented by such organisations as the Pan-Presbyterian Alliance or the Evangelical Alliance, or, in a lesser degree, the world-wide Y.M.C.A.

It was not given to Calvin to see his ideal realised, but there was a time when it seemed within sight. In 1549-50, such a close rapprochement was made between the evangelical Churches of France, England, Poland, Bohemia, the Netherlands, S. and W. Germany, and Geneva, the mother Church of most of them, as flattered the most sanguine hopes. Only the seed-plots of Lutheranism, Saxon Germany and the adjoining Danish territory, stood outside the confederation. But disruptive influences intervened, and the realisation of the ideal receded once more into the dim distance, nor did it return to the foreground of 'practical politics' till last century, when it took shape in the above-mentioned Christian Alliances and Unions,

CHAPTER IX

THE SACRAMENTS

I

THE Sacraments occupied a central place in the thought and practice of the Roman Catholic Church. Almost it might be said that the Church existed to administer them. All lines of mediaeval thought, says Seeberg, converged on the doctrine of the Sacraments. It was not on the ground of any Roman Catholic overestimate of their essential place and value that Protestantism made its attack upon that doctrine, but because it was driven by a revolt of mind and soul from the irrational theories on which their importance was based. The reverent regard in which the Reformers held them is amply proved by the fact that it was disagreement among themselves regarding the view to be taken of their nature and operation which effectually prevented the realisation of a united Protestantism. There was a moment when union was within sight; it only required that Melanchthon should make public declaration of his agreement with Calvin at the time of the dispute with Westphal; but his timidity kept him disastrously silent. The reaction from the Roman Catholic doctrine carried the three leaders to varying distances. The Genevan Reformer recognised that Zwingli's view virtually deprived the Lord's Supper of intrinsic value as a special means of grace. On the other hand, Luther's view was vitiated by the subtleties so heartily detested by Calvin who regarded it as likely to restore the old pernicious notion of some magical efficacy resident in the consecrated elements. He believed that the simpler the view taken of the Sacrament, consistent with the significance attributed to it by Scripture, the greater would be its potency, the more would it be a real means of grace ; also the more likelihood would there be of general agreement. To bring a scholastic disposition to its discussion, as men like Westphal did, was " to cast about them firebrands to involve all Europe in a conflagration."[1] By devising a doctrine which, while true to Scripture, would be of such a reasonable kind as to make it possible for all alike to embrace it, Calvin captured the sympathies of great numbers of religious people who would let the Sacraments speak for themselves and answer the needs of the individual soul that partook, men such as Count Erbach, brother-in-law of the Elector Palatine, and Matthäus Zoll who vehemently affirmed that the devil had brought all the brood of scholastic terms out of hell.[2]

II

What are called specifically the Sacraments are only special forms of the method which God uses in His intercourse with men to communicate certain truths or to impart or intensify certain spiritual impressions or feelings. Calvin took a large view of what may be included under the term. Anything may be called sacramental by which God in some peculiar and especial way excites devout feelings and touches men's souls to a lively sense of Himself and His grace. That embraces " all the signs that ever God gave men to certify and assure them of the truth of His promises." For example, the tree of life was a sacrament to Adam and Eve, as the rainbow was a sacrament of God's mercy to Noah. It is out of regard for our constitution that God speaks through these things. Man is a being compounded of spirit and flesh, and every spiritual communication, if it is to have its full effect upon him, must be sensibly and materially mediated. So Calvin defines a sacrament as " an outward sign by which the Lord seals on our consciences His promises of goodwill towards us in order to sustain the weakness of our faith."[3]

[1] Letter to Swiss Churches, Oct. 6, 1554.   [2] *v. supra*, p.
[3] Instit. IV. xiv. § 1.

THE SACRAMENTS

But the sacrament is one thing; the power of a sacrament another. It is "an empty and trifling thing" unless the Spirit of God works through it[1] and unless there be a receptiveness and responsiveness on the part of those upon whom the Spirit seeks to operate. When these conditions are fulfilled, the sacrament assuredly fulfils its purpose in imparting spiritual energy or stirring the affections or sanctifying the soul. But where they are not, especially where there is not that true faith which prepares the heart to receive, "it can avail no more than the sun shining on the eyeballs of the blind or sounds uttered in the ears of the deaf."[2] It is not in the Sacraments that confidence should be placed, but only in the God who gives grace through them. Grace comes with the Sacraments, not from them. It is not always joined with the visible sign, nor does God limit himself to these ways of giving it; He can and does work without them. These views regarding sacraments in general are fundamental to Calvin's whole position with regard to the Sacraments in particular.

Elsewhere he puts it in a way illuminative of his attitude to the whole self-revelation of God to man. He holds that "the substance (of the Sacraments) is Jesus Christ, for being separated from Him, they lose their efficacy."[3] This saying is not limited in its application to the specifically Christian symbolic rites. He declares that the ancient people of God were partakers of the same Sacraments as ourselves, the difference between us and them being only one of degree, of "more or less." In such a sacrament as that of the rock of which the Jews drank in the wilderness, he interprets Paul's teaching in 1 Cor. 10 to mean that what these people partook of was actually to them the flesh and blood of Christ, otherwise there could have been nothing really sacramental about it nor could they have participated in the benefits of redemption. "Certainly they ate in another way and measure than we do; in the present day it is substantial, which it could not have been then." Their reception of redemptive benefits was "the secret work of the Holy Spirit, who wrought in them in such a manner that Christ's flesh and blood, though not yet

---

[1] *Ib.* § 9. [2] *Ib.* § 9. [3] Cf. Instit. IV. iv. § 16.

created, was made efficacious in them." The sense of absurdity attaching to such a view will be modified when we come to examine Calvin's notions regarding Christ's flesh and blood. Essentially what he wished to assert was that everything that can be called a Sacrament must be somehow related to Christ, inasmuch as it presupposes Him, for Christ is the only real Mediator between God and man. Without Him there would be no Sacrament of any sort.

He is concerned, moreover, to maintain that a genuine Sacrament is never an empty symbol, but beneath it and with it there is given the reality of what it signifies. It is never a mere sign; if it were only that, it would not be even that. It is not even a sign to those who partake without faith. Where a rite is a true Sacrament, it is more than a symbol of something not present; it carries and conveys that which it represents. Baptism, properly performed and rightly received, does not merely declare certain truths; there is present in it an efficacy of the Spirit to perform the work that God purposes through it. The Supper is not a mere memorial feast; it is a genuine spiritual banquet.[1]

In this appears his radical divergence from Zwingli. As Prof. Lindsay puts it,[2] Zwingli called the elements signs which represent what is absent; Calvin, signs which exhibit what is present. Zwingli taught that the sacraments are "signs and seals of the fact that Christ died for us, that He is ours and we are His, that we are partakers of His benefits." Calvin would accept all that, but he would add that we are partakers also of Himself. It is at this point that Zwingli is sharply divided from Calvin. He taught that "the spiritual partaking of the body of Christ is nothing else than the casting oneself in spirit and soul on the mercy and goodness of God through Christ, *i.e.* becoming certain with unshakeable faith that God has given us the forgiveness of sins and eternal blessedness for His Son's sake who altogether has become ours, is offered for us, and has reconciled the divine justice for us." On this view the Sacrament merely provides an objective

---

[1] Letter to Melanchthon, Aug. 27, 1554.
[2] Lindsay's *Hist. Reform.* ii. 55 ff.

THE SACRAMENTS

assurance of objective facts, namely the facts contained in the Gospel. Calvin, of course, accepted this significance, but regarded that as only part of the whole truth. The Sacrament gave not only the assurance of the benefits won by Christ, but Christ Himself. It not only advertised a truth, but conveyed a Spirit.

It may be well here to refer to a difficulty which assailed Calvin's doctrine of the Sacraments from the side of another doctrine, that of election. The efficacy of the rite must be denied in the case of the non-elect; it conveys no grace to them. That of course was easily explicable in view of the condition requiring to be fulfilled on the human side. Only in the elect was that faith possible without which the sacraments could be nothing more than empty signs,[1] which was the view taken by the Consensus of Zurich. In this Calvin had the advantage of Luther whose theory compelled him to agree that the flesh and blood of Christ were partaken of by all alike, as the Formula of Concord asserts. But Luther held that in the case of unbelievers, instead of being efficacious for good, they have the reverse effect, as the sun will melt tar but harden clay. This was an evasion, and Calvin rightly declared that such a view really involved that the unbeliever did not partake of Christ's spirit at all, but only of His body, that is, it was a purely fleshly partaking, which was an impossible position. His own view was that unworthy or unbelieving recipients, the non-elect, repel from them the grace with which the Sacrament is charged. He offered as an explanatory illustration the fact that the sun shines on all alike, but only benefits the living, while in dead bodies it induces corruption.[2]

III

Calvin consistently asserted the importance and value of the sacraments especially that of the Supper. Such benefit did he attribute to participation in the Supper that he would have had it celebrated every Sunday, or at least once a month, and it was much against his desire that it was appointed by the Council to be observed only four

---

[1] Cf. Instit. IV. xiv. § 17.   [2] Defence against Westphal.

times a year. His view was not that the Sacraments imparted a different grace from that which faith received at any time of need, but that they served the purpose of providing an indispensable assurance not otherwise to be gained, which counted for much with Calvin. The non-sacramental communications which Christ gave of Himself through the Holy Spirit were such as often failed of their purpose through spiritual unresponsiveness or unpreparedness and also because of their being purely subjective in their operation, their efficacy depending on the emotional conditions present in the recipient. Feelings due to purely inward causes are notoriously fluctuating and often indefinite in their witness. In the sacraments the visible symbols provide an objective epitome of Christ and His benefits of such a kind as to seal assurance about them on our hearts. Not to partake was to forfeit special grace. It was great folly to absent oneself from the Table because of the unworthiness of others who partook; the apostle does not tell us to examine others but ourselves. Calvin contended against that other wrong-minded view, (in later days so often illustrated in the Scottish Highlands) according to which one who felt weak in faith or too little advanced in the Christian life abstained from 'coming forward.' That, he said, was exactly the same as if one would not call in a doctor because he was ill.[1]

IV

The efficacy of the sacraments according to Calvin is due to two essential factors which must co-operate if they are to be of any value, namely the Holy Spirit and the Word. The latter was as indispensable as the former, so much so as to justify Häring's saying that "the power of the sacrament is the Word in the sacrament."[2] "Without

[1] In Comm. on Col. ii. 17, Calvin illustrates the value of the sacrament by this analogy: "As painters do not in the first draught bring out the likeness in vivid colours and with close resemblance, but in the first instance draw rude and obscure lines with charcoal, so the representation of Christ under the law was unpolished, and was, as it were, a first sketch, but in our sacraments it is seen drawn to the life."

[2] Haering, ii. 743.

the Word," said Calvin, "the sacrament is but a dumb show; the Word must go before."[1] This implies that nothing can be properly a sacrament unless it is expressly appointed to be so, which qualifies Calvin's general view of a sacrament. No one can originate a sacrament except God; it is the word of His appointment by which it is constituted. The repetition of the words of institution and the pronouncement of the baptismal formula are essential to make these signs sacramental. No other outward accompaniment or manner of observance is essential in either rite. Sprinkling or immersion may be practised indifferently, and "whether the wine be white or red, is of no consequence."[2] The actual symbols appointed to be used may be pictorial of what they represent, but they are quite arbitrary for all that; Christ might have chosen others. It is the Word associated with them that makes them means of grace and they become so the moment it is pronounced. Calvin agrees with the early Fathers that the bread devoted to the Sacrament becomes after consecration different from ordinary bread, that is, it is to be considered in a different light from common food, though it does not become another thing.

V

It is difficult to determine whether Calvin regarded participation in the sacraments as necessary to sharing in the benefits of Christ. He could not well do so consistently with his doctrine of election, inasmuch as the cardinal element in salvation was the choice of God. Seeing that to be baptized or to communicate did not argue election, so neither could failure in either of these things necessarily argue non-election. The Helvetic Confession declares that "this eating and drinking of the body and blood of the Lord is so necessary to salvation that no one can be saved without it." The rigorous force of this uncompromising assertion, however, is greatly modified by the qualification which is immediately added;—" but this spiritual eating and drinking happens also apart from the Lord's Supper,

---

[1] Instit. IV. xvii. § 39.   [2] Instit. IV. xvii. § 43.

and as often as or wherever a man exercises faith towards Christ." Obviously the qualification negatives the necessity of participation in the actual Supper, making, as it does, the eating and drinking of the elements equivalent to the exercise of faith independent of the observance of any rite. This position is simply a reassertion of the unguarded utterance of Augustine, Believe and thou hast eaten.

The indecision of Calvin's mind on the matter is specially apparent in his attitude to baptism. The frequent death of unbaptised infants forced him to declare his mind upon the subject. He could not in loyalty to what he believed to be the Lord's express command say outright that baptism was not essential to entrance into the Kingdom, and yet he could not say that the nature of God's decree regarding any infant was evidenced by the fact of its baptism or non-baptism. That position was held by many Protestants, therein agreeing with Roman Catholicism. It seemed to them that the experience of a child in this matter was declaratory of God's will regarding it. The Lutheran doctrine of baptismal regeneration (taken over from Catholicism) logically restricts salvation to baptised infants, though modern Lutherans like modern Anglicans would repudiate that conclusion. Zwingli was the first to assert that baptism was not indispensable, and to embrace the belief that all children dying in infancy were saved. He squared this with his doctrine of election by the assumption that their early death was the proof of their election, being in itself the token of God's mercy. He is not staggered by salvation being bound up with faith, inasmuch as election precedes faith and therefore the absence of faith is no ground for regarding children who have not arrived at it as condemned. The Second Scotch Confession (1590) found it expedient to condemn " the cruel judgment against infants departing without the Sacrament."

No one attached higher value to the rite than did Calvin ; " we ought to fight even to the death for the ceremony itself of baptism," he wrote, " inasmuch as it was delivered unto us by Christ, rather than that we should suffer it to be taken from us."[1] There are utterances which seem to

---

[1] Comm. Acts viii. 38.

set him by the side of Roman Catholicism and of Luther. " It is true," he says, commenting on John iii. 5, "that by neglecting baptism we are excluded from salvation and in this sense I acknowledge that it is necessary." But he finds himself unable to hold that view, in fact he flatly contradicts it in a letter in which he says that " salvation does not depend upon the baptism of the child." Elsewhere in plain words he admits that it is no more always necessary than it is always efficacious.[1] As a Scriptural theologian he could do nothing else when he recalled the thief on the cross and many others who " went unbaptised into heaven." He refuses to regard such a text as John iii. 5 as compelling to the belief in its necessity ; he cannot bring himself to believe that Christ is here speaking of baptism at all. " Water," he holds, " stands there for the same thought as ' Spirit,' the connecting particle ' and ' being often used for ' is ' ; water therefore indicates the nature of the Spirit's work, *i.e.* it cleanses and imparts energy." He points out that in the following verse the newness of life is ascribed to the Spirit alone so that " water must not be separated from spirit." It is with evident satisfaction that he is able to give a distressed parent the hearty assurance that his child is not prejudiced in the eyes of God by not having been baptised before its death. Baptism is only the visible sign and seal of that promise of God to children which constitutes its substance. We are thereby enrolled in the Book of Life by the gratuitous goodness of God. On this ground he denounces the administration of the ordinance to a child *in periculo mortis* by a midwife as a desecration of the Sacrament and a concession to superstition. He denies to all women the right of administration because they are not expressly authorised in Scripture.

VI

If then the Sacraments are not strictly necessary, what exactly are the benefits they confer ? On what ground are they to be regarded as of such vital importance and

[1] Instit. IV. xiv. §§ 14, 17.

inestimable value? The benefits, it must be remembered, are only available for the elect.

Calvin is concerned to make it plain that the Sacraments are not the cause of anything. There is nothing of magical efficacy or potency in them to effectuate what they symbolise. They are no more than signs, signs, however, which are the vehicles or manifestations of spiritual realities or the attestations of spiritual facts. It is by the will of God expressed in the words of institution that they occupy a primary place in the life of the Christian. But it must not be imagined that God has deposited or is constantly depositing in them virtues or potencies which operate upon the mere act of administration, as though one opened the sluice of a millpond. They are not to be thought of after that fashion at all, but only as divinely appointed modes of putting men in possession, in a peculiar and especial way and measure, of blessings whose source is Christ and whose real channel is the Holy Spirit.

As for baptism, Calvin's loyalty to what he accepted as early Church practice, normative for all time, compelled him to accept infancy as the proper period for its administration. He was consequently involved in difficulties with regard to the significance to be attributed to that rite in the case of those of tender age, difficulties which do not trouble Baptists but have involved in perplexity Presbyterians and other Paedobaptists ever since. By baptism, he taught in his work against the Council of Trent, all the guilt of sin is actually taken away, so that sin afterwards committed is not imputed. Regeneration is begun though sin remains, but condemnation ceases because guilt is no longer charged. This would seem to imply that baptism establishes a new condition of soul and a new relationship between God and the child, not actual or existent before its administration. In the Institutes, he describes baptism as a token of our cleansing from sin, not only of sins past but throughout our whole life. It is like " a sealed charter by which God gives confirmation that all our sins are so erased, cancelled, and blotted out, that they may never come in His sight nor be rehearsed or imputed." It does not rid faithful men of original sin but certifies them against condemnation. These benefits, however, are already be-

THE SACRAMENTS

stowed apart from baptism and do not require baptism to make them real. The Sacrament only gives them a reality to our consciousness and sense of need which they might not otherwise have.[1] In that its value consists; its worth is purely experimental; it provides a concrete basis on which to build the life of Christian assurance. We can look back upon it for reassurance when our sins press heavily upon us and our souls are cast down and disquieted within us.[2] Also when the child grows up, it will be animated to " greater zeal for self-renovation, the token of which it will learn that it received in earliest infancy in order that it might aspire to it during its whole life."[3] The rite is a source of comfort to parents, " confirming the promise that God will show his goodwill to the child."[4] The benefits of infant baptism, indeed, are in Calvin's view largely just these two practical ones, (1) the ratification to pious parents of the promise of God's mercy to their children and the sharpening of their sense of responsibility as to their religious education, (2) the introduction of the children into the Church and the stimulus it later brings to bear upon them to be true to the baptismal vows taken on their behalf. Whether the other benefits which baptism symbolises are actually given at the time is known only to God. Apart from whatever benefits it may confer, he argues for its administration on the ground that " if infants be partakers of the thing signified, why should they be debarred from the sign ? The sign is subordinate and subservient to the Word. If the word of baptism (*i.e.* the accompanying promises) is destined for infants, why should we deny them the sign which is the appendage of the word?"[5] " If it be meet that infants be brought to Christ, why is it

---

[1] In the baptismal service prepared by Calvin he says : " We are benefited in two ways by God in baptism ; (1) we have in it the most certain witness that God wishes to be in place of the most propitious father to us and that He will not impute our sins to us, and (2) that He will always be with us by His Spirit so that we may be able to resist and repel the devil, sin, and the lusts of our flesh until we obtain the victory, so that we may live in the liberty of His kingdom which is the kingdom of righteousness. When these two things are fulfilled in us through the grace of Jesus Christ, the truth and substance of baptism are sufficiently embraced and completed " (Ed. Amster. viii. 33).

[2] Comm. Gal. iii. 27. [3] Instit. IV. xvi, § 21.
[4] *Ib.* § 9. [5] *Ib.* § 5.

not also meet that they should be received to baptism, the sign of our communion and fellowship with Christ ? "[1] " No more of present effect is to be required in the baptism of infants than to confirm and sanction the covenant which the Lord has made with them. The rest of the meaning of the sacrament will follow at the time which God has provided."[2]

The chief difficulty for Protestant supporters of infant baptism arises when it is examined in the light of the doctrine of justification by faith. Zwingli cut the knot by asserting that election came before faith and therefore the absence of faith is no ground for regarding children who cannot yet make any profession as condemned. Calvin refused to find refuge in such an evasion. He boldly accepted the inevitable logical conclusion that elect infants must possess saving faith in some wise, faith being the only way of life. Baptism profits nothing unless and until what is promised in it is embraced by faith. He argued as against Zwingli that, if a child is elect, we must suppose that God somehow infuses faith. The fact that Christ was sanctified in His infancy is proof that the age of infancy is not unfit for sanctification. Circumcision also, he points out, was a sign of faith and repentance. As to how the infant can have faith, he, like Luther, confesses himself unable to understand. Luther " lets God take care of that," though the difficulty was less for him, inasmuch as he asserted that baptism conveys grace in and with itself apart altogether from faith. Calvin so far disarms the charge of irrationalism by saying, " I do not mean that faith begins at the moment of birth, but that all the elect enter life through faith, whatever be their age," adding, " if we cannot comprehend this, yet let us recollect how glorious are all the works of God and how secret is His counsel." If we were to ask why infants should not be given the Lord's Supper in view of this presumptive faith, he has his answer ready,—because they cannot examine themselves and so comply with the conditions of worthy participation. (1 Cor. xi. 28.)

Some light upon Calvin's view of baptism is shed by the

---

[1] Instit. IV. xvi. § 7.   [2] *Ib.* § 21.

answer he returned to a query of John Knox, after consultation with the other Genevan pastors. He expresses approval of the baptism of the children of idolaters and excommunicated persons, arguing that God's promise is not only to children but to children's children to thousands of generations. So then those who are descended from holy and pious ancestors, however remote, belong to the Church, though their fathers and grandfathers may have been apostates. The impiety of some progenitors must not be allowed to deprive their descendants of such means of grace. He is careful to add the caution that it is indispensable for them to have sponsors in the meantime, for nothing is more preposterous than that persons should be incorporated in Christ of whom we have no hope of their becoming His disciples.[1] From this it is evident that Calvin perceives and confesses that the efficacy of the rite depends in large degree on the effectiveness of the care exercised by those who present the child. Baptism does not ensure future discipleship; in itself indeed it would be of no certain efficacy but for the human agents who carry out the vows of which it is the occasion,—one might even say, except through the carrying out of the vows taken by those who make themselves responsible for the child.

VII

The differences with regard to the sacrament of the Lord's Supper which split Protestantism into three camps are generally familiar. Zwingli stood for the view that the symbols represent what is absent; Calvin, that they exhibit what is present; Luther, that they "envelop"[2] what is unseen but real. It must not be supposed from Luther's dramatic ultimatum at Marburg that these differences arose out of a mere matter of words. It may be true that Luther took his final stand on the literal meaning of the word " is " in " This is my body "; that Calvin and Zwingli contended that in accordance with numerous

---
[1] Letter, Nov. 7, 1559.
[2] Calvin described Luther's view as meaning that the body of Christ was "envelopped by the bread." (Letter to Bucer, Jan. 12, 1538.)

Scriptural analogies " is " stood for " represents," and that the battle raged round these positions. But they would still have held their respective views, were it true, and they had known it, that in the Aramaic sentence which Christ spoke on that occasion there was no word corresponding to " is " at all. The real ground of difference lay much deeper, and is to be found in the views they held as to our Lord's glorified body. It was admitted by all that in the Sacrament Christ gave Himself in some fashion, or at least that He was somehow present to the believing communicant. The question whose answer divided the disputants was, How did He so give Himself? How was he present in the Supper?[1] This question resolved itself into the ultimate one, Where is Christ? How are we to conceive the manner of His existence now?

Luther's doctrine of consubstantiation necessarily involved a view of Christ's glorified humanity which approximated to an assertion of its ubiquity. Only on that assumption could there be any intelligible meaning in the proposition that His flesh and blood (or His body) were under or in the consecrated bread and wine. This might appear to dissipate Christ's humanity altogether, resolving it into something that had no form or substance, reducing it to some mode of pure spirit, and so eliminating what was specifically human. Luther found the solution of this apparent contradiction with Scripture (which asserted the retention of His humanity in all its component parts) in a theological postulate. Christ, he said, had sat down at the right hand of God. But the right hand of God was everywhere, the phrase being simply a figure for the power of God, and that was omnipresent. Therefore it must be so with Christ; wherever the Godhead is present, there is Christ. If you ask how that can be as regards the human element or side of Him, he answers that Christ's flesh is born of spirit; it is spirit-flesh. Deity is resident in His humanity and the two elements so inhere in one

---

[1] The point of difference between Calvin and Luther is stated by Calvin thus: " We are in complete agreement as to this, that Christ's body and blood are truly offered to us in the Supper to feed our souls; only over the manner and way of receiving and enjoying (*in modo manducationis*) do we differ."

THE SACRAMENTS 175

another as to be inseparable in their activities. He denies the conceivability of Christ being in one place only after the manner of humanity, the divine part of Him, as it were, having separated itself from His manhood, leaving it behind as (to use his own illustration) " Meister Hans puts off his coat and lays it by when he goes to sleep." Christ, he insists, is a simple, single Being, his Godhead and manhood being inseparable. " His manhood is in closer union with God than our skin is with our flesh, yea, nearer than body and soul."

Luther's idea of the ubiquity of Christ's body cannot be understood unless his assumption is remembered that there is nothing of materiality in it. He did not conceive it as being indefinitely extended in some mysterious way. Christ's humanity is no longer associated with a body. At the Ascension, to which Luther consistently refused to attach a literal meaning, Christ's body ceased to exist as a bounded, local thing. Practically he adopted and republished the view of Origen followed by Gregory of Nyssa that that body after the Resurrection was spiritualised and deified after such a manner that it escaped from all the limitations of the earthly nature and was henceforth in all parts of the world as well as in heaven.[1] Consequently " where God is, there is Christ's humanity, and where Christ's humanity is, there is inseparably joined to it the whole Deity."

It becomes evident from all this that Luther used the term " body " in reference to our Lord's glorified condition as equivalent to " Menschheit " or " humanity," *i.e.* that congeries of qualities, mental and spiritual, which go to make up man, made in the image of God who is invisible. The material framework by which these are supported, or the material element of His earthly life through which these evinced themselves under earthly conditions, ceased to exist with His transference from the earthly sphere, because inconsistent with Deity and unable to share the attributes of Deity. There is no correspondence between Christ's present " body " and ours, the virtues and qualities

---

[1] Luther ridiculed as childish the popular notion of heaven being some definite locality in the skies.

of personality resident in His flesh and blood alone abiding as an immortal element in His divine being.

Luther's use of words, unqualified and undefined, is apt to give false impressions, as when he instructed Melanchthon at the conference with Bucer at Cassel (1534) to stand for the literal mastication of Christ's body in the sacrament, "that it is partaken, eaten, and chewed with the teeth."[1] If such a crude and crass expression was not the result of passing aberration, it must be read in the light of His conception of the nature of that body. Obviously then it means and can mean nothing more than what is implied in such a phrase as "drinking in the spirit of the past," or "enjoying a feast of reason and a flow of soul." Or else we may regard Luther as conceiving of the communicant partaking of Christ's body after the manner in which a man, when eating, might be described as "chewing air." It is difficult to take any other meaning out of the declaration of the Formula of Concord which repudiated indignantly the idea that there was physical eating with the teeth ("a malignant and blasphemous slander"), yet taught the oral manducation of both substances of Christ's being, the human and the divine by all alike, unbelievers as well as believers. Yet that Luther attributed substance of some sort to Christ's body appears from his adoption (in defence of his view) of the scholastic theory as to what is meant by a thing being present in space. It may be so in either of two ways,—as excluding from the space it occupies any other body, or as occupying the same space with another body. It is after the latter fashion that the glorified body of Christ is to be understood as present under and in the elements. "It is in the table on which I write," said Luther, "in the stone I throw into the air." That

---

[1] Schaff, *op. cit.* 317, note 2. Unfortunately this outrageous declaration of Luther provided ammunition for combatants of a later day who took up positions which seemed to be authorised by the great Reformer, and effectually prevented the realisation of Protestant unity which the other leaders fervently desired and untiringly sought after. Westphal, an arch-offender, demanded assent to the assertion that the body of Christ was masticated with the teeth. The literalness with which these words were intended to be taken appears from the modification made upon them by Husshius, another of that party, who held that "the body of Christ may be eaten with the mouth, but not touched with the teeth!"

THE SACRAMENTS

is how Christ's sudden appearance to His disciples in a room of which the doors were shut is to be explained. The doors and walls were no obstacle to Him; He could pass through by simply sharing in His passage the space occupied by them.[1] It might be objected that, according to such a view, Christ's body, being ubiquitous, is eaten at every meal. Luther would not deny that, but he would distinguish its being eaten then from its being eaten in the Supper when the word of consecration, according to the promise of God, gives to the body in and with the elements a distinctively sacramental power and virtue.[2]

Now Calvin joined issue with Luther on the presupposition of his whole doctrine, namely, his views as to the present mode of existence of Christ's humanity. He is not sparing in strong language to characterise these, "string of absurdities," "grossest trifling" and so on. That he did not clearly understand Luther is not his fault any more than it is Luther's, whose unguarded utterances were most misleading and perplexing. Calvin could not understand how that which is divine could be eaten and swallowed in earthly elements. The disagreement between them seemed fundamental, but, as will appear, it was more apparent than real, more due to the manner of statement of their respective views than to any intrinsic contradiction or

---

[1] Lindsay, ii. 57.

[2] It may help to bring out the peculiarities of Luther's doctrine to indicate the subsequent development it received. Martin Chemnitz, one of the chief authors of the Formula of Concord, interpreted the ubiquity of Christ as meaning a multipresence depending on His will. "In glory Christ's body is finite and somewhere. Nevertheless, while seated at the right hand of God, He may be present where he chooses to be" (as to Paul on the way to Damascus, and in the Eucharist). This view involves the difficulty of attributing a simultaneous presence of Christ's body in many places, practically amounting to an omnipresence, which is inconsistent with the nature of body. John Brentz, the most prominent of the German theologians after Melanchthon, found speculative ground for asserting Christ's omnipresence. The divine substance and fulness were infused into His human nature. "Wherever, therefore, the divinity is, there also is Christ's humanity, not in the way of local extension and diffusion, but in a celestial, supernatural manner, by virtue of the real communication of the properties of the divine nature to the human." The states of humiliation and exaltation are not successive, but co-existent. "Heaven, moreover, is no particular place, but a state of entire freedom from space." (Schaff, *History of Creeds*, i. 291-3.)

variance. In their practical conclusions they were to all intents and purposes identical. Where there was wide disagreement was in their thought of the way in which Christ's body now existed. Calvin would not allow that it had been in any sense swallowed up of the Godhead. He rejected most emphatically the view that the qualities of Christ's divine nature were transfused into His human, and he roundly accused Luther of resuscitating the Eutychian heresy, which confounded the properties of the two natures, and which had been condemned by the Nicene Council whose authority they both accepted. If Luther followed the lead of Origen, Calvin held the position taken up in the earlier Church which was expressed succinctly and unequivocally in the Letter to the Smyrnaeans attributed to Justin Martyr (second century), " I know that after His resurrection, Christ was in the flesh and I believe that He still is." Sufficient proof is found in the Scriptural statement that he ate and drank after He rose again. Calvin asserted his belief that Christ retained a body of real flesh and blood in heaven, which in consequence he must have conceived of as a place. Acts i. 11 implies that He was removed to some place beyond the world. " It is evident that heaven whereunto He was received is opposite to the frame of the world (*universi mundi machinae opponi*)."[1] Christ remains as His disciples last saw Him. He exists in a certain definite place; the idea that His body was ubiquitous was to Calvin " monstrous." We cannot doubt that " he has limits according to the perpetual nature of the body of a man "; " Christ's humanity is bounded, according to the invariable rule, in the human body and is contained in heaven, where it was once received and where it will remain till He come to judgment."[2] He lays it down as an axiom that " no property may be assigned

---

[1] Comm. Acts i. 11.

[2] Instit. IV. xvii. § 12. All the Reformed Confessions agree with the Calvinistic assertion that the glorified Christ is and remains in heaven, which is regarded as a definite locality. The Consensus Tigurinus affirms that Christ, so far as He is man, is nowhere else than in heaven. Cf. Scotch Confession of Faith (1560): "... notwithstanding the farre distance of place, which is betwixt his bodie now glorifeid in heaven, and us now mortall in this earth, ..." Cf. explanation appended to the Communion Service in the Ch. of England Prayer Book.

THE SACRAMENTS

to the body of Christ inconsistent with His human nature,"[1] in contrast to Luther's postulate that nothing remains in Christ inconsistent with Deity. That rules out any view which " divests Him of His just dimensions," or makes His body capable of occupying a variety of places at the same time, or " assigns Him a body of boundless dimensions, diffused through heaven and earth."[2] To say that God can make the same flesh occupy several different places so as not to be confined to any particular place and so " to have neither measure nor species is to say that the power of God can make a thing to be at the same time flesh and not flesh."[3] " The condition of flesh is that it should have one certain place, its own dimensions, its own form." From which it appears that, if Luther interpreted the crucial text on which he took his stand with slavish literality, Calvin took as literally the statements of the Resurrection narrative, such as Luke xxiv. 39 and Acts iii. 21, on which he took his stand. He would not concede that any change had passed over Christ's body such that it could pass through walls or doors at will, conjecturing that Christ made a passage for Himself into the Upper Room by the exercise of divine power. He would not allow that, wherever Christ's divinity is, there is His flesh, which would be to make Christ by the union of the natures a kind of alloy, so that He is neither God nor man. He quotes with approval the doctrine of the schoolmen, not scorning any more than Luther the assistance of a subtlety, much as he professed to hate them, to the effect that, although the whole Christ is everywhere, yet everything that is in Him is not everywhere.[4]

Yet in spite of this view, Calvin taught that the flesh and blood of Christ were really partaken of in the sacrament. On occasion he uses language that might have satisfied the exacting demands of Luther. He retorted [5]

---

[1] *Ib.* § 19.   [2] *Ib.* § 19.   [3] *Ib.* § 24.

[4] Instit. IV. xvii. 20. Calvin's jealousy for this view was due in no small degree to his anxiety to conserve the doctrine of Christ's Second Coming to Judgment, taken literally, and also to retain Christ's risen body as the exemplar and prophetic pattern of our Resurrection-form.

[5] Letter to Swiss Churches, Oct. 6, 1554. Cf. the conviction of a modern author : " I believe that whatever change may have glorified the Risen Body (of Christ) when it passed beyond the cloud into a new

upon Westphal's charge that he did not " discern the real body "—" As if forsooth we conjured up a phantom instead of a body ! We, on the contrary, when we know that there was but one sole body of Christ which was offered up as a victim to reconcile us with God, assert at the same time that that very body is offered to us in the Lord's Supper, because, in order that Christ might communicate to us the grace of the salvation which he has procured, it behoves that body first to be appropriated by us and the flesh of Christ to be made vivifying to us, since from it we draw spiritual life."[1] He speaks of this as a " capital point." He is not blind to the apparent inconsistency, recognising that it " might seem incredible that the flesh of Christ, while at such a distance from us in respect of place, should be food to us " ;[2] but he is ready with a method of reconciliation and solution.

Duns Scotus had long ago asked the question, Cannot God add to the properties of matter the power of being in many places at once ? Calvin answers in the affirmative at least in respect of Christ's body. In its simplest form, his solution ran thus. " As distance of place seems to prevent the power of Christ's flesh coming to us, I solve the knot thus,—that Christ, although He does not change His place, descends to us by His power." Such a proposition when carefully studied in relation to his other assertions previously instanced, involves the identification of the body or the flesh with its " power." That is what Calvin's view reduces itself to. He conceives of the essence of " substance " as consisting in its " power," so that wherever anything acts, there it is. The substance of Christ's body is its vital and vitalising properties, which can be communicated without the actual partaking of it and in such wise that the partaking of them is equivalent to the

mode or sphere of existence, the earth has ever since the Ascension been the lighter by so many pounds' weight, and the sum of matter in the world the less by so many cubic inches of volume." (R. A. Knox, *Some Loose Stones*.)

[1] " The whole question hinges on this point, whether the material body of Christ be not given to us for nourishment, and as if life were to be sought for from anything else than from a material body." (Letter to Peter Martyr, Jan. 18, 1555.)

[2] Instit. IV. xvii. § 10.

partaking of it. That is in fact the only effective partaking. "The flesh itself is of no value to us since it received its origin from earth and was subjected to death."[1] It is the virtues inherent that are of worth to us, and these Christ can communicate wherever He pleases by the secret power of His Holy Spirit. "His flesh is in no sense projected into us (*caro ejus nequaquam in nos trajicitur*) that we may live thereby, but He poureth into us by the secret power of his Spirit His force and strength (*vim*)."[2] He illustrates by his favourite analogy (a very ancient one) of the sun sending forth its rays and in a manner transfusing its substance into the fruits of the earth. So "the radiance of the Spirit conveys to us the communion of Christ's flesh and blood."[3] What is received, constitutes the whole of Christ, not just a selection of His properties. There is no reserve; Calvin is never weary of reiterating that "by the working of the one Spirit, we possess the whole Christ (*totum Christum*) and have Him dwelling in us."[4]

It is evident how closely this view approximates to that of Luther in essential significance.[5] What Luther calls the body of Christ is identical with what Calvin defines as the substance of that body. The practical agreement appears from his endorsement of Luther's interpretation of the phrase "the right hand of God" on which Christ sits, as signifying, wherever He exercises His power, *i.e.* everywhere. As has been shown, Luther's conception of Christ's

---

[1] Instit. IV. xvii. § 24. [2] Comm. Acts i. 11.
[3] Instit. IV. xvii. § 12. [4] *Ib.*

[5] The approximation becomes very apparent in the change made by Melanchthon on the Article regarding the Supper in the Lutheran Confession of 1520. In the original version, the words ran, "the body and blood of Christ are truly present (*vere adsint*), and are distributed to those who eat." For this in the edition of 1520, Melanchthon substituted, "With the bread and wine are truly offered (*vere exhibeantur*) the body and blood of Christ to those who eat them in the Lord's Supper." Luther must have been aware of this change, and he made no objection. On the other hand, Calvin declared in 1554 that there was nothing in the Augsburg Confession, the Lutheran Symbol, that was contrary "to our doctrine." Craig's Catechism (thoroughly Calvinistic), published in 1581 in Scotland, puts the matter thus: Question. Then we receive only the tokens and not the body? Ans. We receive His very substantial body and blood by faith. Ques. But His natural body is in heaven? Ans. I no doubt; but yet we receive it in earth by faith.

body is that of the qualities and properties which go to make up the humanity divested of its materiality, and it is of these that the communicant partakes, which corresponds in all essentials with Calvin's teaching as to what is received in the Sacrament. The real difference between them lies in their views as to the present manner of existence of Christ's humanity. Calvin localises it in a definite place called heaven; Luther gives it the omnipresence of Deity.

Differences are to be found in their respective views of the way in which the benefits of Christ are enjoyed. Both of course insist on the necessity of faith for beneficial participation. Luther however would say that the unworthy communicant also partakes of the "body" but to his detriment. That was a necessary inference from his doctrine of ubiquity. Calvin held that only true faith really partook of the "flesh and blood." It did so in either of two ways;—(1) either the localised body of Christ radiated its power so as to penetrate and fill the heart prepared by faith to receive it,—a suggestion in consonance with his theory as to how Christ's body is associated with the elements; or (2) the soul of the believer is raised by the Holy Spirit to the glorified body of Christ in heaven and so united with it as to receive of its life.[1] Strangely enough, the latter is the view he generally takes of the matter, a preference he bequeathed to the Reformed Confessions. "Christ is absent from us in the body, but, dwelling spiritually within us, so lifts us up towards heaven as to transfuse into us the vivifying power of His faith, just as we are nourished by the vital heat of the sun by means of its rays."[2] This last quotation is evidently a combination of both views, inasmuch as it is not necessary that we should be lifted up to the sun to enjoy the benefits of its rays; they act

[1] "In order that we be capable of this participation, we must rise heavenward. Here therefore faith must be our resource, when all the bodily senses have failed." (Comm. 1 Cor. xi. 24.) Cf. John Knox's Liturgy included in the *First Book of Discipline* (Calderwood's *Hist. of the Kirk of Scotland*, ii. 114): "The onlie way to dispose ourselves to receave nurishment, releefe, and quickening of his substance, is to lift up our minds, by faith, above all things worldlie and sensible, and thereby to enter into heaven, that we may find Christ where he dwelleth undoubtedlie, verie God and verie man, in the incomprehensible glorie of his Father."

[2] *Reply to Westphal*, ed. Amster. viii. 658.

THE SACRAMENTS

upon us where we are. Calvin indeed seems to have swung hesitatingly between these two views of representing the manner in which Christ operates on us, now imagining that we are mysteriously transported to heaven by the power of the Holy Spirit to be united with the body of Christ resident there and receive directly its energising virtues, now conceiving of the benefit being transmitted through the intervening space by His power of radiating wherever He pleases these virtues and communicating them to any heart prepared by faith to receive them.

There is another consideration which attaches Calvin to this conception of the mode in which the sacrament "works." It recalls the Early Church contention that the Son of God had to assume flesh if that element of the human personality was to be redeemed and sanctified. Calvin himself held that the fault which had been done in our nature could only be repaired in the same nature. In pursuance of this idea, he adopted the notion that if our flesh was to share in sanctification, which it must do if the whole personality was to inherit eternal life, Christ must retain His flesh so as to communicate its particular qualities to that which is corrupt. "The Sacrament not only gives our minds assurance of eternal life, but also secures the immortality of our flesh since it is now quickened by His immortal flesh."[1]

All through the chapter in the Institutes runs this thread of endeavour to establish incontrovertibly that Christ is resident in heaven in the same body as He had on earth. (Calvin will not commit himself to locating Christ in a certain region of heaven. That is "a curious and superfluous question," he answers with Augustine.) Back of all other reasons, of course, is his belief that this is the teaching of Scripture.[2] His theory or doctrine is the outcome of an

---

[1] Instit. IV. xvii. § 32.

[2] In this as in other doctrines, in basing his view ultimately on Scripture, Calvin set the example to those who followed him in it. At the Colloquy of Maulbron (1564), the Reformers took up that position, finding their ultimate referendum in passages of Scripture which seemed to demonstrate that Christ's body must be resident in a particular place, e.g. John xiv. 2-4, 28; xvi. 3, 7, 18; Acts i. 11; iii. 21. In a letter to Bullinger (April 8, 1563) Calvin reports an incident which indicates that the Reformers regarded their view as in accordance

attempt to square this Scripturally-authenticated fact with the fact, also attested by Scripture, that Christ's body is somehow in the bread and wine. It is not to be thought that he was deliberately seeking a *via media* between Zwingli and Luther or a reconciling mean. (Bohatec calls him " the theologian of the diagonal.") He is stating his honest convictions as to what we must believe in deference to all the data of Holy Scripture. He does not conceal from himself or his readers that he is anything but satisfied with his doctrine as an adequate explanation or solution. Over and over again he reminds you that after all we are dealing with unfathomable mysteries. "I will not be ashamed to confess that it (the mode in which Christ is present in the sacrament) is too high a mystery for my mind to comprehend or my words to express ; and, to speak more plainly, I rather feel or experience it (*experior*) than understand it."[1] This mystery, he says at another time, transcends in its depths the measure of our capacity and the whole order of nature.[2] It can only be apprehended by faith. Summing up his doctrine, he says,—" We say that Christ descends to us as well by the external symbol as by His Spirit, that He may truly quicken our souls by the substance of His flesh and blood." Then he adds, " he who feels not that in these few words are many miracles is more than stupid, since nothing is more contrary to nature than to derive the spiritual and heavenly life of the soul from flesh which received its origin from earth and was subjected to death, nothing more incredible than that things separated by the whole space between heaven and earth should, in spite of the long distance, not only be connected, but united, so that souls receive nourishment from the flesh of Christ."[3] No wonder he says that the question

with the primitive one. " When the Cardinal came there (to Deux Ponts), Beza says that at a public banquet a very ancient and broad cup was produced, on which were carved verses which confirm our doctrine respecting the Lord's Supper, and that the Cardinal gazed at the sight for a long time like one almost thunderstruck."

[1] Instit. IV. xvii. § 32. Cf. Letter, May 4, 1555, "this deep and incomprehensible mystery."

[2] Calvin's last farewell to the ministers of Geneva.

[3] Instit. IV. xvii. § 24.

THE SACRAMENTS

here is not, What could God do ? but, What has He been pleased to do ?

No sense of the insoluble mystery and the incredibility surrounding it lessened Calvin's estimate of the incomparable spiritual value of the Sacrament. It was a rite so holy that the utmost vigilance must be exercised to protect it from desecration by unworthy would-be partakers. It was the business of the faithful pastor to defend it at all costs. The scene is historic in which he risked his life to prevent scandalous Libertines from carrying out their intention of forcibly partaking of the sacred feast. Only over his body should they make their way to the holy Table of the Lord. It was Calvin who instituted " tokens " to provide some sort of a pass-port or recognition of worthiness. He would not deprive any one of the benefits because they could not partake at the stated celebration in the sanctuary, and heartily approved of private communion. ". It has been my wish," he wrote to a learned German divine, " that an attestation of what I desired on that subject (the administration of the Supper to the sick) should go down to posterity."[1] He argued for the practice on the ground that the early Christians had no churches and met in private houses. He went the length of saying that there was not much to object to in the practice of giving the Sacrament to condemned criminals if they desired it and seemed properly prepared. But in every such case he insisted on the condition being observed that there was really a communion, *i.e.* that the bread be broken in an assembly or company of believers. The crowning proof of his esteem for the Sacrament is provided by his making excommunication, *i.e.* deprivation of the right to communicate, the supreme ecclesiastical penalty.

[1] Letter of 1558.

CHAPTER X

CHURCH AND STATE

I

IN our study of the relationship that obtained in Geneva between Church and State, this cardinal fact must be kept in mind that the Reformation had been adopted by the citizens convened in general assembly after public debate and through a deliberate resolution. Geneva thereby definitely embraced that form of the Christian religion known in its general features as the Reformed, and accepted the decision as binding upon all its people in the same way as any other regularly enacted law. Those within its borders who asserted different principles or doctrines were regarded as offenders against the expressed will of the commonwealth and liable to be treated as criminals. Malcontents were bidden find a home elsewhere, while heresy and schism became penal offences. It is significant that the names of the heretics, Gruet, Bolsec, and Servetus, arrested and tried in Geneva, appear not on the records of the consistory, but on those of the civil courts. The old laws of pre-Reformation days remained on the statute book, the council now taking over and exercising the authority of the bishop. Geneva therefore proclaimed that the Church established was coterminous with its boundaries. Geneva indeed was a Church as much as it was a State; to belong to the one was to belong to the other. In the proposals first put forward by Calvin and Farel in 1536, they demanded that all the inhabitants of the city should signify their adhesion to the Confession agreed upon " so that it may be known which of them desire to be of the kingdom of the pope rather than of our Lord Jesus Christ." The Council were minded to agree on political grounds, inasmuch as such a Confession would discover any enemies of the city's independence within its walls. The first Catechism which Calvin drew up for Geneva concluded with a short Confession of twenty-one articles which was to be binding on all citizens.

It can be seen therefore how the ecclesiastical court and the civil magistrate had precisely the same area of jurisdiction, all alike coming under the authority of both. As the consistory, constituted according to the Ordinances, claimed to exercise supervision over life and conduct in all its details, to forbid, censure, or denounce for civil punishment any who failed to comply with what they regarded as the requirements of Holy Scripture, it was impossible to distinguish its province from that of the magistrate. Indeed there was no definition of its sphere of action. As the magistrate intruded upon the purely spiritual sphere, the officials of the Church took into their cognisance matters which not even the most liberal interpretation of their functions could bring within the circle of their proper oversight.[1] In fact, by sending frequent remonstrances, counsels and requests to the civil administration on purely civil affairs, it conducted itself very much as an advisory board whose views were entitled to the respect due to those looking at things in the light of the revealed will of God.

II

The later Middle Ages saw the rise of a new sense of nationality, which amongst other things, affected the conception of the Church. Hitherto it had been regarded as one and indivisible, a divine institution presided over by the vicegerent of God at Rome, ramifying into all lands and countries, professing one creed and bowing to one

[1] In 1557, the *consistory* resolved that two of its number should make a general visitation of the whole city and " among other things see that fires were not kindled in rooms where there were no proper fireplaces, that all chimneys were swept, that the streets were kept clean of slops, and that nurses did not take infants to bed with them."

supreme authority. In every kingdom the Papacy was an Imperium whose subjects stood in an immediate relation of subjection to the occupant of St. Peter's chair. As the sense of nationality awoke and gathered strength, this conception of the Church became notably modified, especially in the Germanic States with their native Teutonic self-assertion. The substitution of civil law based upon the law-books of Justinian for the canon law founded upon the Decretum of Gratian resulted in a new view being taken of the relation of the Church to the State.[1] It came to be looked upon as a department of the State, a constituent element of its essential life, partaking of the peculiar characteristics which belonged to it as a nationality. If it was an arm of the Roman Church, it was first and foremost an organ of the State. Its immediate head was the Prince or Lord of the territory in which it stood, and its allegiance as an ecclesiastical body was primarily due to him. It was for him to guarantee its integrity and its competent support, to protect and aid it in the discharge of its spiritual functions, while the Church on its part must submit to the laws of the realm and exert its authority to secure their observance.[2]

This conception passed over into the Reformed Church of Germany. Luther reversed the Roman Catholic idea according to which the Church was divinely empowered to dominate the State. He not only freed the State from this domination but put it in control of the Church in respect of all matters that were not purely spiritual, while entitling it to discharge its own office without let or hindrance from any alien ecclesiastical authority, whether pope or bishop, monk or priest. The Church thus became part of the organism of the State and a national institution.

It was left for Calvin to define a different relationship between them. He was the first to claim and assert for the Church freedom from any kind of subserviency to the State within its own domain, so constituting it an independent, though not separate, entity. According to Luther, the Church was practically the State discharging religious functions; according to Calvin, it was the associate and

---

[1] Lindsay, *op. cit.* i. 44.
[2] Seeberg, *Dogmengeschichte*, iii. 3; also 22 ff.

CHURCH AND STATE

ally of the State in securing the moral regulation of the community. For Luther the Church was the keeper of the State's conscience ; for Calvin, it was the instructor and regulator of that conscience. Luther asserted the right and duty of the State to intervene in ecclesiastical concerns of whatever nature ; Calvin demanded that the Church should exercise its purely spiritual functions unhindered, unhampered, and uncensured by the State.

In Calvin's view, however, Church and State have an intimate relationship, which might roughly be described as of the nature of two intersecting circles. They serve the same ends and both hold divine commissions. Both minister and magistrate are appointed by God to discharge their proper functions, and these functions are complementary to one another. Church and State can as little do without one another as body can do without soul or soul without body. But the Church should brook neither interference nor dictation from the State in things spiritual. Its creed was a matter for its own decision, though the State might afterwards confer its imprimatur without right of review, so formally bestowing upon it legal recognition and status. The Church claimed autonomy in the exercise of discipline and the imposition of ecclesiastical penalties in accordance with the laws of its constitution, also without review on the part of the State. Within these provinces it was self-governing, acknowledging no earthly master and bowing to the behests of no worldly authority. But it claimed the co-operation of the State in carrying out its resolutions and fiats, and in securing obedience and submission to them. The State must be ready to follow its counsel in respect of disciplinary measures or penalties rendered necessary in the moral interests of the community regarded as synonymous with the Church. The magistrate must, if need be, supplement ecclesiastical penalties by civil ones for the effective restraint of wrong-doing. While the civil power had no right to make laws concerning religion and divine worship, it must keep the Church purged of offences by punishment or coercion. It is the business of the State " to foster and maintain the external worship of God, to defend sound doctrine and the condition of the Church, . . . to see that no blasphemy against the name of God, no calumnies against His truth nor other offences against religion, break out and be disseminated amongst the people ; . . . in short, that a public form of religion may exist among Christians and humanity among men." (Instit. IV. xx. § 2, 3.)[1] While only the ecclesiastical court could pronounce sentence of excommunication, the State might be asked to banish the excommunicated persons for a term or until they repented. It was for congregations to choose and appoint their ministers, but the State must secure them in their positions.

In respect of Church property, the State had the same office to discharge as in the case of other property. In no sense could it claim to be joint proprietor. Calvin held steadily to the principle that what had once been devoted to Christ and His Church belonged to it absolutely and in perpetuity. That applied to what had belonged to the Roman Catholic body to whose property the Protestant Church in any locality had succeeded, having become its rightful heir. To alienate it from the purposes of religion (in which he would include care of the poor, and the maintenance of schools) was nothing less than sacrilege, " liable to anathema and the curse, because it profanes what is sacred." The Church officers, not the State officials, were its proper trustees and administrators, always in subjection of course to the laws which apply to those discharging such functions. It was for the State to see that these laws were duly observed ; only so far did it have right of entry into this sphere. " The rule of reformation which King Josiah prescribed is the best," wrote Calvin, "that the magistrates have the power of inspection and that the deacons be the administrators."[2] Where, however, this arrangement was for any reason impracticable or disputed, (as in the case referred to in the letter just quoted) he expresses himself " content

---

[1] " The civil magistrate may not assume to himself the administration of the word or sacraments, or the power of the keys of the kingdom of heaven ; yet he hath authority, and it is his duty, to take order, that unity and peace be preserved in the Church, that the truth of God be kept pure and entire, that all blasphemies and heresies be suppressed, all corruptions and abuses in worship and discipline prevented or reformed, and all the ordinances of God duly settled, administered, and observed." (West. Confession, xxiii. 3.)

[2] Letter, Oct. 1542.

CHURCH AND STATE

that the magistrate may have the full power of administration, provided he faithfully dispenses the annual income and neither diminishes nor dilapidates the property."

III

Calvin, however, found it impossible to carry these principles into effect. From the moment of his entry into Geneva, he found himself confronted by a theory and a practice antagonistic in many points to his own. The influence of Berne with its Erastian views of the relationship of Church and State had shaped existing ideas on the subject in Geneva. The civil authorities assumed the right of intervention and control in practically any matter that concerned the Church, and they refused to relinquish it. Calvin fought many hard battles with them in the attempt to vindicate his principles and secure their acceptance. He would have had Communion celebrated at least once a month ; the Council decided that it should be observed once a quarter. It was they also who abolished traditional festivals and determined which were to be kept. Later on (1538), in an attempt to secure conformity throughout Switzerland in the matter of ecclesiastical practices, when Berne requested that Geneva should conform to its practice of observing Christmas, Easter, Ascension, and Pentecost, and also should use baptisteries and unleavened bread for the Lord's Supper, the Council without consulting the Reformers acceded to the request and ordained accordingly. It was this action which brought about a temporary severance between Calvin and Geneva. He was no fanatic about these matters, but he stood for the right of the Church alone to decide concerning questions falling within the strictly ecclesiastical sphere, and he demanded that a synod be summoned to authorise such a step. A synod was convened at Lausanne and endorsed the Council's action, but the Reformers had not been allowed to speak. Calvin therefore refused to recognise the legitimacy of such a resolution, and demanded that the matter should be referred to a synod properly constituted and empowered to come to a regular ecclesiastical decision. To that he would submit, the position and dignity of the Church having thus been safeguarded. Berne refused to agree, and Geneva sheepishly followed suit. When all Calvin's vehement protests were unavailing, he and Farel shook the dust of the city off their feet and betook themselves into not unwelcome exile.

It became obvious to him that compromise was inevitable, and the constitution and practice of the Church which afterwards obtained offer abundant proof of how far it departed from his ideal. He failed to secure that elders should be elected by the congregation. The consistory was composed of the ordained ministers of the city and a number of elders appointed by the various Councils,[1] the proportion of laymen to ministers being twelve to five. The consistory was thus to all intents and purposes a sub-committee of the Councils. The regulations governing its procedure emphasised the subordinate relationship it held and practically obliterated any real distinction between the civil and ecclesiastical powers. Calvin never succeeded in establishing in Geneva a synod for the review of the consistory's judgments. That court reported the result of its deliberations to the Council of 200, which thereupon initiated such action as seemed requisite. The elders formed the means of communication between the Church court and the civil courts on which they sat. A syndic [2] also presided over the consistory. The State claimed to pronounce final judgment even on the adoption of a creed involving consideration of dogmatic questions. The appointment of ministers was in the hands of the State, only subject to the veto of the people. They were paid by the State out of its own resources, the Church possessing no treasury of its own. If application was made by churches elsewhere for ministers, it was by authority of the Council that they were sent, and their appointment was chronicled in its registers. No minister could absent himself from his parish for any length of time without leave of the Council. In 1549, we find the

---

[1] It may be suggestive of the spirit of these elders that the first question they asked at the first meeting of the consistory was what their wages were to be! It was settled that they should be paid out of the fines, two sous for each day's attendance (Reyburn, 117).

[2] A city magistrate.

CHURCH AND STATE

Council ordering the ministers to preach every day and to repeat the Lord's Prayer and the Ten Commandments frequently during service. Calvin, it may be said, protested against the former as impossible, and against the latter as savouring of superstition and incantation. The Council disputed the claim of the Church to be the sole arbiter and inflicter of the extreme penalty of excommunication. Only in this matter did Calvin win anything of the nature of a decisive victory. There was always, however, a party in the Council ready to challenge the exclusive right of the Church to excommunicate, and such appeals to it as that of Philip Bertelier, an excommunicant, asking that he be restored to membership, stirred smouldering dissatisfaction into angry flame.

The relationship between Church and State which Calvin sought to realise could scarcely result otherwise than in their becoming so entangled as they subsequently did. It was not to be expected that the State would consent to be the blindly obedient executioner of the Church's verdicts or the caretaker of the Church's body of doctrine without demanding the right to use its own judgment as to the justice or expediency of what it was asked to do. If the magistrate had to impose penalties for ecclesiastical misdemeanours, he must be put into a position to do so with a mind thoroughly informed and fully alive to the nature of the offence. That granted, an entrance was given him into the spiritual sphere, out of which he was theoretically ruled. He might sit on the consistory as an elder, but he deliberated as one who could not forget that he presided in another court, possessed of power denied to the ecclesiastical one. Secular authority always tends to take an ell, if it be allowed to encroach an inch upon ecclesiastical preserves.

It is not surprising that in the period following Calvin's death, during the regime of Beza, the magistrates filled the role of supervisors after a manner which certainly was not contemplated by the Reformer, and would indeed have staggered him. The representatives of the Council animadverted upon the errors of the candidates for the ministry presented to them for approval and subjected by them to examination, took it upon themselves to declare whether they were "well-founded in doctrine, whether they had sufficient knowledge and were able satisfactorily to expound Scripture." They laid an embargo upon too long sermons, forbade the pulpit to give voice to matter which they considered would provoke scandal rather than provide edification, claimed to sit in judgment upon any proposed innovation in the Church, and allowed no change to be made, whether in doctrine, service, or constitution, which had not received their approval. This was the inevitable outcome of a union which started by making the State the servant of the Church and ended by making it the master.

CHAPTER XI

CHURCH ORDER AND WORSHIP

I

IT was no easy business to reconstruct the Church from its foundations, and that was the task laid upon the Reformers and particularly upon Calvin, the master architect of the new structure. It might seem sufficient to take the primitive uncorrupt Church as model, but it was obvious to such as he that it offered on many points uncertain guidance and indeterminate example. " All parts of divine worship were clearly unfolded in the sacred oracles of the Lord who is the only Master to be heard in this matter," he says, but in the case of external discipline and ceremonies, He has not prescribed every particular that we ought to observe. Calvin inferred that He anticipated the varying needs of changing times and foresaw that one form would not suit all ages, from which the conclusion followed that such things might be altered or abrogated and new forms be introduced according as the interests of the Church required. To stereotype thought was to stagnate life, and Calvin's constant aim was to create a Church that was ever heartily and healthily alive. Caution, however, must be exercised in proposing innovations rashly or incessantly or for trivial causes.[1] Moreover, churches in different places might find it

---

[1] Instit. IV. x. § 30. In his deathbed instructions to the ministers of Geneva, Calvin said : " I pray you make no change, no innovation. People often ask for novelties. Not that I desire for my own sake out of ambition that what I have established should remain, and that people should retain it without wishing for something better, but because all changes are dangerous and sometimes hurtful."

necessary or expedient to adopt different forms of external discipline or ceremony, and no church ought because of that to look askance on another. For guidance in these matters at any time " we must have recourse to the general rules which (the Lord) has given." The main thing to keep in view is Paul's principle that all things be done decently and in order. Sacred things ought to be treated " with great modesty, seriousness, and reverence," and ceremonies should lead us directly to Christ, if they are to be exercises in piety.[1]

A Church Order of a definite nature is necessary if confusion, barbarism, contumacy, turbulence, and dissension are to be avoided.[1] If these matters were left to the free determination of individuals, the Church would become " a seed-bed of quarrels "[2] instead of the abode of peace which it should be. " If in every human society some kind of government is necessary to ensure the common peace and maintain concord, if in transacting business some form must always be observed, which public decency and therefore humanity itself require us not to disregard, this ought specially to be observed in churches, which are best sustained by a constitution well ordered in all respects, and without which concord can have no existence."[3] No policy will secure respect which is not fortified by laws, and rites will have no proper observance unless fixed forms are prescribed. Ordinances too are bonds of union. Whatever may be appointed for the regulation of Church worship and life " it is the duty of Christian people to observe, with a free conscience indeed and without superstition, but also with a pious and ready inclination to obey."[4] It is of no consequence what the days and hours of worship are, what the nature of church buildings is, and what psalms are sung on each day. " But it is proper that there should be certain days and stated hours, and a place fit for receiving all, if any regard is had to the preservation of peace." Moreover, there are practices which from their nature tend to infuse a certain dignity and reverence into the services, such as praying on our knees and with our head uncovered, employing some degree of solemnity in the

---

[1] Instit. IV. x. § 29. [2] Ib. § 31. [3] Ib. § 27. [4] Ib. § 31.

burial of the dead, quietness and silence during the sermon, respect for the prohibition of Paul against woman teaching in the church and so on.

Nevertheless such ordinances must never be regarded as though observance of them was necessary to salvation or binding upon the conscience; nor on the other hand must their observance be made a substitute for true piety. They are not of fixed and perpetual obligation. Exceptions may constantly require to be made according to circumstances which render it impracticable or inexpedient to adhere to them. "What?" he exclaims, "is religion placed in a woman's bonnet, so that it is unlawful for her to go out with her head uncovered? Is her silence fixed by a decree which cannot be violated without the greatest wickedness? Is there any mystery in bending the knee, or in burying a dead body, which cannot be omitted without a crime? By no means. For should a woman require to make such haste in assisting a neighbour that she has not time to cover her head, she sins not in running out with her head uncovered. And there are some seasons when it is not less seasonable for her to speak than on others to keep silent. Nothing forbids him, who, from disease, cannot bend his knees, to pray standing. It is better to bury a dead body quickly, than from want of graveclothes, or the absence of those who should attend the funeral, to wait till it rot away unburied."[1]

A very striking exception to the imperative of any such ordinances is provided by the assumption of ministerial status on the part of Calvin himself and others without the appointed formalities.[2] His position in regard to that appears from a letter[3] he wrote regarding the action of a party at Frankfurt, who demurred to the ministry of their pastor, Poulain, on the ground that he was not elected

[1] Instit. IV. x. § 31.
[2] Calvin never received consecration to the ministry by ' the laying on of hands." He was called to Geneva according to proper form by the votes of the consistory and magistracy, the people giving their consent. Farel, also in the same case with the addition of not even having received a proper call, held that his position had been regularised by the summons of Oecolampadius (who had been regularly ordained), " with the invocation of the name of God." (*Doum.* ii. 407 ff.)
[3] Dec. 22, 1555.

formally, and demanded that he should resign and be elected anew. Calvin pointed out that where a man had practically made a congregation, it was right that he should be regarded as its properly ordained minister, even though not appointed according to church order. Otherwise, what of the baptisms he had performed, the Sacraments he had dispensed? Where there has been a definite constitution, order ought to be observed. "But it is a different matter where all lies waste. Those who first worked there to plant the Gospel ought to be accepted as pastors without further formalities." The exordium of the Ecclesiastical Ordinances drawn up by Calvin gives concisely his views of this whole matter. "In the name of God Almighty, we, the Syndics, small and greater Councils with our people assembled at the sound of the trumpet and the great bell, according to our ancient customs, have considered that the matter above all others worthy of recommendation is to preserve the doctrine of the holy gospel of our Lord in its purity, to protect the Christian Church, to instruct faithfully the youth, and to provide a hospital for the proper support of the poor,—all of which cannot be done without a definite order and rule of life, from which every estate may learn the duty of its office. For this reason we have deemed it wise to reduce the spiritual government, such as our Lord has shown us and instituted by his Word, to a good form to be introduced and observed among us. Therefore we have ordered and established to follow and to guard in our city and territory the following ecclesiastical policy, taken from the gospel of Jesus Christ."

II

Two main principles determine the system of Church Order which Calvin proposed and which he succeeded only partially in realising in the Ecclesiastical Ordinances. As we have already seen, he asserted the absolute independence of the Church in regard to matters of faith and discipline, and its right to self-government within its own proper spiritual sphere. This constituted a new departure which proved to be fruitful in momentous consequences. In

CHURCH ORDER AND WORSHIP

England, Henry VIII. had substituted himself for the Pope, and installed the reigning King as head of the Church in all things. The Anglican Church therefore as now constituted is empowered by the Crown to exercise such spiritual authority as it possesses, while it must bow to the decisions of the State. Zwingli made the civil power the supreme court of appeal in matters of religion. Luther left the Church under the domination and protection of the ruler of the State in which it was. Calvin saw clearly what the dangers of such a relation would be while he was fully alive to the advantages of the position held by the Pope through his freedom from State control. The subsequent history of established Churches has amply proved the sagacity and farsightedness of his judgment.

But no less epoch-making was the second principle asserted in his system. Early in the history of the Church, a cleavage appeared in its membership which resulted in those who held office being put into a class by themselves distinct from all the rest. The advance of sacramentarianism and State establishment intensified the distinction which thus arose between clergy and laity or priests and people. The direction of ecclesiastical affairs, the discharge of ecclesiastical functions, the cure of souls, fell entirely into the hands of the former, laymen being left without say or control. This condition of affairs was modified to a certain extent in Germany and England at the Reformation, but the layman was still grudgingly conceded a very subordinate and meagre share in the regulation of church affairs. Calvin was the real pioneer in a new departure which completely altered this aspect of things ecclesiastical. Consistently with his view regarding the common priesthood of believers and the absence of any special 'character' conferred by ordination upon ministers, he restored to laymen a position in church government which they had not held since primitive days. He gave them seats of equal authority with the clergy in the church court which supervised and directed the religious life of the community. By doing so, he practically obliterated the distinction between clergy and laity in regard to the conduct of church affairs, the determination of creed and policy, and the supervision of church life. He thus laid the foundation of Presbyterianism and its foster children. In view of the part played by those educated in the methods and ideals of Presbyterianism, the importance of the service rendered by Calvin to the world in this respect can scarcely be exaggerated. He set free the enormous power contained in the membership of Presbyterian and other democratically organised Churches to enter effectively into the prosecution of religious work. He gave laymen that living, active interest which comes of the sense of responsibility, and the call to exercise their private judgment and combined sagacity upon the discharge of the divine commission entrusted to them as members of that Church which is the organ of Christ. The danger of spiritual tyranny was reduced to a minimum; the relations between pastor and people became those of brethren, of teacher and scholar. The Church was no longer merely a city of refuge whose gates opened and shut at the nod of Peter with his keys, but an organised body of people instructed in sacred things by the men of their choice to the end that together they might work to establish Christ on the throne of all men's hearts.

III

In estimating the church order and system which Calvin constructed, certain principles, qualifications, and caveats must be kept in view. Only from what is directly imposed by the Word of God may there be no departure. In regard to all the rest, much was simply legislation necessitated by the existing condition of affairs in Geneva, and therefore susceptible of change if circumstances rendered it no longer desirable. As a matter of fact, the Ecclesiastical Ordinances which Calvin drew up in 1541 underwent with his cordial approval a thorough revision twenty years later. Moreover, these Ordinances, in the form in which they became law, do not represent what Calvin himself would have liked to put in operation. He did not have a free hand in the matter, and was compelled to sacrifice the ideal to the possibilities of the situation. He had to accommodate his proposals to the powers claimed by the civil authorities and to customs and traditions ingrained in the political life of the community. The result was an unsatisfactory compromise for which he must not be held responsible.

The necessity of compromise and the result of it appeared in the mode of electing ministers. As to that, Calvin recognised that the primitive Church had transmitted no certain rule applicable for all time except that the congregation should be consulted in the matter. The general rule indicated in Scripture for such a business, therefore, along with local circumstances, must be determinative of procedure. " Whether it was better to elect the bishop by the voices of all the members of the congregation, or only by those of a few, or by the advice of a magistrate, cannot be determined by law. We must be guided in this respect by times and circumstances. Cyprian strongly urged that the election is legitimate only when all the members give their assent. History also shows that this rule held good in many places. But as it is scarcely to be expected that so many people would have the same mind (*i.e.* in choosing a minister), it seems to me desirable that the magistrate, or the Council, or the elders, should undertake the election, and that certain bishops, known for their rectitude and piety, should be called to their aid." (Calvin held that the word 'bishop' is synonymous with 'minister' or 'pastor.' "In calling those who preside over churches by the names of bishops, presbyters, and pastors, without any distinction, I have followed the usage of Scripture. To all who discharge the office of the ministry it gives the name of 'bishop.'" Instit. IV. iii. § 8.) Yet he laid it down that at least the people's approbation of their choice must be secured, as the people's consent must be given to a minister's deposition.[1]

In practice, the Ordinances laid down the following procedure. The candidate for the vacant charge was examined as to his ability to interpret Scripture and his

[1] Cf. the answer given to a question of the King by a General Assembly of the Church of Scotland in 1597. " The electioun of pastors sould be made by them who are pastors and doctors lawfullie called, and who can try the gifts necessarilie belonging to pastors by the Word of God. And to suche as are so chosin, the flocke and patron sould give their consent and protectioun." (Calderwood's *Hist.* v. 586.)

knowledge of the principal heads of doctrine by the ordained ministers. He had also to preach a sermon before them and two members of the Council. If he satisfied these tests, he was thereupon recommended to the Council as qualified, and their approval and confirmation of his election were requested. It was in their power to refuse, but it does not seem that they ever exercised that right. Thereafter the minister-designate preached before the people and their opinion of his fitness was asked. They were also invited to lodge objections, if any, to his life and character within eight days. If none were forthcoming, the ordination was then proceeded with. At this time, Calvin omitted the laying on of hands because of the danger of perpetuating Roman superstition connected therewith, but he himself desired it to be part of the ordination ceremony. The apostles, by the laying on of hands, intimated that they made an offering to God of him whom they admitted to the ministry. Though there was no fixed injunction regarding the matter, yet as it was the uniform practice in consecrating pastors and teachers, elders, and deacons, to their offices, it ought to be regarded by us in the light of a precept. " It is certainly useful that by such a symbol the dignity of the ministry should be commended to the people, and he who is ordained reminded that he is no longer his own, but is bound in service to God and the Church." The laying on of hands, however, belonged not to the whole people nor to the elders, but only to the clergy.[1] (Instit. IV. iii. § 16.)

Calvin would have had the elders elected by the people directly, but he had to yield on this point too. It was decided by the Council that twelve should be chosen to sit on the Consistory which supervised the religious and ecclesiastical affairs of the city, two from the Council of twenty-four, four from the Council of sixty, and six from the Council of two hundred. A Syndic or magistrate was always to preside over that body, though as an elder and

---

[1] Q. " Is he a lawfull pastor who wanteth *impositionem manuum* ? " A. " Impositioun, or laying on of hands, is not essentiall and necessar, but ceremoniall and indifferent, in admission of a pastor." (Questions proponed by the King, to be resolved at the convention of the Estats and Generall Assemblie [of the Church of Scotland] 1596.) Calderwood's *Historie of the Kirk of Scotland*, v. p. 586, 711, 723.

not as a civic official. No minister was allowed to preside in this, the only church court,—the reverse of the practice which obtains in modern Presbyteries, wherein it is always a minister who is moderator.

The order of deacons was modelled on the primitive prototype. They were elected in the same manner as the elders. It was their function to take care of the poor, the sick, the widows, and to visit the hospitals. It was also their business to put a stop to mendicancy by the judicious distribution of alms in cases of real necessity, but this duty seems to have been assigned to another class of the order. Deacons had no share in the oversight of the Church.

There were three Churches in Geneva, St. Peter's (where Calvin officiated), the Magdalen, and St. Gervais. The city was divided into three parishes corresponding to these, to which certain ministers as well as elders were specially assigned, "there always being danger of confusion when the people have not their own minister, and when the minister does not know his proper charge." To overtake the work, five ministers with three assistants were appointed, though afterwards this number was augmented. Every house in each parish was to be visited yearly before Easter by a minister accompanied by an elder. Household servants were to be specially watched over. It was no perfunctory or merely friendly visit that was paid. The family were assembled and carefully catechised as to their faith and doctrine, and suitable admonitions addressed to them, a practice followed till last generation in the Scottish Church. The sick were to receive special attention; it was ordered that no one should lie ill for three days without sending for a minister. In his liturgy Calvin gave a separate article to the visitation of the sick. It is worth quoting to show the high sense of responsibility and the seriousness of purpose which Calvin sought to import into this work. " It is the duty of the minister not only to preach the truth, but as far as possible to warn, encourage, and comfort every one. This spiritual instruction is then most needful to a man when the hand of the Lord is upon him, and he is visited with pain and sickness or other distresses, and especially in the hour of death. He then feels himself more than in any other moment disturbed by his conscience as well on account of the judgment of God, before whom he is about to appear, as through the assaults of the devil, who then employs all his strength to overpower the poor creature, and to bow him down in shame and misery. It is the duty therefore of ministers to visit the faithful, to comfort them with God's Word, and to show them how all that they suffer comes from His hand and His good providence, and that He allows nothing to happen to His own but what may conduce to their benefit and salvation. In all these cases the minister should choose the most careful expressions. If he sees that death is approaching, he must act towards the dying according to the state of their souls: should they be oppressed with terror at the near approach of death, he must show them that death has really nothing terrible in it for Christians, seeing that they have Christ for their guide and protector, and that He will conduct them to that eternal life which He himself has already entered. In this manner should the preacher subdue that terror which dread of the judgment of God may have inspired. But should they not be sufficiently alarmed by a sense of sin, he must then explain to them what the judgment of God is, and how they can only stand before it through His mercy, and by embracing Christ as their salvation. If again they are disturbed in conscience, and bowed down by the feeling of their defects, then he must represent Christ to them in clear and lively colours, and make them understand how all poor sinners, if only they mistrust themselves, may find in Him refuge and consolation."

IV

The chief function of the pastor was to preach. He is primarily the minister of the Word, not the dispenser of sacraments. Calvin laid immense stress on this department of his duty. In writing to the Duke of Somerset on matters requiring reform in the English Church, he urges him to pay special attention to the provision of satisfactory preaching, of which there seemed to be very little in the kingdom. " There is some danger," he wrote,[1]

---

[1] Letter to Protector Somerset, Oct. 22, 1548.

CHURCH ORDER AND WORSHIP

" that you may see no great profit from all the reformation which you shall have brought about, however sound and godly it may have been, unless this powerful instrument be developed more and more." The central place occupied by the mass in the services of the Roman Church was taken by the sermon in those of the Reformed. Teaching was the pastor's great business; the service was indeed often called the preaching or the sermon. That was intended to be indicated by the gown he donned for the pulpit, which was the robe of the doctor, not a symbolical vestment such as the Romish priest wore. Calvin was not the first to give preaching this central place ; it had already received that centrality from Farel in the Order of Service which Calvin found in operation on his arrival in Geneva. But by devoting himself to the production of sound, strong preachers, he won for the sermon that position of prime importance which it has ever since continued to hold for good or evil in Presbyterianism. It has been suggested that the reason for Presbyterian churches being closed except during the hours of divine service is that their whole purpose was discharged in providing a place for the preaching of the Word. In the absence of the minister to whom that function alone belonged, no profit or advantage was to be gained by those who might frequent them.

With a wisdom which the modern world has only in part yet attained, Calvin provided against the risk of the people losing interest in the preaching through hearing the same voice for too long a period, by arranging for a change of preachers from time to time.[1] But it was not left to the minister to keep his church filled by the attraction of his pulpit gifts. Attendance was made practically compulsory. Before Calvin's day, the Council had ordered all shops to be closed on Sundays during the time of 'sermon.' All disturbance of the service through the

[1] Ten sermons altogether were preached in the churches every Sunday, and two on each week day. Vergerio, a refugee in Geneva, describes how at the first stroke of the bell, all hastened to church with a little book in their pocket containing the Psalms set to music, which they sung with great heartiness in their mother-tongue both before and after the sermon. So crowded were the churches that according to a minute in the State records Calvin urged the authorities to build another church as there was no room for all in the present ones (Stähelin, i. 482).

crying of wares in the street, as by pastry cooks, was prohibited. Regulations were now made more stringent. The civic officers who had hitherto patrolled the town to arrest idlers and the contumacious, were now authorised to invade private houses and take to task those whom they found playing truant from church, and in defect of any sufficient excuse to carry them off to prison. Strangers came under the sweep of those regulations, and if they failed to attend church after three warnings, they were liable to expulsion from the city. Human nature having remained much the same, we are not surprised at the busy time the officials had, and at the nature of the excuses given by defaulters. We are still familiar with the absentee who had to stay at home to look after a child too young to understand the sermon, and the other who is too deaf to catch what the preacher is saying, and that considerable company who shelter themselves behind the sad deterioration in the preachers of the day.[1] Delinquents were summoned by the messenger of the civil court to answer for themselves before the Consistory, which met every Thursday to consider such cases along with other business.

Calvin sought to surround the high occasions of baptism and marriage with an appropriate sanctity and solemnity by urging their celebration in church in presence of the congregation.[2] He strongly objected, however, to funeral solemnities and services for the dead, which he regarded as 'abominations' and founded on falsehood, and as "doing dishonour to the meritorious sufferings and death of our Lord Jesus Christ." What he implied was that they tended to fasten upon the Church the superstition of deliverance from a purgatory by the power of the prayers uttered on the occasion of burial. He did not object to an appropriate address being given, but that should be in the churchyard rather than in the church, within which he objected to interments being made.[3]

Calvin appreciated the peculiar comforts imparted by

[1] Reyburn, John Calvin, p. 118.
[2] Engagements of marriage became religious acts, parties making their vows before the minister and witnesses, and their future duties being earnestly impressed upon them.
[3] Letter to Farel, 1543.

the mass to those who heartily believed in it, and he would have provided that those of the Reformed Church should have the same help provided for them by the celebration of the Lord's Supper every Sabbath after the Apostolic fashion. That being found impossible, he proposed that it should be observed at least once a month in each of the city churches in turn ; but the Council decided that once a quarter was sufficient, at Christmas, Easter, Pentecost and on the first Sunday of September.[1] At the Communion, the practice was at variance with that now obtaining in the Presbyterian Church, the ministers distributing the bread and the elders and deacons the wine.

There were two services on Sunday, one in the early morning, the other in the afternoon, with a children's service between. There were also services early on Monday, Wednesday, and Friday, for which candles were provided that the people might see. At all of these sermons were preached, and whilst they were going on, no ordinary work might proceed. Attendance was no more voluntary than at those on Sunday, the civic officers seeing to it that all alike with their servants were present. It might be suggested that those services took the place of the family prayers now practised in Christian households. Bells were not considered necessary to call people to church on Sunday. The Reformers did not view their use with approval,[2] and those of St. Peter's were ultimately melted down to form cannon.[3] It would seem however that the great bell was employed to summon people to service on other days, when

[1] During the week before the celebration, every house in the town was visited by a minister accompanied by an elder. The inmates were carefully examined as to their spiritual state and religious knowledge. If any were found ill-prepared to partake worthily, they were warned in a fatherly way to absent themselves. The timid and sin-burdened were comforted and encouraged, and all were pointed to the plenteousness of the divine mercy, and the conditions on which it might be received. (Letter of Vergerio, a refugee in Geneva, descriptive of the state of things he found there in 1556.)

[2] " You need not protest any further against the use of bells, if the prince (of Würtemburg) will not consent to your wishes." (Letter to Farel.)

[3] After the Franco-German war, many of the cannon balls were remade into church bells. After the Boer war, many of the empty cases of shells were turned into dinner gongs.

there might be more excuse for neglect or oversight. It was open to any one after the sermon on Friday to make observations upon it or discuss it with the preacher, the object being to stimulate and keep alive the people's interest in the subjects of discourse. Whether this resulted in the opportunity being abused or for some other reason, a new regulation was afterwards introduced, according to which these sermons could only be reviewed at the meeting of the clergy.

To keep the ministers on their part in a state of satisfactory efficiency, a weekly meeting of both those of the city and the country was held at which each in his turn expounded the portion of Scripture appointed for the day. Thereafter his exposition was subjected to the review or censure of his brethren. No one was allowed to absent himself from those meetings without adequate excuse. Another meeting was held before the quarterly celebration of the Lord's Supper, when the ministers were expected to pass each other's life and conduct under review and every one was under obligation to report upon anything objectionable, or any neglect in pastoral visitation, or any suspicion of error or heresy in another's teaching.[1] The Venerable Company, as they were called when thus assembled, took action upon any matter brought under their notice as falling within their province.[2]

It is notable that Calvin, who founded Presbyterianism with its native dislike of ritual and its devotion to 'free prayer,' should himself have advocated the use of a liturgy. His advocacy was no doubt due to his recognition of the incompetency of many of the ministers to give satisfaction in the public devotions. With his reverence for the usages of the primitive Church, he was doubtless influenced by

[1] Calvin had no high opinion of most of his colleagues, at least to begin with. In a letter of March 14, 1542, he says: "Our other colleagues are rather a hindrance to us than a help; they are rude and selfconceited, have no zeal and less learning. But what is worst of all, I cannot trust them, for they give scarcely any indication of a sincere and trustworthy disposition. I bear with them, however, for I dread the factions which must always necessarily arise from the dissensions of ministers."

[2] Children also came within the sweep of this principle of review. They had to submit to catechisings in church four times a year, having to answer the questions of the minister in presence of the congregation.

the considerable element of the liturgical which entered into its worship. He himself was accustomed to repeat the same prayer before and after sermon. Knox, his pupil, compiled a liturgy for the Scottish Church. But liturgies were already in use in the Reformed Church ; Calvin found the congregation at Strasburg in possession of one, and simply modified it into the form of prayers which he prepared in 1542, leaving out the chanting of the Ten Commandments. Farel had already introduced a liturgy into the Church at Geneva. In his Order for Public Worship, there was a strong element of the formal, the Lord's Prayer being repeated twice, once before and once after the sermon ; the Ten Commandments and the Apostles' Creed being also repeated. Calvin adopted this form of service as it stood, as appears from a letter in which he assures a correspondent that he introduced no change into Geneva, and that the usages in connection with the Supper, with marriage, and the feasts were the same now as formerly. The only difference he made was to introduce congregational singing. He desired to insert a formula of absolution into the service, but was advised that such an innovation might cause scandal and he did not insist. He was strongly in favour of the people hearing and joining in the prayers while on their knees, holding that such a posture was so instinctively human as to argue divine suggestion. The service was by no means all of a liturgical cast, opportunity being given for ' free prayer.'

APPENDIX TO CHAPTER XI

Examples of Calvin's Prayers

1. *MORNING PRAYER*

(1-5 are appended to the Genevan Catechism.)

My God, my Father and preserver, who by Thy grace towards me hast brought me through the night that is past to this new day, grant that I spend the whole of it in the service and reverent fear of Thy most holy majesty. In every thought, word, and deed may I seek to submit myself to Thee and do only Thy will. May all my actions conduce to the glory of Thy name and the welfare of my brethren, and by my example may they be led to reverence Thee. And as Thou dost illumine this world by the splendour of Thy sun to further the business of life, so enlighten my mind by the illumination of Thy Spirit and guide me through Him in the way of righteousness. To whatsoever thing I apply my mind, may it always be my aim to serve Thee and Thy honour. May I look for all happiness only to Thy grace and kindness, and may I undertake nothing at all which is not pleasing to Thee. Grant that, while I labour to provide for this life and attend to these things which pertain to the sustenance and care of the body, I may yet lift up my soul above these things to the blessed and heavenly life which Thou hast promised to Thy children. I beseech Thee to protect me in soul and body, strengthening and confirming me against all assaults of Satan and delivering me from all the dangers which do continually threaten us in this life. But since it is little to have begun well unless I persevere, I pray thee,

APPENDIX TO CHAPTER XI 211

O Lord, that thou wouldst be my guide and ruler not only this day but that Thou wouldst keep me in Thy faith to the end of my days, so that my whole course of life may be finished in Thy favour. And seeing that it is profitable for us, increase the gifts of Thy grace to me from day to day, while so much the more I cleave to Thy Son Jesus Christ, whom we justly call the true Sun perpetually shining in our hearts. That I may obtain so many and so great benefits from Thee, remember not my sins and pardon them by Thine infinite mercy, which Thou hast promised to do for those who call upon Thee from the heart. Amen. Psalm cxliii. 8.

2. *EVENING PRAYER*

O Lord God, Who hast appointed the night for the rest of man as Thou didst create the day in which he may give himself to labour, grant, I pray Thee, that so my body may rest this night that my soul may not cease meanwhile to watch for thee or my heart fall faint or be overcome by torpor but rather continue uplifted in Thy love. Help me to lay by my cares and so to be able to relax and relieve my mind that meantime I may not forget Thee or let go from my memory what ought always to be firmly fixed in my mind, the recollection of Thy goodness and grace. As thus my body rests, so may my conscience also enjoy its rest. Forbid that in taking sleep I should indulge the cravings of the flesh, but may I only allow myself so much as the weakness of nature demands, by which I shall be the better fitted to serve thee. Finally, be pleased to keep me chaste and pure, not only in body but in mind, and safe from all perils, so that even my sleep may yield glory to Thy name. But since this day has not passed without my offending Thee in many ways in which I am prone to evil, as all things are now covered by the darkness of the night, so let whatever there is of sin in me be hidden by Thy mercy. Hear me, O Father and Saviour, through Jesus Christ Thy Son, Amen.

3. *PRAYER FOR ONE GOING TO SCHOOL*

(Repeat Psalm cxix. 9.)

O Lord, who art the fountain of all wisdom and knowledge, since by Thy singular goodness Thou hast granted that my youth should be imbued with good arts which may help me to live godly and honestly and also may enlighten my mind which labours under blindness with regard to many things, grant at the same time that I be fit to apprehend what I am taught, and strengthen my memory that I may retain faithfully the instruction I receive; and finally, so govern my heart that I may willingly and eagerly set myself to profit lest the faculty which Thou hast given me may perish through my indolence. Father, pour out Thy spirit upon me, Thy spirit of understanding, of truth, of judgment, and of prudence, lest my study be without profit and the labour of my teacher with me be in vain. Whatever manner of study I undertake, may I remember to direct it to a right end, namely, that I may know Thee in Jesus Christ thy Son. And so whatever I learn, may it help me to follow a right rule of piety. Since Thou dost promise that Thou wilt enlighten even the poor and humble with wisdom and the righteous in heart with Thy knowledge, but Thou dost threaten to cast down the proud and the wicked, and deprive them of their understanding, I pray Thee to create in me a true humility, by which I may show myself docile and obedient first to Thee and also to those who exercise Thy authority over me, and also that Thou wouldst dispose my heart earnestly to seek Thee, purging me of all evil desires. May I ever keep one end before me, so to prepare myself in this my tender age that when I become a man, I may serve Thee in whatsoever estate Thou dost appoint for me. Psalm xxv. 14.

4. *GRACE BEFORE MEAT*

Psalm civ. 27. O Lord, Who art the only fountain of all good and its inexhaustible spring, pour forth Thy blessing upon us and bless for our use the food and drink which are gifts of Thy kindness towards us, so that using them

APPENDIX TO CHAPTER XI

temperately and frugally, as Thou biddest, we may eat with a pure conscience. May we always recognise Thee as our Father and the maker of all good with a sincere gratitude of mind, making confession with our mouth: and so may we enjoy bodily nourishment that yet we aspire with the chief affection of our hearts to the spiritual bread of Thy doctrine, by which our souls are fed unto the hope of eternal life through Jesus Christ our Lord. Deut. viii. 3.

5. *BAPTISMAL PRAYER*

O Lord God, eternal and omnipotent Father, since Thou hast promised us of Thine infinite mercy that Thou wouldst be our God and our children's, we pray Thee that Thou wouldst deign to confirm that benefit in this infant, born of these parents whom Thou hast received into Thy Church, and, as he is offered and consecrated by us to Thee, that Thou wouldst receive him into Thy guardianship, proving Thyself his God and Saviour, pardoning and remitting his inborn sin (*peccatum originis*), seeing that all his race bears the guilt of Adam, and sanctifying him by Thy Spirit, so that when he has arrived at an age capable of judgment and understanding, he may recognise Thee to be alone his God and Saviour and reverence Thee, giving Thee praise and glory all through his life, that he may always receive from Thee the pardon of his sins. But that he may be able to receive from Thee these benefits, deign to receive him into the communion of our Lord Jesus Christ, so that he may share in all His blessings, as one of the members of His body. Hear us, O Father of mercy, so that the baptised, whom we present to Him according to Thine appointment, may show forth His fruit and power.

6. *PRAYER WITH WHICH CALVIN HABITUALLY BEGAN HIS LECTURE*

Le Seigneur Dieu nous doient tellement traiter les mystères de sa sapience céleste, que nous profitions vrayement en la crainte de son sainct nom, à sa gloire et à notre edification. Ainsi soit-il.

7. *PRAYER WHICH HE ORDINARILY MADE BEFORE THE BEGINNING OF HIS SERMONS*

Let us call upon our good God and Father, praying Him to vouchsafe to turn away His face from the great number of faults and offences whereby we cease not to provoke His wrath against us; and forasmuch as we be too unworthy to appear before His majesty, it may please Him to look upon us in the face of His well-beloved Son our Lord Jesus Christ, accepting the merit of His death and passion for a full recompense of all our sins, that by means thereof He may be favourable to us and vouchsafe to enlighten us by His Spirit in the understanding of His word, and grant us the grace to receive the same in true fear and humility, so that we may be taught thereby to put our trust in Him, to serve and honour Him by glorifying His holy name in all our life, and to yield Him the love and obedience which faithful servants owe to their masters, and children to their fathers, seeing it has pleased Him to call us into the number of His servants and children. And let us pray unto Him as our good Master taught us to pray, saying, Our Father etc.

8. *PRAYER WHICH CALVIN ORDINARILY MADE AT THE END OF HIS SERMONS*

Let us fall down before the face of our good God, with acknowledgment of our sins. (Here he added petitions suitable to the matter of his discourse. Then he continued.) That it may please Him to grant this grace not only to us, but also to all people and nations of the earth, bringing back all poor ignorant souls from the miserable bondage to error and darkness to the right way of salvation, for the doing whereof may it please Him to raise up true and faithful ministers of His word that seek not their own profit and vain-glory but only the advancement of His holy name and the welfare of His flock; and to root out all sects, errors and heresies, which are seeds of trouble and division among His people, to the end that we may live in good brotherly concord altogether. And that it may please Him to guide with His Holy Spirit all kings, princes and magistrates that have the rule of the sword, to the end that their government be not by covetousness, cruelty, tyranny or any other evil and disordered affection, but in all justice and uprightness, and that we also, living under them, may yield them their due honour and obedience, and in good peace and quietness may serve God in all holiness and honesty. And that it may please Him to comfort all afflicted persons whom He visits after divers manners with crosses and tribulations, all people whom He afflicts with plague, war or famine, or other of His chastisements; also all persons that are smitten with poverty, imprisonment, sickness, banishment or other calamity or vexation of mind, giving them all good patience till He give them full deliverance from their miseries. And specially that it may please Him to have pity upon all His poor faithful ones that are dispersed in the captivity of Babylon under the tyranny of Antichrist, chiefly those which suffer persecution for the witnessing of His truth, strengthening them with true constancy and comforting them, and not suffering the wicked and ravening wolves to execute their rage against them, but giving them such a true steadfastness as that His holy name may be glorified by them both in life and death. And finally, that it may please Him to strengthen all churches that are now in danger and assaulted in the defence of His holy name, and overthrow and destroy all the devices, practices and attempts of all His adversaries, to the intent that His glory may shine over all, and the kingdom of our Lord Jesus Christ be increased and advanced more and more. Let us pray Him for all the said things in such wise as our good Master and Lord Jesus Christ has taught us to pray, saying, Our Father etc.

Also let us pray our good God to give us true continuance in His holy faith, and to increase it from day to day, whereof we will make confession saying, I believe in God etc.

His customary benediction was: The grace of God the Father and the peace of our Lord Jesus Christ, through the fellowship of the Holy Spirit, dwell with us for ever, Amen.

9. *PRAYER TO BE SAID BEFORE A MAN BEGINS HIS WORK*

O Lord God, most merciful Father and Saviour, seeing it hath pleased Thee to command us to labour that we may relieve our need, we beseech Thee of Thy grace so to bless our work that Thy blessing may extend unto us, without which we are not able to continue; and that this great favour may be a witness unto us of Thy bountifulness and assistance, so that thereby we may know the fatherly care thou hast over us.

Moreover, O Lord, we beseech thee that Thou wouldst strengthen us with Thine Holy Spirit that we may faithfully labour in our lot and calling without fraud or deceit, and that we may endeavour ourselves to follow Thy holy will rather than to seek to satisfy our greedy affection or desire of gain. And if it please Thee, O Lord, to prosper our labour, give us a mind also to help them that have need according to that ability that Thou of Thy mercy shalt give us. And knowing that all good things come of Thee, grant that we may humble ourselves to our neighbours, and not by any means lift ourselves up above them which have not received so liberal a portion as of Thy mercy Thou hast given us. And if it please Thee to try and exercise us by greater poverty and need than our flesh would desire, that Thou wouldst yet, O Lord, grant us grace to know that Thou wilt nourish us continually through Thy bountiful liberality, that we be not so tempted as to fall into distrust, but that we may patiently wait till Thou fill us, not only with corporal graces and benefits, but chiefly with Thine heavenly and spiritual treasures to the intent that we may always have more ample occasion to give Thee thanks and to wholly rest upon Thy mercies. Hear us, O Lord of mercy, through Jesus Christ Thy Son our Lord, Amen.

CHAPTER XII

DISCIPLINE

It may be said that Calvin's supreme aim was to produce a Church that deserved the name of holy. Religion to him was an essentially moral thing, vindicating its claim to authority over the minds and souls of men only by its ethical effects. Roman Catholicism judged the worst offences lightly, provided that the offender gave submissive ecclesiastical obedience. Calvin would palliate or tolerate no wickedness within the Church. Morality of the highest and purest kind was of the first importance, and the Church was endowed with spiritual forces and energies for its promotion. Calvin once committed himself to a definition of a Christian (*Comm. John*, i. 47), and it runs,— "it is integrity of heart before God and uprightness before men that makes a Christian." To him the Gospel in its last analysis was a new law designed to be embodied in a new life, individual and social. From the beginning of his public career he had steadily kept before himself the problem as to how the expression of faith in life was best to be secured. He had been impressed by the fact that the transference of sympathy and attachment from the old Church to the new had failed to result in a corresponding change of life. Reformed life was not specially characteristic of the Reformed Church, and to make it so became his great aim and endeavour. Doctrine was only contributory to the furtherance of that aim, giving inspiration and direction. Thought must ever be the servant of life. It is significant that in the first edition of the Institutes (whose comparative brevity permits its intention to stand out in clearer relief than in later expanded editions) the emphasis is laid not on doctrine, but on morals. To this attitude Calvin adhered all through his career. It was ultimately in the interests of morality that he waged his life-long struggle against the manifold agencies and forces enlisted on the side of unbelief or error. When he was recalled to Geneva by a penitent people, he laid it down as a first condition of consenting to return that a satisfactory system of discipline should be instituted, such as should effectually curb or suppress the prevalent disorders and scandals which disgraced alike the Church and the community. To the hands of the Church had been committed the task of securing the conformity of men's thoughts and conduct with the principles and truths of the revealed Word. It was false to its divine commission if it did not sedulously prosecute this great business. With it was deposited the revelation of God's will for man, and its chief function was to declare that will and in His name command the obedience of all. To the ministers all must listen as to God Himself. (Instit. IV. i. § 5.)

Whatever may be thought of the methods and measures Calvin adopted to secure that life and conduct should be truly Christian, it was a movement urgently required. The sweets of freedom from the fetters of Roman Catholic bondage created a taste for intellectual liberty of the most unrestricted kind and a corresponding absence of all moral restraints. There were many who, after throwing off one yoke, strongly resented being compelled to pass under another in some ways more burdensome. If its exactions were less, its restrictions were greater. If conformity of belief was demanded by the old Church, that was easier to submit to than the conformity of life demanded by the new. The threat of future punishment uttered by a Church which claimed to hold the keys of heaven and hell affected but little their secretly sceptical souls. But they could not be contemptuous of the civil penalties inflicted at the nod of a Church which could make it extremely unpleasant for them here and now. Those in Geneva who went by the name of Libertines or Patriots had embraced the cause of the Reformation with eagerness but with no love for the doctrines it asserted.

DISCIPLINE

It was to them the engine which was to break down the barbed wire of ecclesiastical tyranny that gallingly fenced them in, and lead them into a liberty which had no law but its own pleasure. Calling sin an illusion and a negation, they would destroy the hedges of God which kept the wayward propensities of men from paths of folly, vice and shame. Supervision and restraint were hateful to them; shame was a weakness and repentance a stupidity and folly. The system of indulgences and the complaisant tolerances of priestly absolution which could be bought and sold had widely enfeebled the conscience and blunted the moral sense of men to the distinctions between right and wrong. Emancipation from the rule of the Church was accompanied too often by the refusal to allow of any authority in the region of conduct. We will have no man to rule over us, was the watchword of many to whom life was but a generous opportunity for unrestrained self-indulgence.

The foundations of a healthy and stable society were gravely threatened. Calvin's brief experience in Geneva during his first stay was sufficient to inform him that measures of the most drastic and peremptory kind would be requisite for the restoration of the moral tone of the community as a whole. He spoke of the spirit of Libertinism as " the most pernicious and execrable which ever existed in the world, a fire kindled to scathe and destroy everything, a contagion which will infect the whole earth unless some remedy is found." The whole aim of these men, he asserted, was " to destroy all religion whatsoever, to efface all knowledge of the spiritual nature of man, to deaden his conscience, and obliterate all distinction between men and brutes." Compared to them the Pope was a virtuous character; the intensity of Calvin's hatred and dread of Libertinism may be gauged by contrast with the hearty recognition he offers to the good things to be found in the body whose head he regarded as Antichrist. The men who espoused it, he held, must be brought back to the recognition of the 'categorical imperative,' to submission to the authority of God's will, explicit in the Scriptures. Society would need to be reconstructed on the basis of a morality enforced by all the sanctions of a religion whose word was law and whose assertions were truth. The Reformed Church could only fail miserably in its function of Christianising the community unless it were authoritatively entrusted with the exercise of a salutary discipline backed by the power of the State. If the institution of discipline is the characteristic work of Calvin, with him rests the credit of saving not only Geneva but emancipated communities elsewhere from moral anarchy and the decadence which inevitably ensues.

Discipline, of course, in its proper ecclesiastical sense, was applicable only to members of the Church, but in practice it merged imperceptibly into legislative disciplinary measures for the whole community, as we shall afterwards see. Strictly speaking, it meant the supervisive control by a church court of those who had made profession of faith, and was intended " to protect the Church from contamination and profanation, to guard individual members against the corrupting influence of constant association with the wicked, and to bring the offender to repentance that he may be saved and restored to the fellowship of the faithful." [1] The consistory, to whose hands its exercise was confided, sat in judgment upon the conduct of all such, taking cognisance of whatever in their lives infringed the revealed law of God. They did not hesitate, however, to deal with whatever was offensive to their private moral judgment, though no Scripture could be adduced in condemnation, giving the force of law to their arbitrary view of conduct or acts to which no Biblical test could be applied. *E.g.* they vetoed the marriage of a 'small and infirm' girl of fourteen as premature. They refused permission to a man to marry a woman who had been banished for sorcery. Reprimand and censure, private or public, according to the adjudged needs of the case, were the ordinary inflictions. The only positive penalty at the disposal of the ecclesiastical court was excommunication, that is, exclusion from the Lord's Supper. As it was not within its province or power to inflict any other sort of punishment, it consigned

---

[1] Schaff, *Swiss Reformation*, ii. 487 f.

DISCIPLINE

any offender for whom some other form was needed to the civil courts to be dealt with in accordance with their judgment of his deserts. The consistory assumed the right to pronounce the verdict, while they required the magistrates to inflict the appropriate penalty. For example, the police court records of 27th April, 1546, attest that a man was imprisoned for four days because he persisted in calling his son Claude instead of Abraham, as the minister wished him to do, and for saying that rather than change he would keep his son unbaptised for fifteen years.[1] Condemned heretics, such as Servetus, were handed over to the civil courts at the recommendation and behest of the Church for punishment suitable to their guilt. It was the business of the State so to assist the Church in protecting purity of doctrine. Frequently the magistrate was called upon to pronounce sentence of banishment from the city upon those whom the consistory regarded as dangerous to the religious welfare of the community. The same sentence was pronounced upon any one who showed despite to the sacrament by failing to attend once at least in the year.

The sole positive punishment open to the ecclesiastical court to inflict, that of excommunication, was only imposed in extreme cases of misdemeanour; it was "the last thunderbolt of the Church." So serious a matter, Calvin held, must not be entrusted to the hands of any one man; it was only in the power of the consistory acting as a body. "I have never thought it expedient to entrust the right of excommunication to single pastors," he writes, "for the thing is odious, of doubtful example, apt to merge into tyranny, and the apostles have transmitted to us a contrary practice."[2] The accepted gravity of the penalty is evidence of the central place held by the Lord's Supper in Calvin's system. The principal object of such discipline, he asserted, was to preserve the Supper from profanation. But to be deprived of that special grace

---

[1] Letter, Aug. 27, 1554. In 1558 and 1559 there were 414 trials for such offences as laughing at Calvin while he was preaching. The penalty for that offence was three days in prison and having to ask pardon of the consistory.

[2] Letter, Aug. 27, 1554.

of which it was the channel was a profoundly serious matter. It was tantamount to being dissevered from Christ, for only through the Church and its Sacraments was union with Him mediated. (Instit. IV. xi. § 2.) Possessed of the power to effect this severance, the Church, represented by its court, was enabled to vindicate its authority and command respect. Where its view of the Supper was implicitly accepted, the possibility of being subjected to what might imperil eternal life acted as a wholesome restraint upon rebellious spirits. Incorrigibles like Philip Berthelier were as anxious to be restored to full church privileges as to civic rights. It was not to be thought, however, that the excommunicate were thereby expunged from the number of the elect and therefore to be despaired of as irretrievably lost. Of that, God was the sole judge. We ought to pray for them, said Calvin, this man of pitiful heart, and by every way of gentleness we must woo them back to holiness, taking care lest by lack of forbearance we turn discipline into torture. He urged that unless tenderness were exercised by individual members as by the Church collectively with a view to promote reformation and return, discipline would be in danger of degenerating into cruelty. "We may lawfully judge (the excommunicated) as aliens from the Church and so aliens from Christ. Let us not consign to destruction their person, which is in the hand and subject to the decision of the Lord alone." (Instit. IV. xii. § 9.) There was indeed a still graver form of ecclesiastical punishment, that of anathema, which differed from excommunication in that it completely precluded pardon, dooming and condemning the individual to eternal perdition. Such being its awful nature, it was rarely if ever to be used by fallible men. Excommunication had the intention of forewarning the guilty of the doom that awaited the impenitent and so restoring them to a right mind and a place within the walls of salvation.

Calvin found justification for resort to this form of punishment in the practice of the primitive Church of which it was one of the outstanding features and therefore one to be perpetuated under a due sense of responsibility. But the power to inflict it was really held only by the legitimate successors of that Church. There was nothing therefore to fear from its imposition by the Papal body, inasmuch as it had forfeited the claim to be regarded as a true Church of Christ. " Nor ought we to dread being banished from their assembly," he says, " since Christ, who is our life and salvation, is banished from it." (*Comm. John*, ix. 22.) Those who are not subject to Christ are deprived of the lawful power of excommunicating. It was for the Reformed Church to restore the ordinance to its primitive purity " that it might be in full vigour among us."

Calvin had a severe struggle with the civil authorities to secure to the Church the exclusive right of the power of excommunication. The Libertines, spying a danger to their liberties in such a power exercised by an unsympathetic body that frowned upon their ways, loudly protested against its being in the hands of the consistory, on the ground that thereby would be set up a tribunal within the State, an " imperium in imperio," whose decisions the magistrates had neither the right nor the power to review or veto. It is interesting to see how Calvin, when replying, draws his arguments from the Old Testament, in which alone, of course, he could discover precedents for procedure in a theocratic State. Other Reformers were not of the same mind with him in this matter. Zwingli and Bullinger held that excommunication should be in the hands of the State when it was governed by Christian magistrates. They admitted that it was the Church that exercised it in primitive days, but then it could get no assistance from Emperors who were pagans. Their view that the civil authorities, where Christian, were alone competent to inflict it effectively, was confirmed by the troubles occasioned by the Anabaptists, who acknowledged no jurisdiction on the part of the Church and cared nothing for its censures. Backed by such an influential opinion, in Berne, Zürich, and Lausanne, the State arrogated to itself the right of excommunication, and Berne, in its zeal for conformity, instigated Geneva to follow suit. But on this point Calvin, who compromised or yielded on so many others, was adamant. Holding that discipline was ' the nerve of the Church ' and excommunication 'the nerve of discipline,' he flatly declined to let this most sacred and responsible function of the Church be usurped by any secular tribunal. It might be said in a general way that the Reformed Church split over this point according to racial affinities, the German-Swiss sections taking the one side, the French-Swiss the other. How much stress the latter laid upon excommunication appears from the fact that rather than be deprived of the right, Viret and his ministerial colleagues at Lausanne resigned their charges and left the city, with the consequent dispersion of the Church.

There was reason in the contention of both sides. Where the Church is regarded as distinct from the State, with its own proper constitution, organisation, and life, the exercise of discipline rightly resides in the ecclesiastical authorities, who thereby safeguard its character and defend it against prejudicial influences emerging within itself. It is legitimate when exercised upon those who become members of such a religious society by profession of faith, and who therefore voluntarily subject themselves to its laws and regulations. But where the Church is practically identical with the State, that is, where every individual born in the community becomes a member simply by virtue of birth and nationality, as in Geneva, the case is different. Then the State which is responsible for putting him into such a relation to the Church is accountable, and ought to deal with him for infringements of laws of the Church which are really laws of the State. It is the business of the State, on the other hand, to safeguard the person, property and liberty of anyone arbitrarily menaced by the Church authorities on account of mere doctrinal deviations or ecclesiastical transgressions which are not, at the same time, civil offences.

CHAPTER XIII

INTOLERANCE AND SERVETUS

I

ONE fruit of Calvin's zeal for unity and his profound regard for the integrity of the Church along with his reverence for it as a divine institution was the intolerance he displayed in certain directions. To anything in doctrine which threatened to be disruptive of the Church he was fiercely hostile and inexorably merciless to those who asserted it. What was inimical to the Church's welfare was to be determined by the application of the test of Scripture. The Church was founded upon the Word of God, and anything destructive of the foundation was fatal to the whole superstructure. Calvin exposed himself to the charge of constituting himself judge of what was or was not consistent with its teaching; but one who had expounded with such particularity all its books with few exceptions in a series of commentaries accepted by the Protestant world as authoritative, might well feel that there was none to dispute his supreme competency and right to decide. His views on the great doctrines of Scripture were generally held within the Reformed Church as substantially sound. He allowed for variety of opinion as to the exact way in which some of these were to be stated and interpreted. It was in connection with their outright denial or what in his opinion amounted to that, or the assertion of others incompatible or contradictory that his intolerance blazed forth in all its grim fury. In the lengths to which it carried him, Calvin did not secure the sympathy of other leaders. The Berne ministers addressed a letter of severe remonstrance on the matter of the unmitigated and passionate severity of his attitude to Bolsec, who had joined issue with him on the doctrine of predestination.

If his vicious vehemence was sometimes inexcusable, it must be said that he had good ground for the dread which fired it. He was consumed with concern for the moral well-being of the community, and experience as well as history had taught him that the upshot of serious doctrinal deviation was moral mischief. The Libertinism which pervaded Geneva with a moral miasma was rooted in a creed which radically departed from the fundamentals of the Christian faith. Its adherents rejected the Evangelists, denied the Resurrection, jeered at the Apostles, characterising each of them by a nickname,—Paul, pot-cassé, Peter, renonceur de Dieu, and so on. Instigated by this irreverent spirit, they sought to convert immorality into a system.[1] Towards such men Calvin demanded that no tolerance should be shown. "There be many crabbed philosophers," he said, "who would have these furious giants soothed by flattery. Such did never taste what that meaneth, the zeal of thine house hath eaten me up. Let us, bidding adieu to their coldness or rather sluggishness, be carried even to the highest pitch of fervour, as becometh us in maintaining the glory of God."[2] Into his conflicts with them Calvin went with ungloved hands, intent on nothing short of their suppression or extinction. "It is a cruel kind of mercy," he said, "which prefers a single man to the whole church." He paraphrases Paul's words in Gal. v. 12 thus :—"Ought not my care of the Church to lead me to desire that its salvation should be purchased by the destruction of the wolf? Yet I would not wish that a single individual should perish in this way ; but my love for the Church and my anxiety about her interests carry me away into a sort of ecstasy so that I can think of nothing else." With such zeal as this, he adds, every true pastor of the Church will burn. It may moderate the summary and wholesale condemnation that has been meted out to Calvin on this account if the opinion

---

[1] Strype's *Annals*, ii. p. 2. ii. 287 ff.   [2] *Comm. Acts*, xiii. 10.

of Harnack, who cannot be accused of partisanship with the Reformer, is quoted. " If one considers that the principal anti-Trinitarians . . . allowed themselves to become parties to a bad morality, we must judge that tolerance opposed to them would have probably led forthwith in the sixteenth century to the dissolution of the evangelical faith in the Calvinistic countries."

It might be objected that, whatever could be said for intolerance within the Church, it had no right to assert jurisdiction over any outside its membership, as in the case of not a few like Servetus and Bolsec. But that is a modern notion. Since the time that Christianity became the law of the State or part of its constitution, according to the maxim, *cujus regio, ejus religio*, any one within its borders who professed heresy put himself among the criminal classes. Augustine endorsed that view, and it was an accepted axiom of the Middle Ages. The supervision which had been exercised by the Roman Church over the whole community was claimed also by the ruling courts of the Reformed Church. The consistory of Geneva regarded all within the city walls as under their ecclesiastical care. Practically they identified the Church with the community, and brought to book all alike who infringed the moral law of which they were the appointed guardians or who attacked the creed which was the foundation of the Church. If the soul of the Church was purity of doctrine, and the soul of the community was a pure Church, then it followed that purity of doctrine must be safeguarded in the interests of the community. But any one who intruded upon the sphere of theology, the peculiar province of the Church, might be regarded as *ipso facto* including himself within the Church, otherwise he had no right of entry. Either it must be ' Hands off ! ' altogether, or submissive and tacit acceptance of the articles by which the Church was constituted. A belligerent outsider was capable of doing as much injury as a rebellious insider. No one therefore could be allowed to attack the Church with impunity, as though it need fear no harm from him. But while measures of controversial defence are taken now-a-days against such external foes, the Genevan Church demanded that the State authorities should intervene and enforce the verdicts pronounced by the ecclesiastical courts. A theological error thus became a criminal offence, liable to the pains and penalties of all lawbreaking.

II.

During the celebrations of the Calvin quatercentenary at Geneva in 1909, there was unveiled a monument whose character stamps it as unique in history. It consists of a rough-hewn, upright slab of stone, with inscriptions on both sides which indicate its purpose. On the one side are inscribed the words, Fils respectueux et reconnaissants de Calvin, notre grand Réformateur, mais condamnant une erreur qui fut celle de son siècle, et firmement attachés à la liberté de conscience selon les vrais principes de la Réformation et de L'Évangile, nous avons élevé ce monument expiatoire, Le XXVII Octobre MCMIII. On the other side are engraved the words, Le XXVII Octobre MDLIII MOURUT SUR LE BÛCHER À CHAMPEL MICHEL SERVET DE VILLENEUVE D'ARAGON, NÉ LE XXIX Septembre MDXI. Doumergue, whose elaborate work on Calvin will form a quarry for all subsequent investigators, at whose instigation this expiatory monument was erected, informs us that the inscription originally proposed ran, A Champel Servet monta sur le bûcher le 27 Octobre 1553, victime de l'erreur de Calvin et de son temps. Les protestants reformes du vingtième siècle ont dressé cette pierre en témoignage de leur profond respect pour la liberté de conscience et à l'honneur des vrais principes de la Réformation et de l'Évangile. This makes more explicit the feeling and views of those responsible for it, and proves that the prolonged and often acrimonious controversy on the deplorable occurrence may be now considered settled by the verdict, consented to by the adherents of the Reformers, that Calvin was guilty of a grave fault, whose only extenuation was that he was instigated by the spirit of the times. It adds to the significance of this monument that there is none to Calvin himself; he appears only as one of a sculptured group of Reformers. Doumergue thinks that he would himself desire no better one than this of expiation.

Though the controversy may now be regarded as closed, any review of Calvin's attitude to the great problems of life would be incomplete without some account of the miserable story. There have been those who have taken their view of Calvin from his association with Servetus, of whom a somewhat extreme example is quoted by Cunningham as saying, " It (the execution) stamps his (Calvin's) character as a persecutor of the first order, without one humane or redeeming quality to divest it of its criminality or to palliate its enormity " !

III.

It is of the irony of things that the man whose fate more than anything else has given ground for odium against Calvin and his Church, was a native of Spain, the one European country which Calvinism barely touched. Servetus was born the same year as the Reformer himself in Villeneuve in Aragon, whence was taken the pseudonym under which his first book was published, Villanovanus or Villeneuve. Like Farel, he was of noble family, and, like Calvin, his father was a lawyer. Also like his great antagonist, he began his career by studying law at the University of Toulouse. There a copy of the Bible came into his hands, and its perusal, as with Luther at Erfurt, began his emancipation from the bondage of Rome. He was present at the Diet of Augsburg in attendance upon a friar who was confessor to the Emperor, and a mind like his, already disposed to revolt, would inevitably receive a strong impulse along the way his face was set by what he heard from the lips of Melanchthon and the other Reformers attending the Diet. But he identified himself with no party or sect, remaining a theological freelance to the end of his life, approaching now one side, now another, although he remained nominally within the Roman Church and conformed to its rites. His portrait represents a man with face lean and pale, of something of a Shakespearean cast, peaked beard, brooding, melancholy eyes that might flash into passion or melt into self-pity or droop with timid self-consciousness, the pouting lips of the ready speaker, the large nose commonly indicative of pronounced character, if not of strength of mind.

Servetus was only twenty-two when his first book appeared, that on the Trinity, which immediately brought him into prominence and made him a marked man. He had indeed a precocious and versatile mind with something of the instinctive insight into things which characterises genius. Perhaps through his association as proof-reader with a famous firm of printers at Lyons his attention was early turned to the study of geography, and at the age of twenty-six he issued a splendid edition of Ptolemy's geography, whose preparation proved his capacity for strenuous labour and real scholarly work. His essay in this new field brought him well-merited reputation; so highly was the volume esteemed that a second edition was soon called for. His characterisations of the various nations are often just, penetrating and shrewd. Of the races embraced by Germany he says (to some extent repeating the views of Tacitus), "Hungary is said to produce oxen; Bavaria, swine; Franconia, onions, turnips, and licorice; Swabia, harlots; Bohemia, heretics; Switzerland, butchers; Westphalia, cheats; and the whole country, gluttons and drunkards. . . . The Germans, however, are a religious people not easily turned from opinions they have once espoused, and not readily persuaded to concord in matters of schism; every one valiantly and obstinately defending the heresy he himself has adopted." Regarding his fellow-countrymen he is candid and in part the reverse of flattering. " The Spaniard is of a restless disposition, apt enough of understanding, but learning imperfectly or amiss, so that you shall find a learned Spaniard almost anywhere sooner than in Spain. Half-informed, he thinks himself brimful of information, and always pretends to more knowledge than he has in fact. He is much given to vast projects never realised; and in conversation he delights in subtleties and sophistries. . . . Spaniards are notably the most superstitious people in the world in their religious notions; but they are brave in the field, of signal endurance under privation

INTOLERANCE AND SERVETUS

and difficulty, and by their voyages of discovery have spread their name over the face of the globe." Scotland was beyond his ken, but from his information he drew this picture. " The people of Scotland are hot-tempered, prone to revenge, and fierce in their anger, but valiant in war and patient beyond belief of cold, hunger, and fatigue. They are handsome in person and the clothing and language are the same as those of the Irish, their tunics being dyed yellow, their legs bare, and their feet protected by sandals of undressed hide. They live mainly on fish and flesh. They are not a particularly religious people."

Servetus now gave himself to the study of medicine, taking his degree at Paris. Such was his industry and quickness of mind that within a year from his graduation he published a learned treatise on Syrups, whose usefulness and accepted trustworthiness were proved by the issue of four editions in ten years. But his chief claim to a permanent place among the world's men of light and leading rests on his discovery of the circulation of the blood, in which he anticipated Harvey by nearly a century. The Englishman, however, is entitled to the credit of independent discovery, inasmuch as neither he nor in fact more than a few of the medical profession have ever been aware of Servetus's priority. The explanation of the announcement leaving so slight a trace in the scientific world is probably to be found in the fact that his discovery was intimated as a kind of *obiter dictum* in his theological treatise on *The Restitution of the Christian Religion*. Meanwhile he was applying himself with tireless industry to other departments of study, and succeeded in acquiring at least a competent knowledge of Greek and Hebrew, French and Italian, besides Latin with which every educated person was more or less acquainted. Along with the acquisition of these languages, he plunged into the study of theology and philosophy, exploring many of the classics of both Plato and the Neo-Platonists, some of the early Christian Fathers and the later schoolmen. It was on the strength of this array of acquirements that he assumed the insufferable air of arrogant superiority which he displayed alike to his professorial colleagues in the

University of Paris and to the Reformers whom he set out to reform, earning the hearty dislike of both. It may be said that, while he made enemies wherever he went, he made no such friends as Calvin attracted and rejoiced in. He seems to have been one of these hedgehog natures which find their own company sufficient and secure all the satisfaction they desire in the admiration they extort or the commotion they occasion. What help he did need to sustain him in his tempestuous career was received from his religious faith, which was undoubtedly a staff and rod to comfort him, even though it signally failed to guide him.

After leaving the University of Paris in mingled disgust and disgrace, he spend the one quiet period of his life practising as a physician for fifteen or sixteen years mostly in Vienne. During this period, he published an edition of the Latin Bible as prepared by a pupil of Savonarola. Here again credit must be given him for anticipating the results of later thought in that he independently applied to the interpretation of Scripture the historical method which Calvin so fruitfully practised, but he went even further than the Reformer in his application, *e.g.* identifying the Servant of the Lord of Deutero-Isaiah with Cyrus, King of Persia, the liberator of the exiled Jews from Babylon. It was at Vienne, too, that he composed the book which brought him to the stake, *The Restitution of the Christian Religion*.

Such was the man who, after these quiet but busy years, emerged from his obscure retirement, urged by some uncontrollable impulse which he interpreted as a divine call, to disturb the whole Reformed world, and, communicating to it temporarily something of his own aberration, to bring upon himself the most tragic of fates and upon the Protestant Church an indelible stain. The sordid story has been told hundreds of times, and it is sufficient here simply to outline it. Getting into touch with various leading Reformers and finally with Calvin, Servetus sought to convince them of their errors and persuade them to accept his view. He rendered himself equally obnoxious to the Roman Catholics, and on the strength of information lodged by a resident in Geneva who was

INTOLERANCE AND SERVETUS

supplied with data by Calvin himself, he was brought to book and put on his trial in the town in which he had so long practised. Foreseeing condemnation, he cleverly succeeded in making his escape from gaol. He was nevertheless sentenced to be burnt along with his books in a slow fire. It was not the fault of the Roman Catholics that Protestantism was not spared the odium of inflicting on its own account a similar sentence.

Servetus did not learn his lesson and, as though afflicted by a 'fatal madness,' to use Calvin's words, he soon exposed himself again to the very danger from which he had just escaped. He proposed to settle in Naples, there to resume medical practice under an assumed name amongst the numerous Spanish residents. On his road thither, drawn by some fatal fascination, he made Geneva a stopping place for a few days. His vanity would not let him remain incognito; his presence was made known to Calvin who promptly procured his arrest, a most mischievous error of judgment on the Reformer's part. Servetus was not under the jurisdiction of Geneva, and, even if he had been, he had committed no crime within its walls. It may be that Calvin mistakenly presumed that he had come to spread the poison of his teaching through the city, and dreaded the consequences of his success at that supremely critical juncture of Geneva's affairs when he had his back to the wall and was fighting for the very existence of Reform in religion and morals. Unfriendly though the Council was at that time to Calvin, they endorsed his action and put Servetus on his trial. Calvin led in the prosecution from the theological side. The accused was given every facility for preparing his defence, Calvin himself lending him copies of such Fathers as he desired to consult; but he was allowed no counsel. The trial went on for two months and was conducted by a large jury consisting of the little Council, the criminal judges, and the heralds of the city, presided over by the Lord-Lieutenant. It largely developed into a theological tournament between Servetus and Calvin, Servetus showing considerable skill and resource in argument, but proving no match for his opponent either in logic or in learning. In the course of his trial Servetus exhibited that vein of natural timidity which he shared along with Calvin, yoked as it was with a boldness that savoured of insanity. He resorted to all manner of equivocations and sheer lying to escape from damaging charges and facts. The Council corresponded with the judges at Vienne, asking for details of the accusations brought against him there; in response, a commissioner arrived, conveying a copy of the sentence passed upon him and requesting that he be sent back to France to suffer the penalty which had been pronounced upon him. It is to the credit of the Council that they refused to consent, declaring that he would have every justice done him. They certainly went very thoroughly into the merits of the case, traversing the whole ground of the charges against him more than once. It must be admitted, however, that by this time a strong prejudice had formed itself in their minds, as appears from their refusal to grant his request for counsel in accordance with their criminal statutes, on the ground that there was " not one jot of apparent innocence which requires an attorney." Yet he had judges strongly partial to him because of their hostility to Calvin. At their solicitation, Servetus and Calvin prepared documents setting forth grounds of accusation and defence, each being allowed to reply to the other, and these were submitted to the other Swiss Churches for their judgment. In the last of these replies Servetus appears to be of demented mind, such are the violence and coarseness of abuse he heaps on his opponent. Yet he subscribed it as one who had " the most certain protection of Christ." Zürich, Schaffhaussen, Basel, and Berne unanimously declared for his exemplary punishment, whose nature they left the civil tribunal to decide. The partisans of Servetus, foreseeing what the issue was to be, sought to get the matter referred to the Council of 200 and on their failure quitted the Court. Thereafter, those remaining unanimously condemned the accused to death at the stake. The sentence was carried out on the following day, the condemned man displaying frantic terror and yielding up his soul with the suffocating cry, Jesus Christ, thou Son of the eternal God, have mercy upon me.

IV.

Servetus was the fruit of the freethinking of his time grafted upon the basal principle of Protestantism, namely, the supreme and final authority of the Scriptures. He was one with the Reformers in accepting the Canon as the infallible source of all truth, but he differed from them in refusing to submit to the dictation of the great oecumenical Confessions as to what the Bible taught. Indeed he declared that the demise of the Church occurred at the Council of Nicaea, and the reign of Antichrist then began. Athanasius and Augustine, according to him, were disciples of that evil spirit. He took this view of these venerable Councils because they were responsible for imposing on the Church doctrines professedly drawn from the Bible which were to him utterly irrational and therefore incredible. Convinced of the truth of certain theological tenets of Greek philosophy, as appears from his frequent approving references to Plato and the Neo-Platonists, he insisted on bringing them to the elucidation and interpretation of Scriptural teaching.

His first book, that against the doctrine of the Trinity, defined the fundamental ground of his quarrel with orthodoxy. Though he subsequently retracted the views therein expressed, it was not because he had come to regard them as false, but because they were imperfectly stated and " as if by a child for children," to use his own words. He held them unwaveringly to the end of his career and was finally condemned largely on their account. The doctrine of the Trinity, he affirmed, was without warrant of Scripture and without support of reason. He ridiculed it as a piece of nonsense and a fable, describing the God it represented as " a devil with three heads like the Cerberus whom the ancient poets called the dog of hell, a monster." He accused Trinitarians of being believers in three Gods, or alternatively, four, the essence which was the common ground of their Being constituting the fourth. A Being who was three Gods in one was an impossible existence, he held, and therefore he characterised the Trinitarians as really atheists. He himself believed in one divine Being, simple and indivisible, not such a God as the Mohammedans accepted, though he quotes the Koran with approval, but one more nearly corresponding to that of pantheism, pervading and indeed constituting all things, " showing Himself to us as fire, as a flower, as a stone." Evil is subsumed in His essence as well as good. At his trial Servetus assented when Calvin asked him point-blank if God was in the pavement under his feet. "With Simon Magus, you shut up God in a corner," he wrote in prison, " I say that He is in all things." The human spirit is a spark of the divine Spirit. It was in developing this thesis that he entered upon an investigation regarding the vital essences in man which led him to expound his theory of the circulation of the blood.

Yet he did not deny the divinity of Christ; his theology was as Christocentric as that of the Reformers. Jesus was to him the Son of God through whom are all things and for whom are all things, and he worshipped Him heartily, even calling Him God. He might well have passed for orthodox, had he not proceeded to explanation and definition. He parted company with the Reformers in denying that Jesus was the *eternal* Son of God, asserting that He had no previous personal existence as the Second Person of a Trinity, and that He began to be with His conception and birth. Nor, he affirmed, was He an inconceivable compound of two natures, divine and human, each communicating its attributes to the other; that was to make two Sons of God. Jesus underwent a deifying process, exercised upon His whole being by God, a process which resulted in His becoming of the same substance as God and so entitled to the name of God. "The soul of Christ is God; the flesh of Christ is God; the spirit of Christ is God," he declares. Elsewhere he puts it otherwise, thus:—the divine nature coalesces with the human in Christ; His flesh, the earthly portion of His being, is derived from the first pure matter, as it existed before sin, and belongs to the stage previous to that from which ours, corrupted by the fall, is drawn.

It is to be noted that Servetus himself taught a Trinity, but it was a Trinity of manifestation, not of persons. The one God reveals Himself in different ways, in Christ and in the Holy Spirit, the latter manifestation dating from

INTOLERANCE AND SERVETUS 237

Pentecost. He might have adopted other forms, and so there might have been a fourfold or a fivefold seeming personality. He might have manifested Himself in different ways suitable to beings differently constituted from ourselves. The holy Spirit is an energy or 'disposition' in God. The person of Christ, when His work is finished, will cease to be. It was no mere hardened waywardness which made him stand by these views; he was convinced enough to die for them. His expiring breath carried a prayer to "Jesus Christ, thou Son of the eternal God." Even to escape that last bitter agony, he would not address Christ as "eternal Son of God."

While this was the fundamental ground of his condemnation, there were few doctrines of the Reformers with which Servetus did not totally disagree. He repudiated predestination, holding that God is just and merciful to all His creatures and arbitrarily condemns no one, each individual really passing sentence upon himself. God gave freedom of will to every man; it is due to man's own evildoing if he loses in part that freedom. To teach a doctrine of total depravity is to blaspheme God, seeing that the soul is of the same essence with God. Hereditary guilt was a pure fiction. Hereditary sin was a different matter and proved by observation and experience, but it was only a disease for which a child cannot be held responsible. Sin to which guilt was attached began only with the age when responsibility was recognised to begin, *i.e.* about the twentieth year. (He refers for proof to such passages as Exodus xxx. 14; xxxviii. 26; Num. xiv. 29; xxxii. 11; Deut. i. 39.) Faith alone is not sufficient for salvation; it must be supplemented by good works. Baptism is of no efficacy unless preceded by repentance and the illumination of the Spirit, which involves that the subject of it must have reached manhood, and then it confers remission of sin and entrance into the kingdom of heaven. He regarded infant baptism as most responsible, after the doctrine of the Trinity, for all the corruptions of the Church. Singularly enough, he approximates very closely to Calvin in his view of the Lord's Supper, holding that in it we receive the body of Christ in a spiritual and mystical manner, and so are united more and more closely to Him. He advocated a doctrine approaching that of conditional immortality, asserting that the soul is mortal but is put in possession of eternal life by union with Christ; yet he taught that the souls of all the departed continue to exist in Sheol awaiting the judgment. He condemned prayers for the dead on the ground that they do not need our prayers, and that there is no warrant in Scripture for such intercession. After a millennial reign of Christ upon earth, the general resurrection and judgment would follow, the dead being raised in the prime of manhood, which he determined to be the thirtieth year, the age at which Christ was baptised and began His public ministry.

V.

From this rapid sketch of his system of ideas, it will be seen that in many points Servetus was at once an echo of antiquity and a herald of modernity. He claimed to be striving for the restitution of primitive Christianity, as the title of his chief book indicated. Indeed he regarded himself as divinely commissioned to this end, ' the chosen instrument of God to enlighten mankind,' claiming to be either the archangel Michael incarnate or one of his angelic warriors through whom the great dragon, the deceiver of the whole world, was to be cast down. He distinguished himself from Calvin, who, though he too strove to reproduce Christianity in its primitive purity, yet was really nothing more than a reformer of the existing Church, while he (Servetus) claimed to be a restorer of the original Church. Calvin was indeed the heir of traditional orthodoxy, and incorporated it in his system; but Servetus, while repudiating the theologians of the formative creedal period, unearthed again the heresies of these days and fashioned them into an amalgam closely related to them all, but identifiable with none. Calvin himself showed signs of the disposition to break away from the shackles of the great creeds at least in respect of their modes of stating some doctrines. Servetus would wipe the slate clean of all the precipitate of study, discussion, and controversy and go back to quarry directly from the only authoritative sources of truth a system acceptable to reason while consistently loyal to Scripture. The result proved that with the best will in the world no man can divest himself of personal prepossessions engendered perhaps by extra-Biblical study, nor avoid reading them into the assertions of the Bible. Moreover to ignore the fruits of previous controversy is to destroy guide posts which keep inquirers from straying into inviting but dangerous ways already fully explored by competent minds. The man who derides the value of early dogmatic controversy and brackets ecclesiastical orthodoxy with heresy as alike misleading and unworthy of serious consideration is sure to find himself sooner or later on paths marked with the feet of those upon whom he thought he had turned his contemptuous back. If Calvin was a second Augustine, Servetus was a composite of nearly all the heresiarchs from Paul of Samosata, the foppish apostle of a deified man, to Eutyches, the commonplace apostle of a God-man with one nature. The early Church had been given divine wisdom to perceive how disastrous would be the adoption of certain views regarding the fundamental articles of the faith, and the thoughtful informed modern mind has endorsed its apprehension. Even Carlyle, sworn foe of all cant, came to admit that the future might hang on a diphthong. History was repeating itself in Servetus in a concentrated form, and through him the future welfare of the Christian religion, as a uniquely divine revelation and faith, was once more imperilled. That was the immediate perception of all the leaders of the day. Oecolampadius, to whom he first submitted his views, was horrified. Zwingli characterised them as " dreadful blasphemy," a thing insufferable in the Church of God. Martin Bucer pronounced his treatise to be " a most pestilential book," for which the author deserved to be " disembowelled and torn in pieces,"—which from a mild man like him indicates pretty strong feelings. Luther summarily condemned the book as " ein graülich bös Buch," (a shockingly bad book), while Melanchthon spoke of " the horrid blasphemies " of Servetus.

The danger from these views was all the greater that they were advocated by a man who was honestly convinced of their truth. Servetus was no play-actor, strutting the stage merely for fame, though he was not without his ambitions in that direction. He really thought he had exposed the untrustworthiness of the traditional theology and had something more reliable to offer in its stead. His scientific mind would not allow him to acquiesce in what seemed to him the evident irrationalities of orthodoxy. Three ones make three not one, and if the three proceeded from one, why then there were four. The error of Trinitarianism in a nutshell! So he applied arithmetical criteria to theological formulae and proved to his own satisfaction the falsity of a doctrine by a *reductio ad absurdum* which only betrayed how far he was from rightly apprehending it or its value for faith, mysterious though it be. Yet the ultimate consequences of successfully discrediting the Trinitarian doctrine did not come within his horizon, and Christ remained to him practically what He was to Calvin. He had a passionate belief in Him as the foundation and centre of his faith, the only source of all true or reliable knowledge of God, the author of salvation and the giver of eternal life. If He was not God to him in the orthodox sense, at least He had the value of God. Servetus was indeed something of a Ritschlian born out of due season.

With the sincerity of his theological convictions, he combined a genuinely religious soul, that is, a soul to which religion meant much. But his religion was largely a matter of thought and emotion such as expressed itself in the prayers and ejaculations scattered through his books. It did not penetrate or govern his moral life. In spite of disclaimers, it is easy to believe the testimony of contemporaries that his conduct was far from impeccable, in view of his flippant answer to the question why he did not marry,—" because there were plenty women." The identification of such subversive views with a man whose life was of no high character must have greatly contributed to strengthen Calvin's apprehensions regarding the sure issue of their widespread acceptance. There can be little doubt that, if the views of Servetus had gained a wide and sympathetic hearing, a crisis, whose gravity cannot be exaggerated, would have been precipitated upon the Christian world. Many of his opinions may now be held widely and innocuously, but the world was not then prepared for them. Many were only too ready to welcome any view that would justify their breaking away from the restraints and constraints of a faith whose high moral demands were hatefully irksome. The temper of immorality needs the countenance of irreligion to make it blatant. Servetus may be credited with failing to see the issue of a general acceptance of his propositions; a second Arius would not consent to the verdict of history upon the first. But believer and unbeliever alike recognise that the success of such an attack as his upon the pillar doctrines of Christianity would have involved, sooner or later, as its implications became apparent, a landslide of faith over the precipice of negation into the welter of natural religions, and therewith the deposition of Christianity from its supreme place as a unique revelation to the level and order of those religions whose comparative merits must be decided by the test of their fruits.

VI.

Nevertheless it was not his views merely that brought Servetus to the stake, (anti-Trinitarianism was rife among the Italian and Polish refugees in Geneva); it was the tone he adopted and the temper he displayed in their advocacy which brought him into such special disfavour. From the beginning he made enemies by his insolent and arrogant bearing. This rendered him so unpopular at Charleroi, a small town near Lyons where he practised as doctor, that he had to leave it. He would own no man as master and he wished to master the minds of all. To Calvin, whose temper was at no time of the sweetest, he assumed the most exasperating air of superiority, urging him to abandon his errors and accept enlightenment. Victim of the conceit of finality, he insulted the intelligence of past ages by writing their thinkers down as fools and appraising himself as the one wise man. Something of a theological anarchist and a religious rowdy, he was ambitious to lead but lacked the qualities of leadership, and so to the end he ploughed a lonely furrow, and that but a zigzag one. The encyclopaedic brain, which might have won him enduring fame, only gained him a fatal notoriety. His really capacious intellect was stultified by his capricious character. If he did not get fair play, he invited and incited the implacable hostility which glared at him from all points of the compass. Fortune and the world favour the brave, but at the insolence of a freakish and presumptuous audacity they are more likely to turn their thumbs down. Of not one can it be said with more truth, that he made the bed on which he had to lie. He played for high stakes, knowing and approving of the rules of the game and the penalties of such failure as would be his if he did not win.[1] But he was too much of an egotist to believe that he could fail, or too much of an opportunist to anticipate that issue. He counted on a sympathy which was actually already prevalent, but not in such strength as to succeed in averting his fate. His fate indeed contributed in no small degree to the growth of a new spirit, for the stake of Servetus became one of the main roots of the world's tolerance. The smoke of his pyre, if it did not extinguish, at least greatly moderated the flame of the fanaticism which saw no good where it saw no truth.

As he was the ripe fruit of the intellectual libertinism to which the Renaissance and the Reformation had together given birth, he was the incarnation of the spirit of self-assertive, self-confident youth, conscious of its strength, dogmatic in insistence on its rights, regarding with hostile suspicion traditional views presented for its unquestioning acceptance, delighting to apply the acid of doubt to all that called itself orthodox. "He gave the impression of being an undisciplined presumptuous boy," says Schaff, "who, with the most froward effrontery, indulged himself in whatever passed through his head and then shrank from chastisement, rather than of a man who ventures

[1] " Hoc crimen (heresy) est morte simpliciter dignum." (*Restit.* 656.) Cf. Gentilis, who attacked the doctrine of the Trinity, and was condemned and beheaded at Berne three years after Calvin's death. He had challenged the ministers of Gex to a dispute " under the condition that he who could not support his opinions by God's word should be beheaded as a deceiver."

INTOLERANCE AND SERVETUS

deliberately on the highest and serves a holy conviction with his life." In an age of hard hitting and strong words he shocked all alike by the coarseness of the language he employed in seeking to turn to ridicule the most sacred objects of faith. At times it sounds like the ravings of a mind temporarily deranged. But this much may be said in extenuation, that what sounded blasphemies to others were not so to him. He was slinging his muddy missiles at what in his view were non-existences, imaginary divine beings. He might have been speaking of one of the creatures of Lewis Carroll's agreeably grotesque fancy. His very blasphemy, as others regard it, might, from his side be regarded as evidence of his absolute assurance of the truth of his own views. He was all reverence for the Christ in whom he believed. Nevertheless a man of fine feeling or even of no more than discreet judgment would have avoided such crass and coarse jocularity in dealing with matters which lay close to the heart of the faith of others. That was to excite in those whom he would win an antagonism which made them indignantly deaf to all his reasonings. It is the reverse of politic first to incense a man whom you would convince. Plausible as many of his ideas were and sound as some of his views would now be considered, it is significant that none stood up in defence of them at his trial, and the protests that were raised against his treatment proceeded not from any ardent sympathy with his teachings but were inspired by a righteous hatred of persecuting intolerance.

VII.

If Calvin's share in his execution cannot be excused, at least it can be explained. The peculiar asperity and hostility which he displayed to Servetus had a temperamental origin. Each was an egotist of the first order, and saw in the other a rival, in the one case to be dreaded for the mischief he might work, in the other to be hated for the prominence he had attained. High austerity on the one side was ranged against moral laxity on the other. Protest as he may and did, Calvin cannot be acquitted of allowing his personal antipathy to bias his judgment. One cannot help feeling as if he had been actuated by a remorseless and vindictive resolution to crush out of existence this serpent in his path. He pressed pitilessly for the issue he frankly desired and with a kind of self-congratulation actually claimed credit for the sinister part he had played.

In a strange way their lives collided and rebounded again and again from the time when they studied concurrently at Paris. Under an almost demoniac impulse, Servetus had set himself from the first to bait and harass Calvin. It looked as if Servetus discerned by some prophetic instinct the great role Calvin was to play, and his envious ambition sought to secure that prominence for himself. He challenged the student Calvin to a disputation at Paris, but himself failed to appear. A few years later when he concluded that his first baptism was of no value and he thought it necessary to be re-baptised, he sent two letters to Calvin fatuously urging him to follow his example. When on the eve of publishing the book which damned him, he again intruded himself upon Calvin and sought to entangle him in a discussion on various doctrinal points such as the nature of the divinity of Christ and the presuppositions of effectual baptism. Calvin certainly sought to give him satisfaction, but it was not explanations Servetus wanted; it was the discomfiture of one whom he regarded as the main obstacle in the way of the triumph of his views. He bombarded Calvin with letters, to some of which the Reformer replied with exemplary patience and kindly desire for his correspondent's enlightenment. A copy of the Institutes to which Calvin had referred him Servetus returned with copious marginal annotations of such a kind as at last roused the Reformer's ire and disgust which he expressed in no squeamish terms in a letter to Farel. It was in this letter that Calvin made a declaration which in itself prevents his name being cleared of the guilt of the tragic issue, to the effect that, if Servetus came to Geneva, as he proposed to do, " I shall never permit him to depart alive, if I have any authority in this city." He was now driven to the conclusion that Servetus was a heretic of the most dangerous and incorrigible type who might become a centre of widespread and devastating mischief. In the *Restitutio*, Servetus prints no less than thirty letters to Calvin, all couched in a bumptious irritating tone, the deluge having ceased only after Calvin had for some time declined to reply or take any notice. Some of his letters were amongst the most incriminating documents produced at the trial; they were extracted from Calvin after at least a great show of reluctance; but granting the sincerity of his unwillingness, that only proves his recognition of the fact that he was doing a thing which would be hard to justify.

Servetus's arrival in Geneva occurred at a time when Calvin's soul was worn to the raw by the constant friction of conflict with the Libertines who had temporarily won the upper hand in the State. It looked as if the edifice he had so laboriously built up might be on the verge of collapse and the work of a lifetime undone. Servetus could not have chosen a more favourable moment to insinuate himself into the good graces of Calvin's opponents and help to oust him from his seat of authority. His appearance upon the scene at this critical juncture seemed the very providence of Satan. It might well have reinforced and reinspirited those who would like nothing better than Calvin's downfall. He was fully alive to the ambitious hopes of Servetus and as keenly aware of his high abilities. Here was a man eager to put himself at the head of a party virulently hostile to his regime. A victory for him would mean his own supplanting, and, it might be, his undoing, and that was a prospect which one who regarded himself as essential to the Reformation could not view with equanimity. Calvin's spiritual condition of sensitive rawness was aggravated by the mental sufferings caused by the many letters he was then receiving from those who were submitting to martyrdom in loyalty to the doctrine he had taught them. Michelet says with reason, " One understands how such blows, incessantly repeated, made the man savage, rendered him arrogant, fierce, in defending a dogma which each day drew blood from him. It is so that we can explain the crime of his life, the death of Servetus."

VIII.

There can be no question that Calvin was in hearty sympathy with the sentence pronounced upon Servetus, except as regards the form the execution was to take. Writing to Farel in the course of the trial,[1] he expressed the hope that the sentence would be that of death. He pled however that the sword might be substituted for the stake, but in vain. Not only on his own confession did he work to bring about the fatal issue, but he maintained thereafter an impenitent attitude towards his conduct. He takes a certain evil pride in the retrospect. "In Melanchthon's judgment," he writes, "posterity owes me a debt of gratitude for purging the Church of such a monster."[2] Only once or twice is there a suggestion that something like a suspicion of his having been at fault had entered his mind. He writes to Bullinger, "There are those who assail me harshly as a master in cruelty and atrocity for attacking with my pen not only a dead man but one who perished at my hands. Some even, not ill-disposed to me, wish that I had never entered on the subject of the punishment of heretics, and say that others in the like situation have held their tongues as the best way of avoiding hatred. It is well, however, that I have you to share my fault, if fault it be; for you it was that advised and persuaded me to it."[3] Again in his reply to Balduin, he protests,—"True it is that the unhappy man received the punishment due to his offences; but did this happen merely according to my will and pleasure? It is certain that his arrogance, no less than his impiety, was the cause of his ruin and death. But what of wrong did I commit, when the Council of this city, encouraged indeed by me, but according to the decision of the various churches, took just revenge for the horrible blasphemies of that wicked man? Melanchthon approved of the proceeding and commended the severity of the republic to imitation." Evidently he is quite unconscious of the inconsistency of which he is guilty when in

---

[1] Letter, Aug. 20, 1553.   [2] Ans. to Baudoin.
[3] Letter, April 28, 1554.

the very letter in which he defends the execution he laments that so many Protestants in France were suffering the same penalty. We may acquit Calvin of the spirit of retaliation, but he cannot be pronounced innocent of having allowed himself to be driven by personal antagonism to instigate a deed which he laid at the door of his zeal for the ark of God.

Extenuation has been found for his offence in the spirit of the age which approved of the capital penalty for specially dangerous heretics. Prolonged custom had made it appear right. It dated back to the time of Theodosius the Great (375-395), who ordered it to be inflicted in particular upon those who impugned the doctrine of the Trinity,—the very ground of Servetus's condemnation. The Justinian Code (527-534), which became the basis of all subsequent European legislation (with the exception of English), reenacted the edicts of Theodosius and gave fixity to the penalty of burning at the stake for all heretics. The merciless law remained anything but a dead letter, and was responsible for pyres whose number must have run into hundreds of thousands in the succeeding centuries. It is little wonder that an age-long practice, when encouraged by religious sanctions, cruel as it must always have appeared to some, so gripped the mind of the world that it could not immediately shake itself free from the inbred sense of its rightness, even when the Church which authorised it was definitely repudiated at the Reformation. It was a measure of self-protection whose fundamental inconsistency with elementary Christian principles, not to speak of its fiendish inhumanity, only gradually dawned upon the Protestant mind. In the heat of a life and death struggle, when the eyes of the leaders saw a deadly menace to the infant cause in anything which might disturb the faith of its adherents in the doctrines by which it was vitalised, no measures seemed too severe to stamp out the threatening spark or germ. They appealed for justification to the precedents of God's direct command in both O.T. and N.T. Reference was made, *e.g.* to such passages as that sanctioning the use of the sword by the civil power against evildoers (Rom. xiii. 4) ; and that recounting the judgment on Ananias and Sapphira (Acts v.

1 ff.). Pity for the culprit was swallowed up by concern for the cause and by jealousy for the honour and glory of God, whose vindication and assertion they regarded as committed to their keeping. If they did have qualms of conscience, they rolled the responsibility upon the civil statutes. They regarded it as a much more heinous crime to murder a soul by infecting it with damning heresy than to murder a body, and the criminal as a much more dangerous person to be at large. Even Servetus himself approved of the capital penalty when he challenged his opponents to substantiate their views or else suffer it as in accordance with law and justice.

Nevertheless, a sentiment against its imposition was already abroad amongst large-minded men uninfluenced by the responsibilities of leadership and either less apprehensive of the contagion of heresy or more trustful of the deep-rootedness of the general faith. Outspoken protests were uttered against the subjection of Servetus to such a barbarous punishment, chiefly by Italian refugees who were notoriously tainted with anti-Trinitarianism. Calvin became the target of many anonymous pamphlets in both prose and verse, pillorying him as a new pope and inquisitor, and picturing Geneva as a new Rome. But condemnation was not confined to outsiders ; it was pronounced by many in sympathy with Calvin's views and by such as Nicolas Zerkinden, an old friend who described the whole matter as "hateful to almost all." So widespread and strong was the dissatisfaction that Calvin was stung to make a defence, which took the shape of a lengthy work, endorsed by the fifteen ministers of Geneva. The impenitence of its author is sufficiently attested by the sub-title to the French edition which runs, "Against the detestable errors of Michal Servetus. Where it is also shown that it is allowable to punish heretics, and that righteously has this wretch been executed by justice in the city of Geneva." The hardness of its tone is deplorable ; it was as if Calvin was ready to erect endless stakes, if necessary, beside that of Servetus. If there is to be found justification anywhere for Bossuet's saying, "If the Protestants knew their origins, they would blush for them," it is to be found in such a passage as this. "Whoever shall now contend

that it is unjust to put heretics and blasphemers to death
will knowingly and willingly incur their very guilt. This
is not laid down on human authority; it is God who
speaks and prescribes a perpetual rule for His Church.
It is not in vain that He banishes all those human affections
which soften our hearts; that He commands paternal
love and all the benevolent feeling between brothers,
relations, and friends, to cease; in a word that he almost
deprives men of their nature in order that nothing may
hinder their holy zeal. Why is so implacable a severity
exacted but that we may know that God is defrauded of
His honour, unless the piety that is due to Him be preferred to all human duties, and that when His glory is
to be asserted, humanity must be almost obliterated from
our memories?" When one remembers that Calvin
started out on his literary career with a treatise on *Clemency*,
one can only grieve over the sorrowful change that may
be worked in a noble nature by the influence of fanatical
zeal endowed with power to carry out its will.

The execution itself did more than anything else to
stab men awake to the inhumanity of the statute that
authorised it. Protestants began to see that so to treat
an opponent was to flout the very principle of freedom
for which they stood. If Servetus failed in his life to reform
the Reformation, as he set out to do, he did it at least in
one direction by his death, which gave a mortal blow to
the mediaeval theory that made heresy a capital crime.
It did more; it provoked the very spirit of revolt which
it was meant to quell. The constancy of the victim, the
resolute assertion of his views to his last breath, stimulated
in resentful and horrified minds widespread questioning
of dogmas imposed upon them. The prediction of a
contemporary that numberless Servetuses would arise
instead of the one murdered only exaggerated what actually happened. So is the blood of heretics the seed of
great mischief to the Church.

CHAPTER XIV

LEGISLATION

It has been said by an eminent writer [1] that Calvin's chief title to a place in history rests upon his success as a legislator. As a theologian, he was a follower; as a legislator, he was a pioneer. His system of doctrine was derived, while his political economy broke new ground and based the social edifice on new principles. Certainly he is entitled to the credit of having established a political and legal system on a model of its own which has profoundly influenced, directly or indirectly, all subsequent democratic constitutions. It may be said that in doing so he found his true métier. He was endowed with statesman's gifts of a high order, if they were too much under control of theological principles. His father made no mistake in launching him as a youth upon a legal career. If the world gained a great theologian by his subsequent self-consecration to the Church, his country lost a great lawyer. With a mind instinctively and luminously systematic, rigidly logical, keenly alive to the relations between things, sure of his principles and sagacious in the application of them, he was cut out by nature for the task of reviewing, initiating, and codifying legislation for a community about to make a fresh start in life.

[1] Fairbairn, *Cambridge Mod. Hist.* viii. 364. Lord Morley declares that Calvin presented " a union of fervid religious instinct and profound political genius almost unexampled in European history." " No intelligence was more worthy to be called ' inspired ' than Calvin's," says Principal Oswald Dykes.

LEGISLATION

I.

The paradox of Calvin's career is that he, the arch-inspirer of modern democracies and democratic institutions, was chiefly responsible for changing the democratic constitution of Geneva into a virtually aristocratic one. After Geneva was liberated from the rule of duke and bishop, the direction of affairs fell into the hands of the people, convened from time to time to express their sovereign decisions. Later a system of Councils was devised for the conduct of public business. There was, however, a lack of precise definition of their powers and of coherent working amongst them, with consequent frequent disputes. It was recognised that things could not go on in such a tangled fashion, and steps were taken to bring order out of the confusion. The commission of seven who were first entrusted with the work of producing a satisfactory civic constitution proved unequal to the task and gave up the attempt. It was then resolved to call in the aid of the great legal knowledge and abilities of Calvin.[1] He was at first associated with two others, but the press of their own work left them insufficient time to give the needful attention to such a responsible business. As further delays were dangerous, the whole matter was handed over to Calvin singlehanded. To give him the necessary leisure, he was released from the duty of preaching on Sundays, and for his stimulus he was presented with a barrel of well-matured wine! It was work after his own heart, and with such impetuosity did he labour that within a fortnight he was able to present a draft of his proposed regulations. It was assigned to a committee of the Councils for review, and on their favourable report was adopted by them all. These regulations dealt with the mode and terms of appointment and the duties of the chief civic officials, such as the syndics (corresponding to the magistrates or baillies in Scottish towns), the heads of the police department, the mint, the fire-brigade etc. They constitute a monument to his genius for legislation, the width of his interests, his particularity

[1] Reference is made to the work Calvin did in collating the laws and edicts in various State protocols of the years 1541-43.

of mind, his farsightedness, his ability to gauge political exigencies and to estimate the capacities and needs of the people. It was not a mere revision that he formulated; it was a reconstruction with the aid of selected existing material.[1] His aim was to produce a constitutional and legal system which would be the expression of what he regarded as divine principles and which would be penetrated by the spirit embodied in the Scriptures. He refashioned the whole edifice of government and law and securely rebuilt it on the sound and safe foundation of the Gospel and the revealed divine will.

II.

While this was testimony to his legal capacity, Calvin exercised as profound an influence, though more indirectly, upon the political constitution of the city. The relationships of the legislative bodies to one another and to the people required to be specifically determined. One of the most distinguished lawyers of the day, Germain Colladon (the prosecutor in the Servetus case) was appointed to make a thorough revision of the existing system and propose such alterations as would make the mechanism of State work smoothly and effectually. Colladon entertained the highest respect for Calvin; he was one of his most intimate friends, and was strongly imbued with his principles. The constitution he produced is therefore deeply imprinted with the stamp of Calvin's mind. In the course of its construction Calvin busily engaged himself in compiling suggestions regarding all sorts of administrative details. The width of his purview and the shrewdness of his judgment are evidenced by many documents drawn up in his own handwriting. The result is in the highest degree significant of his personal propensities and preferences.

In the Institutes (IV. xx. § 8) he had passed under exam-

[1] Three elements are distinguishable in the legal system of Calvin: (1) the old laws of the city and the surrounding territory, (2) the Reform principles infused by Calvin, (3) the laws in vogue in the French province of Berry, communicated by Germain Colladon who brought them thence to his new home. (Stäh. i. 346.)

ination the three forms of government. " There are three kinds of civil government," he says, " namely, monarchy, which is government by one only, whether he be called King or Duke or otherwise ; aristocracy, which is a government composed of the chiefs and people of note ; and democracy, which is a popular government, in which each of the people has power. These all have their dangers : monarchy is prone to tyranny ; in an aristocracy, the tendency is not less to the faction of a few, while in popular government there is the strongest tendency to sedition." On comparing the three, he decides that " the form which greatly surpasses the others is aristocracy, either pure or modified by popular government, not indeed in itself, because it very rarely happens that kings so rule themselves that their will never departs from what is just and right, or that they are endowed with so much acuteness and prudence that any one by himself sees all that is needful. Owing therefore to the vices and defects of men, it is safer and more tolerable when many bear rule, so that they may mutually assist, instruct and warn one another, and should any one be disposed to go too far, the others are censors and masters to curb his excess. This has already been proved by experience, and confirmed also by the authority of the Lord Himself when He established an aristocracy bordering on popular government among the Israelites."

This conclusion found practical expression in the constitution with which Geneva was now provided. It proves the truth of what is evident from many statements in his writings that he was no friend of pure democracy. He distrusted and often was outspokenly hostile to anything savouring of the rule of the masses. His influence therefore was all in the direction of limiting rigidly their scope of immediate action, leaving them little more than the occasional exercise of the right of approval or sanction. All legislation was placed in the hands of the three Councils, but in such wise as to put the greatest power into the hands of those farthest removed from the control of the people. The general assembly of citizens met only twice a year, and could initiate no legislation, its rights being restricted to approval or disapproval of proposals laid before it by the largest of the three official bodies. It elected the four new syndics required to fill the places of the four who annually retired out of the eight holding office. The three Councils were composed respectively of 200, 60, and 24 members. Their interrelations were such that the constitution of the 200 as well as of the 60 was largely determined by the 24. The Council of 24, presided over by the syndics, had complete control of the administration, and took the initiative in shaping laws.[1] The range of its activities covered not only purely civic affairs, but military as well, while co-operating through its representatives on the consistory in the administration of the ecclesiastical. Nothing could be proposed in the Council of 200 which had not been before the Council of 60, nor in the latter which had not been examined and approved by the Council of 24. It is obvious how the small Council came to possess or control practically all legislative, judicial, and executive power. It alone had regular meetings, four times a week, while the other Councils met only when summoned for the consideration of special business requiring their sanction, such as any that had to be laid before the general assembly of citizens. The 24 held in their hands the nomination to almost all the high State offices, excepting that of syndic and one or two others. The constitution, therefore, was essentially aristocratic with a specious appearance of being fundamentally democratic. The people were left with little say in matters of government ; at most they were given occasional opportunities of vetoing projected measures at meetings which were only legal when called by the Council of 200.[2]

The general assembly, after it lost its ancient privileges, became little more than a shadow, though the syndic

[1] Corresponding in some degree to the British Cabinet.

[2] The populace were bitterly indignant at " the foreigner who would rob the native Genevese of their ancient liberties." But it is very doubtful whether under former political conditions Geneva would have been able to maintain its independence and self-government, ringed round, as it was, with enemies ready to take advantage of any weakness or disorder in the State. At least such competent judges as Montesquieu and Ancillon were of opinion that because of these political and legislative systems constructed by Calvin, the Genevese might well regard his birthday and the day of his arrival in Geneva as "the most blessed of all days for the Republic." (Stäh. i. 347.)

LEGISLATION

who presided at its annual meetings addressed the citizens as "sovereign lords." It was indeed a phantom democracy which now existed, the rights assigned to the popular assembly only sufficing to maintain amongst the citizens a sense of their civil dignity and their part in the state. The consummation of the process of spoliation was reached in 1570, the year after Calvin's death, when the general assembly was deprived of its right of deliberation and permitted only to give validity by its vote to the laws agreed upon by the two Councils and to choose the syndics from the candidates presented by these bodies. Before this time membership of the Councils had come to be largely recruited from a few families by virtue of the political traditions in their possession. A patrician caste was thus created, proof of the essential nature of the seed which had been sown and the potentialities inherent in it.

Yet, on the other side, it must be pointed out that Calvin introduced the system of legislative checks which characterises all democratic constitutions. The decrees of the consistory were subject to the review of the Councils, as were those of the Councils to the scrutiny of one another. Autocratic or arbitrary power was thus completely barred. If the political machinery in Geneva was not all that could be desired (and Calvin was regretfully aware of it), it was at least an experiment in a form of government which became in its essential elements the pattern for that of the freest, most enlightened, and progressive peoples.

III.

The code of laws established and enforced in Geneva has been described as the apotheosis of grandmotherly legislation.[1] Such a view might easily be supported by

[1] Prof. Lindsay points out (*Hist. Reform.* ii. 108) that Calvin was only carrying out a policy which had been long followed in every mediaeval town. There were laws which "prescribed the number of guests to be invited to weddings, and dinners, and dances, when the pipers were to play, when they were to leave off, and what they were to be paid.... Maid-servants were summoned before the Council (of Nürnberg) for wearing silk-aprons, or a mother for adorning her

examples from its more eccentric parts. For example, it was forbidden to have too many dishes at dinner and to wear apparel cut in certain ways or made of forbidden stuffs; also to adorn one's person with jewellery. Girls of the poorer classes must not wear red. Men must not wear their hair long. Novel-reading, too, and swearing *even* at animals were prohibited. Card-players were exposed in the pillory with the cards hanging round their necks. A woman was publicly whipped for singing a worldly song to a psalm tune. Only a certain number of guests might be invited to a marriage, for poor people not more than ten, for rich not more than twenty, while the noblest were allowed thirty. Marriages between a man of over sixty and any one less than half his age were disallowed, and a woman of over forty might not marry a man of less than thirty-five. Calvin has had to bear the brunt of the blame for suchlike enactments. While he is not to be relieved of the full responsibility attaching to wholehearted approval, he must not be pilloried as the progenitor of the inquisitorial system. A stringent and vexatious Puritanism had been in operation in Geneva before his appearance on the scene. It is significant that, during the interval of his exile, when those hostile to him held command, the same severity of restriction was practised. This at least suggests that the circumstances of the city warranted, in the view of the best and most patriotic minds, measures of a drastic and searching nature. There was something of the Augean stable about the city. Vice flaunted itself unashamed, and the authorities took complaisant cognisance of it in a regulation imposed in 1459, according to which the prostitutes were instructed to elect a queen from among their number (or in default the syndics would do so) who would take an oath upon the Holy Gospel " that she would discharge her functions well and faithfully with all her power, with-

---

daughter too gaily for her marriage." These laws " interfered with private life at every turn, and that in a way which to our modern minds seems the grossest tyranny, but which was then a commonplace of city life. . . . Every instance quoted by modern historians to prove, as they think, Calvin's despotic interference with the details of private life, can be paralleled by references to the police-books of mediaeval towns in the 15th and 16th centuries."

out affection or hate." It was a time of hard drinkers,[1] and the hours of their potations had to be limited. The inns and taverns were ordered to close at 9 o'clock and during the hours of divine service. The number of convictions of all kinds assumed deplorable dimensions. The fact that the general assembly endorsed the laws dealing with these conditions is strong proof of the general recognition of their necessity among responsible and decent-thinking people.

It is easy to hold up many of these enactments to ridicule and reprehension, but behind those which seem to be most questionable in their wisdom, if not censurable, there were reasons which in the circumstances of the times must be admitted to be not without their cogency. It must be remembered that social customs and fashions, apparently un-moral and innocent, if frivolous, may indicate a spirit likely to produce morally reprehensible fruits, if not nipped in the bud. If you cannot cure a moral disease, you must at least seek to reduce its symptoms or evidences which may in themselves be socially dangerous. To speak disrespectfully or satirically of individual ministers of religion may not be in itself an offence deserving much attention, but where the moral interests of the community are bound up with respect for those whose business it primarily is to look after them, such conduct, if unchecked in a society full of elements susceptible to contagion, may gain such a boldness and grow to such magnitude as to be disastrous to religion itself and with it to the morality for which it provides the main authority and most effectual sanctions.[2] Preventive measures to be effective must be searching and drastic. Evil cannot be allowed sanctuary anywhere; you cannot circumscribe its action; you cannot isolate it; you cannot draw a cordon round it and prevent its malign atmosphere suffusing itself abroad. To let even the home be exempt from regulation and control, to let its doors shut out law, is to

---

[1] *v.* Reyburn, 123. In one of the districts of the town, there was a tavern for every three houses.

[2] In Jan. 1555, during the height of the Libertine rebellion, the streets were illuminated one night and a mock-procession took place, in which the hymns of the Church were ridiculed in vulgar parodies.

let that sphere of life which is most influential of all become a possible centre of intense moral contagion. The home is either the nursery of virtues or the spring of evils. The legislator cannot afford to leave it outside his province. If he places restrictions on what may enter a home, he may also do so on what goes on within the home.

Calvin's legislative system was the practical counterpart of his theological presuppositions. Such laws would not be objected to by the really regenerate; they would regard them as an often necessary guide and safeguard and a no less necessary spur. As for the reprobate, goodness was impossible to them by nature, and it was not made possible for them by grace. Hence arose this apparent antinomy of Calvin's system, that for the protection of the Christian community from the corrupting influences of the reprobate, the State must compel them to do what God would not give them the will to do. Legislative compulsion alone could procure in them the external conformity and compliance to which the influence of grace inwardly moved others. Where grace failed, law must abound.

Modern legislation, by whatever political party imposed, evinces the working of Calvin's principles. That you cannot make men sober by Act of Parliament has ceased to be an axiom of domestic statesmanship. If men cannot resist temptation, then the temptation must be taken away. Again, with all the difficulties surrounding the exercise of a literary censorship, its necessity is generally recognised. If you cannot enter the parlour or study and snatch pernicious literature out of the hands of those who avidly devour it, you effect your purpose equally well by forbidding its publication. To prohibit the sale and use of cigarettes in the case of boys under sixteen, to penalise those who take children with them into public houses, to purge shop windows of indecent picture postcards, to make the use of foul and profane language in the open street a police offence, these and suchlike measures are approved by the strengthening moral sense and social wisdom of the community, and they are essentially of a piece with the policy of which Calvin was the outstanding exponent and determined pioneer.

It was Calvin's mission to assert that a State has no right to the name of Christian unless it consistently and constantly aims at procuring the moralisation of the society and community under its control in accordance with the ethical code revealed in Scripture. The highest interests of the State must not be jeopardised by the lawless vagaries of individual liberty. If righteousness alone exalteth a people, the civil authorities must exercise their God-given functions and powers to procure the suppression or excision of all that puts the public welfare in peril by alienating the favour of God, sovereign over all. The promotion of the health and true wealth of society is a matter of prime concern to each of its members. As the unit lives by the whole and should live for the whole, so the whole will only maintain a robust existence if it exercises a vigilant supervision over all the units that compose it. Every man is his brother's keeper. The wisdom of the community must impose restraints and constraints on the wickedness and folly of individual members. A community will only be the unity it should be if a common ideal possesses it and authoritative control be exercised over recalcitrant elements. Immorality is treachery to the body politic and must be dealt with stringently. Whatever weakens the moral and spiritual fibre of civic life, whatever introduces poison into its veins, whatever threatens insidiously to sap the stamina of the people as a whole, comes within the cognisance of the powers designated by them to look after their interests. Calvin's conception of the State was simply that of the organ through which God ruled the nations for the advancement of His kingdom of righteousness.

Public opinion is the greatest of repressive and regulative influences in regard to things which do not properly come within the scope of statutory law. The conjunct sentiment of the community, gradually gaining definiteness of conviction, acts upon the minds of its members with an immediacy and force which legislation in general fails to attain. That is true of a society homogeneous in its constitution, with a history continuous in the development it records. Geneva in Calvin's day conformed to neither of those conditions. With an increasingly heterogeneous population composed of varied nationalities, with a constitution of recent origin, penetrated by the new and heady spirit that appeared with the expulsion of the Roman Catholic regime, communal feeling had not developed that strength which makes legislation in certain directions unnecessary. A healthy public opinion had to be developed and educated, and for lack of agencies such as the newspaper by which in modern times that work is industriously prosecuted, there was no other way but that of tuition by the enactments of laws whose expediency or necessity in the circumstances was recognised by those to whom the care of the social wellbeing was committed, viz. the Church and the State acting together. In ordinary circumstances law is mostly the precipitate or embodiment of prevalent public opinion. The legislator registers the judgment or verdict of the community. But in Geneva law had to occupy a different place and discharge a different function ; it had to act as the tutor of the public mind, directing its attention to evils requiring restriction or regulation ; it had to educate, consolidate, and unify the moral sentiment of the community ; it had to vivify and mould a new social conscience and endow it with such authority as would gradually render inquisitorial laws unnecessary. A community once nurtured into healthy-mindedness comes to exhibit quickly-acting instincts of shrewd insight and foresight with regard to new fashions, customs, and practices, and, guided by these, sets in operation machinery of disapproval and antagonism which speedily procures their repression. Whether consciously devised with that in view or not, Calvin's policy was calculated to secure sooner or later such a condition of affairs.

It must be remembered that a social conscience was then practically non-existent. The Peasants' Revolt in Germany demonstrated how great was the need of one to secure the recognition of the rights of man as man, and to foster the humanity, justice, and public-spiritedness, without which society becomes a cockpit for the merciless struggle of all the selfish and self-seeking elements of human nature. The sense of mutual responsibility, the recognition of social duties implied in social rights, the readiness to submit to the limitation of liberty in the interests of the commonweal,—these and much else whose operation is now taken for granted, were largely the product of the political and legislative experiments made in Geneva under the Calvinistic regime, and radiated from it as from a focus where they found concentrated expression.

It may be that Calvin erred by excess of zeal, making such demands on unregenerate human nature as awakened a fury of resentment, forgetting that to attempt to dam up a torrent of evil with suddenly devised and imposed 'Thou shalt Nots' is to cause it to overflow in unforeseeable directions. But that he was on the right lines was recognised by the burghers themselves, who set the seal of their approval in general assembly to the code submitted to their judgment. Singlehanded or backed by his ministerial colleagues, Calvin could not possibly have secured its adoption, much less its effectual operation. Law in restricted and embryonic democratic communities such as Geneva has never more force than that given by the weight of public opinion. There was sufficient sympathy in Geneva with Calvin's aims to secure that his proposals became laws honoured by increasingly general observance as is proved by the decreasing number of breaches committed.

Without precedents to guide and warn him except such as were provided by Old Testament history, with a lawyer's reverence for the law and confidence in its power, with a free hand given him to let his idiosyncrasies and prejudices take shape in statute, it is no wonder if Calvin produced a legal system marked by much imperfection, both in regard to what it included and what it left out. The revision to which it was subjected twenty-six years later with his approval and co-operation is sufficient proof that experience had revealed many defects of which he himself was very sensible. Not the most farseeing wisdom can foretell how the law, theoretically admirable, will work in practice when it impinges upon the incalculable in human nature. It is inevitable that men such as Calvin should provide others with warning as well as with instruction.

IV.

How great a renovation Geneva required to undergo appears from the variety of matters dealt with in the new code which had up till now been without statutory regulation or appointment, from the disposal of sewage to the provision of a fire-brigade. The scavenging of the town was now properly organised and brought about such a sanitary improvement as to stir travellers to admiration. Market wares were inspected and anything bad or rotten was thrown into the Rhone. To prevent the frequent fatal accidents to children due to their falling over windows, an order was issued that a solid balustrade or secure railing as high as the breast must be provided. Calvin recognised the human need of fellowship which was responsible for the frequenting of the taverns, and set himself to provide for its satisfaction in a wholesome and safe way. He instituted five clubs where " young men and fathers of families could meet and discuss matters relating to the war, and other things useful to the commonwealth." They were not forbidden their wine, and at first these clubs were disgraced by excessive drinking and rowdiness, but under the care of the Syndics, who took it in turn to attend, a new spirit was gradually infused, and they became nurseries of patriotism. If card-playing and dancing were forbidden,[1] it was not because Calvin at least regarded them as wrong in themselves, but because of their evil associations and results,[2] the craving for unhealthy excitement stimulated and the waste of time and idleness of spirit occasioned. According to Gaberel, it appears from a memoir which still exists that the dances then indulged in would not be tolerated at the present day in the height of the most disorderly carnival.

[1] In 1506, the Council forbade playing with cards in the open street. Gamblers were set in the public pillory with their cards hung round their neck. In 1546 and 1556, laws were passed prohibiting the manufacture of cards. (Henry I., 362.)

[2] Cf. also his attitude to a prevalent fashion, " We have protested that the slashing of the breeches was a mere piece of foppery which was not worth speaking about, but that we had quite another end in view, which was to curb and repress their follies." " By the loopholes of the breeches, they wish to bring in all manner of disorders." (Letter, July 14, 1547.) This fashion had been prohibited for twelve years past.

To the theatre Calvin was not on principle opposed. The Genevese populace were fond of theatrical representations. Calvin countenanced the occasional performance of plays,[1] recognising their possibilities of edification; for example, where children presented a piece of Terence or Plautus by way of educative entertainment, or when a tragedy, representing the martyrdom of five Lausanne students in Lyons, was acted by boys to celebrate the conclusion of the agreement between Geneva and the Swiss. All depended on the nature of the play performed whether the theatre was to be supported as a desirable institution or not. He approved of a certain piece, "provided one scene was suppressed in which shopkeepers were ridiculed and traduced." Once he consented to postpone the evening sermon to allow of time for the piece presented to be given in its completeness. But a crisis was precipitated by a play entitled "The Acts of the Apostles." After perusal of the manuscript, Calvin said, "Those who desire the performance of this play ought rather to devote their money to works of charity. What I say is not so much by way of censure as of remonstrance." One of the pastors however inveighed against it in strong terms. "The women who mount the stage to perform that false scene are shameless creatures;" he said, "those who are handsome go to exhibit their beauty, and the ugly ones to show off their finery and their magnificent satins and gold. All this display excites evil thoughts and profligate talk among the spectators." On the matter coming before the Council, Calvin expressed agreement with his colleague. The play was, nevertheless, performed, but the magistrates refused to sanction any further representations "until the time was more favourable for them."

The ordinances were not a dead letter. Their provisions in regard to life and conduct were enforced with an even-handed justice that had no respect of persons.[2] Members

[1] Calvin and another minister voted against the proposal of the other pastors to forbid the performance of a morality play in 1546.

[2] A captain in the service of the Genevan Government was discovered to have been condemned for murder eight years previously. At the urgent instance of the ministers, he was arrested and would have been executed but for the intervention of the Council of 200, which banished him for life.

of the leading families, women as well as men, were arraigned before the consistory or council and compelled to satisfy them with regard to their most private affairs. A banker was executed for adultery and died blessing God that righteousness and justice were so well maintained. Informers were employed to report upon cases requiring attention. A species of police saw to it that people attended the statutory services of the Church, or, if they did not, were able to give good reason for their absence. Insolent contempt or anything savouring of ridicule of sacred things was summarily punished. Three children were prosecuted because they stayed outside Church during sermon to eat cakes. A young man was penalised for presenting an account book to his betrothed with the words, "Madam, this is your best hymn-book." So was a peasant who heard an ass braying and called out, "What a fine psalm he is singing!" Also a man found riding through the streets during the hours of divine service, who impertinently answered the question of the municipal officer as to why he was not at church, "Oh! is there room enough in church for my horse and me?" Another, who at such a time was found discharging a necessary domestic task and thought that the provision of firewood for his wife had first claim on his attention, said, "My faith and religion are a block of wood, and I am cutting them into chips." Unguarded utterances like these, if overheard and reported, were promptly chastised. The statutes providing for the punishment of witchcraft by burning and the infliction of torture to extort confession or evidence,[1] as also the old laws constituting heresy a

[1] In a letter to Bullinger, July 1555, Calvin says: "When it was almost palpable that there had been a conspiracy, was it not the business of the judges to have recourse to the torture?" The accused had already been subjected to 'no greater violence' than "having been raised from the ground a little with their arms fastened to a rope." In connection with the execution of certain Libertines in 1555, when in one case the executioner cruelly bungled, Calvin wrote to Farel on July 24, "I am persuaded that it is not without the special will of God that, apart from any verdict of the judges, the criminals have endured protracted torment at the hands of the executioner." A hundred and fifty persons were burnt for witchcraft in Geneva within sixty years. It was described as "crime de lèze majesté divine au plus haut chef." But a century later, Archbishop Leighton, of whom Prof. Flint says that ("a purer, humbler, holier, spirit never tabernacled

LEGISLATION

penal crime, were retained and were frequently put in operation.[1]

Credit, on the other hand, must be given for the severity with which the authorities dealt with those who tried to enrich themselves by exploiting the poor or the stranger within the gates. They were pitiless towards the merchant who defrauded his customers, towards the manufacturer of velvet who made his stuff too narrow by an inch, towards those who gave short measure of coal by constructing with cords the baskets in which it was sold. They brought to book the tailor who overcharged the English exiles, the surgeon who demanded extortionate fees, the butcher who charged more for his meat than the appointed price. A press censorship was established consisting of three men, whose business it was to examine every book before it was printed and to protect the publisher against piracy. Taken all in all, the legislation and discipline enforced in Geneva must have won high and wide approval, inasmuch as the city, instead of repelling immigrants, attracted them in large and increasing numbers.

V

Though political economy can scarcely be said to have been even an infant science, Calvin grasped the principles that lie at its base and sought to apply them, energetically advocating measures which had much to do with raising Geneva to high commercial and industrial prosperity. He did not regard this as outwith his province, inasmuch as he reckoned the occupations of life as means towards the realisation of Christian ideals. When he came to Geneva, there were only small industries, and the handworkers provided scarcely enough for current needs. The political unrest, recurrent epidemics of plague and periods of financial stringency, brought ruin to many. Poverty was increasing amongst the working-classes to an alarming degree, and beggary was rife, while philan-

---

in clay," made no protest against the action of Church courts in consigning witches to the Privy Council to be burnt.

[1] From 1542-6, fifty-eight death sentences were passed.

thropy was not organised to meet the increasing demands made upon it. Calvin perceived the needs of the situation, and on Dec. 29, 1544, he appeared before the Council and made a long statement on the matter, recommending instant measures of remedy. Among others he suggested that a silk industry should be started, his keen eye having discerned that the geographical situation of Geneva was peculiarly favourable for its prosecution. He proposed that public funds should be used to initiate and foster it. So impressed were the Council by his statement that they asked him to draw up a scheme embodying his proposals. This he did, with the result that a factory was established in which work was given to all the idle and those who had been existing mostly on charity. Begging could now be absolutely forbidden, any foreigner found practising it being promptly expelled. A hospital for the indigent sick was built and equipped. The success of these and other such measures awoke the citizens to new possibilities and excited in them a new spirit of enterprise. Such skill did the workers soon attain, especially in making silk and cloth, that their products came to be highly prized throughout Switzerland and France, and brought to the city an unprecedented prosperity.

CHAPTER XV

ATTITUDE TO ART, MUSIC AND SCIENCE

I

IN estimating a personality, one must not assume its lack of certain gifts or qualities because they do not appear in obtrusive exercise. Circumstances may not permit a man to develop himself on all potential sides of his nature. Talents or tastes may remain more or less latent, their possibilities a matter of unverifiable conjecture. Had Darwin not been engrossed in science, he might have proved capable of distinguished achievements in pure literature.

It has often been asserted of Calvin that his was an arid, prosaic soul, unresponsive to the aesthetic side of things, even in extreme Puritan antagonism thereto. To the beauty of nature, to the appeal of music, to the claims of art, his mind was closed, it is said. He lived in a world from which the things that stir the senses were sternly exorcised. Characterised as an incarnate "theological formula," he is declared to have been untouched by the humanising genius of song. He is roundly accused of " never having recognised music as a means of religious expression, or even having appreciated it as an aid to devotion." In still stronger terms, it has been asserted that he was "utterly destitute of musical sensibility, as every page of his works and every element of his character indicates. The musical Luther has filled Germany with rich church hymnody; the unmusical Calvin has so impoverished Puritan and Presbyterian worship that its rugged, slovenly Psalmody has become a byword."

Without denying that there is any grain of truth in

these views, they argue such a defective acquaintance with Calvin's history and writings as to deprive them of any value. As for the general charge that the aesthetic was entirely absent from his nature, is that not negatived by the simple fact of his own personal tidiness, his scrupulous neatness and cleanness of attire? No one, however disposed to flatter him, would claim for him the really poetic temperament of Luther, or that he had musical or artistic gifts or sympathies so strong that, given proper opportunity and stimulus, they might have made him a composer or an art critic. But if careful search is necessary to discover how exactly it was with him in this respect, there is sufficient evidence to show that the somewhat meagre indications of his possessing an aesthetic temperament are due not to his lack of it, but to other causes which are to be found in the character of the work he was called to do. Luther might give his disposition free scope and spread the evangel by his hymns; he had natures to work upon that responded healthily to such appeals. Had Calvin possessed Luther's gifts and used them to the same extent, he might have rendered the Church he founded more popular, but he might have made it less virile, by stimulating in the prevailingly light-minded people with whom he had to do elements that were already to blame for a state of things which was a crying shame. Conditions had changed, too, since Luther lifted up his voice in musical war-cries. A new stage of the conflict had opened, and Luther himself had felt the difference in the moral and spiritual atmosphere. Something of his old blitheness had disappeared, and been replaced by a deepened earnestness, even sternness, which in part may have accounted for the irritable vehemence of his later years. But the Gallic temperament, which hilariously wedded Marot's Psalms to the music of bacchanalian airs, had need to be disciplined and mortified, at least for a time, to reduce it to the gravity in which alone true religion had a chance to take firm root.

Moreover, Calvin was not unlike Darwin in respect that he too would have had to make confession, though perhaps not with the wistful regret of Darwin, that in the press of other higher matters demanding his whole attention and strength, tastes, in whose gratification he would have found a real satisfaction, had suffered a ' sea-change ' or become emaciated and desiccated. Calvin, it must be remembered, was French, and it is characteristic of the French nature, if worldly, to be frivolous, but, if deeply religious, to be passionately earnest, puritanically severe. The task to which he was called was of a nature which did not allow him to break out in any direction to which the mood turned him, and necessitated a vigorous self-control and self-limitation. Immersed in the incessant production of what the times urgently called for, from early morning to late at night the slave of a pen which had few and short intervals of rest, beset by trials and troubles which might well kill the sentimental in him, whatever there was of the aesthetic had little chance to air or express itself. It was his business to lay the foundation of a great and lasting building and determine its general architecture, leaving future generations to overlay its plainness by such elegancies as might give to their developing religious sensibilities a safe and profitable pleasure. Calvin did not attempt to stereotype divine service for all time, but only for such time as the form which he instituted was needed, that is, so long as careful education in true worship was required and the despiritualising extravagances of the new liberty had to be restrained.

What are the facts of the case ? The poetic and the musical cannot be said to be intimately allied or inevitably associated ; Tennyson was lacking in musical sympathies. But at least the penchant for poetry, the ability to produce what approximates to it, evidences an aestheticism which springs from the same general ground in nature as the love of music. Calvin has won no place amongst even the minor poets ; but if he had no genuine poetic gifts, he had strong poetic tastes which early in his career sought expression in religious compositions.[1] There

[1] One of Calvin's hymns has been thus translated ;
"I greet Thee, who my sure Redeemer art,
My only trust, and Saviour of my heart !
Who so much toil and woe
And pain didst undergo

was in him a pathetically passionate desire to give such utterance to the deep feelings of his soul as can only be satisfyingly found through poetry. Like many another youthful aspirant in that direction, he thought he had the divine afflatus, at least in some degree. He says of himself,—" I had naturally rather a turn for poetry, but having bid adieu to it, I have composed nothing since the age of 25, except that at Worms. I was induced by the example of Philip (Melanchthon) to write, by way of amusement, the poem which you have read." (He alludes to the Epinicium Christo cantatum, Geneva, 1541, a song of the victory of Christ over the Pope.[1]) But with the best will in the world, with a copious and facile command of apt and graphic language, with a pronounced and true dramatic instinct, he lacked 'that' which essentially distinguishes the true poet from the mere clever versifier. He had other qualities which spoilt the play

> For my poor, worthless sake ;
>   We pray Thee from our hearts,
>   All idle griefs and smarts
> And foolish cares to take.
>
> Thou are the true and perfect gentleness ;
> No harshness hast Thou, and no bitterness :
>   Make us to taste and prove,
>   Make us adore and love
> The sweet grace found in Thee ;
>   With longing to abide
>   Ever at Thy dear side
> In Thy sweet unity."

[1] In his Comm. on Phil. 1, 7, he quotes two lines of it, in which he had 'imitated' Tertullian's saying, The blood of martyrs is the seed of the Church. It may be interesting to give the original Latin with the corresponding lines in French into which he subsequently turned the poem :

"Sanctus at ille cruor, divini assertor honoris,
    Gignendam ad sobolem seminis instar erit."

(" But that sacred blood, the maintainer of God's honour, will be like seed for producing offspring.")

" Or le sang précieux par martyre espandu,
    Pour auoir à son Dieu tesmoignage rendu,
    A l'Eglise de Dieu seruira de semence
    Dont enfans sorteront, remplis d'intelligence."

(" But the precious blood shed by martyrs,
That it might be as a testimony rendered to its God,
Will in the Church of God serve as seed
From which children shall come forth, filled with understanding.")

of his fancy, which antagonised the Sapphic in him, which clipt the wings of inspiration and made him flutter when he would soar. The concluding lines of the one epic poem he achieved, read in view of the fact that he would not allow it at first to be printed, give evidence that he had become conscious of lacking a native and real poetic gift :

"Quod natura negat, studii pius efficit ardor
Ut coner laudes, Christi, sonare tuas."

Grudgingly at last he had to confess that his grasp exceeded his reach, that the thing he would do was beyond him, and that he must be content to walk along the levels of pedestrian prose. It is to his credit, as it is characteristic of the man all through, that he did not shirk the rigorous and frank self-estimate which blasted his youthful hopes. There was song in his heart, but his tongue could not utter it. He abandoned the effort to make bricks with little straw, and cast away the crown of bays that proved to sit but ill upon his brows.

II

Time and again it has been asserted that there was nothing of the artistic in Calvin's nature. The depressing plainness of many Presbyterian places of worship has been laid to his charge. A critic like Brunetière has the hardihood to declare that " the horror of art is and must remain one of the essential and characteristic traits of the spirit of the Reformation in general and of the Calvinistic Reformation in particular." Even an ardent admirer like Henry echoes the opinion that Calvin was insensible to the beauties of Nature. Michelet asserts (contrary to facts) that " he sought the darkest street in Geneva, from which he could neither see the Lake nor the Alps." Principal Lindsay goes the length of saying that "neither poetry nor art seemed to strike any responsive chord in his soul."[1] Certainly Calvin had more in him of Bernard who, absorbed in meditation, traversed the shore of Lake Neuchatel without being aware of it, than of Luther who,

[1] Lindsay, *Hist. Reform.* ii. 154.

thrilled by the loveliness of a spring day, sighed, "if sin and death were away, we might be well satisfied to remain in such a Paradise." But it is dangerous to draw emphatic conclusions as to a man's appreciation of Nature from the amount of allusion to it in his writings. Henry affirms that the same charge made against Calvin may be brought on the same grounds against all the other reformers, Farel, Wessel, Erasmus, and even Luther, though in less degree. As Dr. Goold says, "Apart from the circle of the poets, in the best authorship of Greece and Rome, how faint the response we find to the charms and glories of natural scenery! In the letters of Cicero, there is but one passage of this character deserving of honourable mention, and in it the fancy of the orator glows not so much under the natural beauty of the Greek isles, amidst which his vessel ploughed its way, as under the strength of historical associations. Becker appeals to one passage in Plato as all that could be adduced from the writings of the philosophic Greek in proof of his love of outward nature; and his taste in this respect was deemed something uncommon by the ancients."[1] Schaff seeks to extenuate Calvin's defect, if it be real, by pointing out that "we look in vain for descriptions of natural scenery in the whole literature of the 16th century." But that Calvin's eyes were not just one blind spot to the beauties of the world, and that he did take a sober pleasure in it, many hints in his works and letters make plain.[2] In one letter he pays tribute to the prettiness

---

[1] Calvin Tercentenary Lecture, 1864, p. 43 f. Cf. Geikie's *Landscape in History*, p. 52: "Even so near our own time as the later decades of the 18th century, men of culture could hardly find language strong enough to paint the horrors of that repulsive mountain-world into which they ventured with some misgivings, and from which they escaped with undisguised satisfaction. . . . Mountain scenery not only had no charm for intelligent and observant men, but filled them with actual disgust." Cf. also, Maeterlinck, *Old-Fashioned Flowers*: "What flowers then blossomed in the gardens of our fathers? They were very few no doubt, and very small and very humble, scarce to be distinguished from those of the roads, the field and glades. Before the 16th century, our gardens were almost bare. . . . Our forefathers were unaware of their poverty. Man had not yet learnt to look around him, to enjoy the life of nature."

[2] Cf. Letters, July 23, 1550; July 27, 1550; March 16, 1558; also Sermons on Job, 33-36, and on Ps. 19, also Instit. III. 10 § 1-3.

of the countryside through which he is passing. Again, he is careful, when selecting a house for M. de Falais, to choose one which had " as beautiful a view as you could well desire for the summer," though " the other rooms have not so pleasant an aspect as I would like." His own house commanded a magnificent panorama of lake and mountain, on which his tired eyes might gratefully rest in the brief moments of relaxation permitted them. No one can read the Institutes with any attention or such passages as his exposition of Ps. 19 without being impressed by evidences of a keen appreciation of the marvels of God's works, an appreciation not merely of a mimetic or conventional kind (Calvin was the last man to echo any one) but proceeding from a lively personal sense of natural beauty. He too regarded Nature as " the garment we see God by."

Calvin was far from being insensible to the magic charm of art or unappreciative of the elegancies and adornments with which the instinct of man from the beginning has led him to embellish his dwelling-place. It is true that the furnishing of his own house was severely plain and simple, but the power of appreciation is by no means always associated with the lust for personal possession. In a passage of the Institutes he describes heaven and earth as being " most richly adorned and copiously supplied with all things, like a large and splendid mansion gorgeously constructed and exquisitely furnished." There is a tradition that he cultivated friendly relations with Titian at the court of Ferrara in the leisure times of his exile there, but it seems untrustworthy. Nevertheless, that he did take an interest in the work of artists seems certain from such a sentence as this,—"As painters do not in the first draught bring out a likeness in vivid colours and like a copy (εἰκονικῶς), but in the first instance draw rude and obscure lines with charcoal, so the representation of Christ under the Law was unpolished and was, as it were a first sketch, but in our sacraments it is seen drawn out to the life." If it is the fruit that proves and tests the root, then it is not without significance that such a competent critic as Taine should commit himself to the assertion that " under the liberating influences of Calvinism, the common but rich human life disclosed to art an entirely new world, and by opening the eye for the small and insignificant, and by opening the heart for the sorrows of mankind, from the rich content of this newly-discovered world, the Dutch school of art has produced upon the canvas those wondrous art productions which have shown the way of all the nations to new conquests. ... When the artist saw how God had chosen the porter and the wage-earner for Himself, he found interest not only in the head, the figure, and the entire personality of the men of the people, but began to reproduce the human expression of every rank and station."

III

It may be true that Calvin had not the musical training of Luther nor the musical temperament of Zwingli, who found recreation in playing several instruments, but no one can speak as he does about music without having some music in his soul. Douen, who summarily rules him out of the circle of the musical, has to admit that "since Plato and Augustine, no one had spoken of music like him, save Luther. No one has better understood its action, whether harmful or elevating." That is a deserved tribute, for though Calvin might not be more than superficially musical, incapable of intensely feeling the emotions which are the peculiar excitation of music, he could shrewdly and deeply enter into the effects it had for good or ill upon the human mind and soul. "Amongst all the things that give men pleasure and satisfaction is music the chiefest or at least one of the principal means," he says, "and we must be convinced that it has come from God's hand for this end. ... As Plato rightly remarks, there is scarcely anything in the world that exercises such an influence upon men and so potently affects and fashions their morals." The introduction to his commentary on the Psalms is marked by the same insight and sympathy. "We all have experienced with what mysterious and almost incredible power music moves our hearts and drives them hither and thither," he observes.

ATTITUDE TO ART, MUSIC AND SCIENCE 275

There is a remark in his commentary on 1 Cor. 1.20 which contains an implicit claim that he did appreciate music:—
"Man with all his acuteness is as stupid for obtaining of himself a knowledge of the mysteries of God as an ass is unqualified for understanding musical harmonies."

But we need not search his writings for proof of his musical sympathies. Convincing evidence is supplied by the action he took in reorganising the services of the sanctuary. Zwingli had omitted singing from public worship, substituting a kind of responsive recitative; Calvin made singing one of its chief features. He was influenced perhaps by the example and success of Luther, who gave vernacular hymns an important place in the service,[1] but he may have been moved too by the extent to which the Psalms of Marot were being sung everywhere,—a witness to the want they supplied. Marot's aspiration was in some degree being realised as he expressed it in a kind of introductory poem to his book of 52 Psalms:

> O bien heureux qui voir pourra
> Fleurir le temps, que l'on orra
> Le laboureur à sa charrue
> Le charretier parmy la rue,
> Et l'artisan en sa boutique
> Avec un PSEAUME ou cantique,
> En son labeur se soulager ;
> Heureux qui orra le berger
> Et la bergère en bois estans
> Faire que rochers et estangs
> Après eux chantent la hauteur
> Du saint nom de leurs Créateur.

These Psalms of Marot were given no special musical setting, popular tunes of the day, commonly those of ballads, being adapted to them, as was also the case with some in Luther's hymn book. Lords and ladies gay had their favourite psalm, which they would sing to the accompaniment of lutes or guitars or violins, Henry II.'s preference being, "Like as the hart," etc., especially when he went a-hunting; Diana of Poictiers doted on "Out of the depths," etc., sung to a fashionable jig; the Queen's favourite was "Rebuke me not in thine

[1] The Kirchenlieder or Church songs issued by Luther in 1524 form the first known collection of Christian hymns and metrical Psalms with music.

indignation," Antony, King of Navarre's, "Revenge my quarrel," sung to the air of a dance. One of the recreations of society life was to join in the singing of these psalms, and thousands of persons of all classes, including royalty itself, would gather of an evening to the Pré aux clercs in Paris, an open space used by the Protestants for their meetings, to sing them together. The enlistment of 'profane' music after this fashion was no new thing. Roman Catholic Churches had rung to the Magnificat or the Credo or the Paternoster sung to the tune of some drinking or love song, *e.g.* Prends, ma Phillis, prends ta verre, or, Suivons, suivons l'amour, or, O Venus, la belle, Adieu mes amours. Michelet speaks of the obscene farce of performing masses of which the Introit was an invocation of Venus. So firm a hold did this psalm-singing take that the Council of Trent in vain protested against it.

In the French Protestant Church a reaction supervened, and resulted at first in the exclusion of singing from the service. But "this infectious frenzy of Psalm-singing" had scarcely begun before Calvin perceived how it might be made to serve the highest religious ends. Farel and he had observed that "the prayers of the faithful were so cold that they might well be turned to shame and confusion." Let them be sung (praise was simply sung prayer to Calvin) and a desirable warmth and passion would be infused into the service. The experiment was resolved upon and Calvin set about compiling the necessary material. He had no objection in principle to what are now called hymns, but the result of a careful scrutiny of current hymnology was to give him a very decided preference for the Psalms. Not only did their divine inspiration argue their providential adaptation to be the most perfect expression of the complex feelings of the human soul, but, apart from all presumptions about them, they appealed to him as incomparably the most suitable to voice the needs of the faithful in the peculiar circumstances of the times. "When we have sought all round," he asserts, "looking here and there, we shall find no songs better and more suitable for this end than the Psalms of David, which the Holy Spirit dictated and gave to him; and therefore when we sing them, we are certain God has put words into our mouths as if He himself sang within us to exalt His glory." (Pref. to Psalms.) Unlike Luther, who did not object to, indeed rather encouraged the singing of Latin and even Hebrew and Greek in the ordinary services of the Church on the ground of the instruction conveyed to the youth by that means, Calvin would tolerate no language in the sanctuary but that of the people who worshipped there. To sing spiritual songs without understanding, as you might " une linotte, un rassignol, un papejay," was " une grande moquerie." In 1538, while at Strassburg, he had tried his hand at translating the Psalms into metre, turning into French verse the 46th and 25th, afterwards the 91st and 138th and others, including possibly the 36th, of which Bovet says that " they have not the elegance nor facility of Marot, but show the clearness and firmness which distinguish all his prose." These (the only French verses of Calvin extant, not discovered till 1873) were published in the first Protestant Psalm book issued in 1539 from Strassburg. Meanwhile Clement Marot, at the instigation of Vatable, Prof. of Hebrew, 'the Reuchlin of France,' had been at work in the same way, and succeeded in making translations which at once captured the popular mind and heart. They were already circulating in MS. copies from hand to hand when Calvin was busy with his own effort. A copy came into his possession and so favourably impressed him that he incorporated eight of them in his Psalm book, subsequently increasing the number to thirteen. In later editions, with a discrimination and self-effacement which does him honour, he replaced his own versions by those of Marot, recognising that he did not have " the true temperament of the poet." Marot translated forty-nine of the Psalms before his death ; the rest were undertaken by Beza at Calvin's request. But the publication of the Psalmbook was not delayed till this work was completed, a small selection being as soon as possible put into the worshippers' hands.

The music was the next consideration and a matter of first importance. Calvin's guiding principle was that "touching the music, it should be simple, to carry weight and majesty suitable to the subject and to be fit to be sung in Church." Such a test could not be met by the frivolous airs to which they were being sung in boudoirs or the streets. At least Calvin did not appropriate them, thinking the Psalms "too good for the devil." He summoned to his aid distinguished composers of the day with Protestant sympathies. The first collection of Psalms, published at Strassburg in 1539, was accompanied by three tunes, but later editions were greatly enlarged in respect of Psalms and tunes.[1] Working under Calvin's direction, on his return to Geneva, Louis Bourgeois, appointed master of singing there, adapted or composed over eighty airs, the freshest and most melodious of which were acknowledged to be his own. Many of them were adaptations of popular songs, "purified and baptised into Christian seriousness." It is said that Bourgeois was threatened with imprisonment for changing some of the notes of the pioneer tunes, in particular that composed for Ps. 119 in 1524 at Strassburg by Matthias Greiter, a monk who turned Protestant.

Beza had been struck by the melody, and under its inspiration translated for it Ps. 68, to which it subsequently became wedded. Words and music fitted it to become, as it did, the Marseillaise of the Reformation. It is to be regretted that Greiter recanted and reverted to the Roman Church; "he who inspired the heroism of the Huguenots, was not a hero." The work of Bourgeois was supplemented by Claude Goudimel, one of the most eminent musicians of the sixteenth century, who was martyred at Lyons in 1572. These two musicians may be regarded as founders of modern congregational singing. Bourgeois adopted the two modes of major and minor instead of the Gregorian previously in use, and also harmonised tunes in four parts. Goudimel is said to have initiated the practice of giving the leading part to the soprano instead of to the tenor who had held it hitherto, as the result of hearing the dominance of children's voices

[1] It is unfortunate that we must remain in ignorance of the authors of the oldest Psalm tunes, as no indication of the composers is given in the Psalm-book.

ATTITUDE TO ART, MUSIC AND SCIENCE

in part singing. It was in a reprint of Goudimel's Psalmody issued in 1565 that the melody was for the first time assigned to the highest voice.[1] Four-part singing was taken up with enthusiasm ; some Scottish gentlemen, passing through Paris in 1557, were astonished at its effect. It formed indeed a very effective ally of the Reform movement, and so popular did it become that the French Parliament, instigated by the Sorbonne, the Roman Catholic college, issued successive interdicts with a view to its suppression.

A vigorous campaign of musical education was undertaken in Geneva. Children were formed into choirs to practise the airs, that through them their elders might be instructed. In the College the curriculum included four hours a week given to the study of music and the practice of the Psalms, of which a large number were sung at the statutory meeting on Wednesday morning and at the services on Sunday. To begin with, in the ordinary diets of worship, all voices joined in singing the melody, as they did at first in the case of Gregorian chants or Plainsong. This was not because Calvin objected on principle to part-singing. Far from it ; in one of his sermons on Melchizedek he gives evidence of his enjoyment of it ; "a man may sing well with one voice alone," he says, " howbeit, there will be no perfect melody, without there be many tuneable voices agreeing together." The difficulty in the way was that of securing the practice necessary for the proper performance of part-singing. Luther was faced with this also, and in Germany at first only the melody was sung. Other considerations doubtless influenced Calvin in enjoining the unison of voices. He had to safeguard against the frivolous spirit so rampant and rife in Geneva, turning that portion of the service into an opportunity for purely sensual enjoyment. Prob-

[1] "The edition of 1567 is of special interest to musicians, since alongside of each note-head the initial letter of the scale-degree is given " M " for Me," " S " for Sol, and so on, thus proving that the " Movable Doh," or Tonic sol-fa system, is not a modern invention, but the revival of an old one. In the edition of 1597 this feature is omitted. For more than a century and a half the book was the Psalm-book of the Reformation." (*London Quarterly Review*, Oct., 1910, p. 291.)

ably he had not overlooked in his reading how Chrysostom had complained of the theatricalities introduced into the singing in his day "when all should be grave and solemn," and how Jerome had to make protest in the same strain, and how Augustine had confessed that at one time he thought more of the sweetness of the song than of the matter that was sung. Calvin, governed in his policy by the supreme aim of deepening and strengthening the spiritual life, was concerned that nothing should enter into the service which might endanger the purity and sincerity of worship. Four-part singing, however, soon became established, and was flourishing in the Protestant congregation at Paris in 1555.

It was the same consideration that influenced Calvin in his attitude to organs. In a homily on 1 Sam. 18 he uses some strong expressions with regard to them, describing them as "a very ridiculous and inept imitation of papal worship." All that is needed in the praise of God, he held, is a pure and simple modulation of the voice. "Instrumental music was tolerated (in the Jewish Church) because of the condition of the people. They were children, Scripture tells us, who used childish toys ... which must be put away if we wish not to destroy evangelical perfection and quench the light we have received through Christ." He makes plain his root objection to organs when he argues that they preoccupy people's minds with external rites and distract their attention from the words.[1] Calvin was not the first to take up this attitude. Thomas Aquinas, who lived not long after their introduction into the Church in the twelfth century, had made the same objection. Luther, instrumentalist as he was himself, wrote no word in praise of them. If Calvin failed in judgment here, forgetting his own commentary on the use of instruments in the Temple as calculated "to excite dull and hard people," he erred in company with others upon whom the responsibilities of leadership fell at a time when circumspect caution had to guard against easy laxity and accommodating concessions. He must not

[1] This seems to dispose of Ritschl's assertion that in the sixteenth century organs were used "only for artistic music," and did not accompany congregational singing.

ATTITUDE TO ART, MUSIC AND SCIENCE 281

be blamed for the excess which prompted the regrettable act perpetrated in 1562, three years after his death, when the tubes of the organ of his own church of St. Peter's in Geneva were melted down and turned into flagons for holding the Communion wine, nor for its church bells being cast into cannon by those whose frenzied zeal deprived them for a time of sweet reasonableness.

The movement set agoing towards congregational singing in the Reformed Church spread rapidly. It has been blamed for kindling the flame of fanaticism in Germany and firing the spirit of insurrection in the cities of the Low Countries.[1] The first Scottish book of praise seems to have been more after the Lutheran pattern. "Gude and Godly Ballates," printed probably as early as 1546, mingled metrical versions of the Psalms with hymns on various subjects, mostly translated from the German, along with ballads satirising the corruptions of the Roman Church. This volume enjoyed great popularity for half a century, but never received the imprimatur of the Church. When the Scotch Reformers took up the task of preparing a Psalter, they followed Calvin in confining themselves to metrical versions of the Psalms. Working upon a book issued in 1556 from Geneva for the use of the English-speaking congregation there, which contained only a portion of the Psalms, they completed the metrical translations and published their Psalm-book in 1564. The Psalms in the original Genevan book were each provided with a tune, twenty-four of them being taken from the French Psalter. In the later enlarged edition this method was not carried out, some of the Psalms sharing a tune in common. Of these tunes a considerable number were taken over into the Scottish book, at least two of which, the old 100th and old 124th being still held in strong affection by the Presbyterian Church.[2] Other fine tunes might have survived,

[1] D'Israeli's *Curiosities of Literature*, ii. 345.

[2] The metrical version of the 100th Psalm was written by Wm. Kethe, one of the translators of the Genevan Bible, an exile in the reign of Queen Mary; the old 124th by Whittingham, who succeeded Knox in the English pulpit at Geneva; the 2nd versions of the 102nd, 136th, 143rd, and 145th by John Craig, once a Dominican monk at Bologna, subsequently minister at Holyrood, one of Knox's most trusted friends. The tunes 'Martyrs,' 'Elgin,' and 'Dundee' (named by

had they not been adapted to metres in which none of the metrical Psalms as now sung are written.[1] It is significant of the different view taken then of the appropriate use of major and minor (doubtless as the result of the influence of Bourgeois) that of 105 melodies, almost half are in minor keys, many of these being assigned to Psalms of a joyful or even triumphant nature.[2] The Scottish Church exhibits the influence of Geneva in respect that for nearly a century it sang the melody alone.[3] A compilation of four-part tunes of the most rudimentary kind was published by Crowley as early as 1549, but it made no impression. In 1615, however, an edition of the Psalms was issued from Edinburgh containing many tunes so harmonised which caught the public fancy. Part-singing seems to have come into vogue by this time, and, in response to the demand for material of a sacred character to practise upon, an edition of the Psalms with four-part tunes was published in 1635. Among the tunes which were taken from the original French Psalter and were found until recently in Scottish Psalmody were, besides Old 100th and Old 120th, Commandments, Old 113th, Old 117th, Old 134th (also known as St. Michael), Carmel and Lausanne.[4]

Burns in the Cottar's Saturday Night as used by his father in family worship) belong to the time of Knox and Melville, and illustrate how minor tunes were then often sung to Psalms of a cheerful or triumphant nature (v. M'Crie, *Public Worship of Presbyterian Scotland*, p. 221, etc., and Bannerman, *The Worship of the Presbyterian Church*, p. 351.).

[1] The metrical Psalms now used were the work of an Englishman, Francis Rous, revised by a Committee of the Church of Scotland. They are all written in 'common metre,' alternatives in five different metres being provided in thirteen instances. In the Reformation Psalm-book no less than thirty metres were employed.

[2] v. The Chorale Book compiled by Sir William Sterndale Bennett, 1863, for numerous examples.

[3] The Reformation was in itself immediately disastrous to Scottish music. The Sang-Schules, connected with Cathedral and parish churches, fell into rapid decay, and in a few years a statute was passed providing for education in music and singing, " quhilk is almost decayit and sall schortly decay without tymous remeid be providit."

[4] "The first *complete* Psalter of which any copy exists, that published by the Englishman, Robert Crowley, in 1549, contains only *one* tune to the whole hundred and fifty psalms!" The first musical edition of Sternhold and Hopkins' psalter was issued from Geneva in 1556. Like the French psalter it contained the melody only. (Cf. *Hymns Ancient and Modern* (historical edition), Introduction. Also Dr. Neil Livingston, *The Scottish Metrical Psalter*.)

IV.

One wonders what difference it would have made in Calvin's views had he lived a generation later when ideas of cosmology had been revolutionised by the doctrine of Copernicus. The acceptance of that momentous theory may be said to mark the beginning of modern science. Calvin had been educated in the traditional views, identified with the Church, which put the earth at the centre of things with the sun and other stellar bodies revolving around it. Those views he held without suspicion of their falsity, and he brought them to bear upon many a Biblical passage that spoke of nature. The heavens to him formed an encircling sphere or a vaulted roof. He thinks it possible that there might have been a rent or opening made in heaven such as allowed Stephen to see through it Christ sitting at the right hand of God, but, doubting if a man's eye could reach so far, he embraces the view that " a miracle was not wrought in the heavens but on Stephen's eyes." Though Copernicus had finished his treatise in 1530 (dedicating it to the Pope), he did not publish it till 1543, six years after Calvin issued the first edition of the Institutes. It is almost incredible that he did not hear of it, for Beza had read it, as appears from his work on the plague. If he had read it, probably enough he would have been as mystified and unimpressed as Beza. Such scientific excursions as Calvin ventures upon, do not dispose one to think that amongst his capabilities he numbered any unusual scientific capacity. Whether he was aware or not of Copernicus' epoch-making discovery, certainly he either did not grasp its significance or refused to take it seriously, for in the last edition of the Institutes he is still found declaring that the whole heavens revolve round the earth. In his *Comm.* on Ps. xix. 4-6, he speaks as if in ignorance of the new astronomy or as ignoring it. Whether his ideas as to the relation of God and man would have undergone revision, had he been compelled to take the new point of view which translated himself and his fellow creatures from the centre of things to a relatively insignificant celestial body, is doubtful in view of the negligible influence which the advance in knowledge had upon subsequent theologians of his school. Against all doubts and questionings Calvin was armour-proof by his implicit acceptance of the teaching of Scripture as final. He may have felt embarrassed by the demands of logic in his occasional excursions into the realm of science, but on withdrawing into the domain of theology he would have denied its relevance or shut it out from consideration as without weight or consequence in face of the assertions of authoritative revelation. It must be remembered, however, that so little value was generally attached to the treatise of Copernicus during his lifetime and for two generations after, that even when its truth was openly asserted by a distinguished man of science in the person of Galileo as late as 1610, he was promptly offered the alternative of recantation or imprisonment for dangerous and subversive views.

Astronomy, as we know it, was really included under astrology, and the distance the world has moved forward is measured by the gulf that separates the science and the pseudo-science now called by these names. The study of the heavens had been diligently prosecuted from time immemorial not for the sake of the knowledge gained in itself but for the ascertainment and determination of what might be learnt as to the influence of heavenly bodies upon human affairs. Astrology was astronomy turned into prophecy. There was no science more assiduously and believingly studied. Not even the most advanced minds had emancipated themselves from this ancient superstition. Melanchthon gave anxious consideration to the meaning of celestial phenomena. When the world was startled by the appearance of a new star in Cassiopeia, Beza regarded it as predictive of the overthrow of all things. Francis I. discharged his physician because, with a caution entirely creditable to him, he declined to read the future out of the stars. The most noted professor of medicine of the day, Nostrodamus, had no such compunctions, and owed something of his distinction to the confidence with which he practised the astrological art, a confidence and distinction due no doubt largely to one or two lucky predictions like that of the death of the King in a tournament.

If Calvin was no more free than the rest from bondage to these beliefs, it may be claimed for him that he was as near being so as any other of that age. His view of the relationship of God to man and the world, his dwelling-place, disposed him to believe that the movements and configurations of the stars, the most striking objects of creation, must bear upon human affairs either by way of influence or prediction or both. " Forasmuch as astrology doth consider the wonderful workmanship of God, not only in the placing of the stars and in such excellent variety, but also in their moving, force, and secret offices, it is a science both profitable and worthy of all praise." (*Comm. Acts* vii. 22.) In his treatise on *Astrology* he concedes that " all earthly bodies are subject to those above." " Natural astrology teaches rightly that the moon exercises an influence on bodies ; that, for example, when it grows or wanes, the joints are more or less affected ; and from this science of astrology physicians derive what insight they possess. We are therefore obliged to confess that there is a certain degree of harmony between the stars and human bodies." Again, true astrology will show why " oysters are full or empty as the moon is full or empty, and why the bones are full of marrow or the reverse as the moon waxes and wanes. It will also show physicians when to let blood, and when to order potions and pills."

So far he is prepared to go, but no farther. He perceived how prejudicial to true religion were the superstitions engendered by this science which intruded itself into all the concerns of life. The heavens were threatening to put their Maker out of sight. People consulted the astrologer about all manner of things,—" what they were to do or suffer, what was to be the issue of their undertakings, nay, about the minutest affairs of existence." He does not hesitate to dub as fools, insolent, and presumptuous, those who believe such nonsense as was served up by professional astrologers. He subjects their contentions and principles to the cool, searching analysis of a hard-headed commonsense. *E.g.* he declines to credit any such asserted predictions as that of the sooth-sayer who warned Caesar to beware of the Ides of March. " I ask you," he argues, " whether there were not many other persons born at Rome and in Italy on the same day and under the same star as Caesar ? Did they all die on the same day and by a similar death ? . . . There may be thirty who have the same nativity ; one may die when he is thirty, another when he is fifty ; one at home, another in battle. Theagenes had foretold Augustus that he would be emperor, having been born under the sign of Capricorn ; but how many poor wretches were there not born under the same sign, who attained to no higher glory than that of being swineherds or cowherds ? If the stars had given the kingdom not only to Augustus, but to all the rest who were born under the same sign, a very little portion of territory would have remained for him." Were the thousands of men killed in the same battle all born under the same star ? The amazing thing is that such a common-sense criticism had not long ago blown the whole science sky-high, but few things are more ineradicable than superstition.

Calvin's objections to this whole science are fundamentally theological. They result from the application of his views of the relations between God, man, and the world, as also from his profound antipathy to anything of the nature of speculation as an irreverent intrusion into the secret counsels of the Most High. He accuses the Egyptians and Chaldeans of " not being content with the simple order of things, and wandering into many foolish speculations," contrasting with their practices the sobriety of Moses who, whether he was infected with their superstitions or not, " contents himself with sincerely and plainly setting before us what should be considered in the frame of the world as appertaining to godliness." (*Comm. Acts.* vii. 22.) What Calvin is concerned to deny is that God ever gives revelations of his intentions or appointments by the medium of natural occurrences interpreted by uninspired minds. It may be asserted with some appearance of probability, he cordially acknowledges, that the stars exert an influence upon the present ; God uses their virtues to this end. They do not play a purely ornamental part in the scheme of things ; and, the earth being the centre of the universe and man the crown of creation, it may well be that they affect human

ATTITUDE TO ART, MUSIC AND SCIENCE 287

affairs. Barrenness may indeed be sometimes foretold by the disposition of the stars; but then there is no certainty in such foretellings. (*Comm. Acts*, xi. 28.) That is as God would have it be; the future is in His hands, and He will not allow Himself to be controlled or trammelled by Nature imposing upon Him any kind of necessity. It is He and not the stars that determine destiny; all is predestinate, as were the widely different futures of Jacob and Esau, born nevertheless under exactly the same celestial conditions. To arrange a journey or any business according to the dispositions of the planets in the hope of ensuring its prosperity is futile. The stars " have not power in themselves to do either good or harm." God governs earthly things at His pleasure far otherwise than can be gathered from the stars. He would have men realise their dependence upon Him and lead them away from " a perverse beholding of stars," even although their foretellings may have their degree of truth. (*Comm. Acts*, xi. 28.) God does not order things so that the appointments of His Providence might be anticipated, heavenly things being a symbolic prophecy of earthly things. Occasionally He might so give warning, but the warning so given would be itself a link in the chain of the working out of His purposes. If the celestial bodies did play their part in the economy of earth, then it was by their becoming the agents of God at whose command they bring their influence to bear upon the world.

Calvin was certainly not free from the credulousness of the times. He was not impervious to the mystical influence of things eerie and weird. Though he vigorously declaimed against the absurdity and injuriousness of presentiments in his work on *Astrology*, that same year he wrote to his friend Viret, " In the packet which you lately forwarded to me, were letters from Poland. They contained nothing new, except the account that a lake had appeared for two days like blood, and that the people had here and there taken up masses of the gore. A fearful wonder, the meaning of which will soon become clear to us." He adds, however, " There being now so many fables abroad, I can scarcely believe it, till our booksellers come back from the fair." There was an element of what has come to be known as the 'clairvoyant' in him, which all his theology could not suppress. Beza tells us that during one of his spells of sickness "he was lying in bed; it was Saturday; the north wind had raged terribly for the last two days; Calvin lifted up his voice in the presence of many persons and said, 'I know not what I ought to think of it, but the whole night through I have seemed to hear a tremendous sound of warlike instruments, and I could not convince myself that it was not so. Let us, I beseech you, pray; for certain it is that some great event is at hand.' And strange to say, on that very day the great battle of Dreux was fought."

It is perhaps not to be wondered at that he refused to 'reckon it as fabulous' that Vespasian opened the eyes of a blind man. But it takes one aback to find him giving ready credence to the following amazing story which is given in detail in the registers of Geneva. A labourer, to whom " God was no more than the vilest part of an old shoe," while lying sick of the plague, was seized by the devil, carried over his mother's head as she sat at the door in spite of all efforts to hold him, then over a broad road with a hedge and ditch on both sides, and finally disappeared in a vineyard on the other side of the road. So the mother and a servant affirmed. No trace of his body could be found. The story was generally laughed at, but Calvin took it seriously, and insisted on an enquiry being made into the case, so that, if it were false, it should be refuted by public authority, and if true, " so signal a judgment of God should not be buried in oblivion." He did not conceal an eagerness that it should be declared true, and raged at the other investigators because of their scepticism. He preached in church about the matter with great violence, concluding, as he tells Viret in a letter, "till hell absorbs you, with your whole families, you will not believe when God stretches forth His hand."

If it is asked what Calvin did *dans cette galère*, it is to be noted that he was in excellent company. Bishop Jewel, in a letter to Bullinger, tells him of the incredibly bad season of sunless days with incessant rain; " out of this contagion monstrous births have taken place; infants with hideously deformed bodies, some being quite without heads, some with heads belonging to other creatures; some born without arms, legs, or shinbones; some were mere skeletons, entirely without flesh, just as the image of death is generally represented. Similar births have been produced in abundance from swine, mares, cows, and domestic fowls " (*Zurich Letters*, p. 116).[1]

[1] For an example of the science of the day, cf. Calvin's explanation of thunder, *Comm. Ps.* xviii. 18, " When the cold and humid vapours obstruct the dry and hot exhalations in their course upwards, a collision takes place, and by this, together with the noise of the clouds rushing against each other, is produced the rumbling thunder peal."

CHAPTER XVI

THE ESSENCE OF CALVINISM

THERE is a widespread popular presumption that Calvinism is a discredited system, a spent force, a burnt-out star. The day of its dominance, commonly regarded as pernicious, is past. The time has come for it to be cast out neck and crop from creed and confession of an enlightened, emancipated age. The genius of Protestant mediaevalism has become the bogey-man of Protestant Modernism. This is an opinion and attitude to be reckoned with in the rapidly approaching era of creedal reconstruction. Practically all Protestant confessions are more or less saturated with Calvinism. Shall we anticipate revisions which will remorselessly extrude its every noxious germ? Is Calvinism to be consigned to the museum of antiquities among the wicked things that have ceased from troubling? Is it breathing its last? Has it no future?

Obviously such a question at once raises the previous one, What is Calvinism? The popular readiness to pronounce upon a subject is often in inverse proportion to its knowledge of it. The judicial " man in the street " is apt to base his opinion of things on his perception of some feature in them which repels or attracts him. Puritanism has suffered from the obtrusive wart on Cromwell's nose. The judgment that is rooted in prejudice is apt to be stubbornly defiant of the most vigorous and indignant spade-work. Calvinism has been the victim of its identification with a doctrine abhorrent to a complacent modern humanitarianism. That which Calvin accepted because it magnified God's glory, it construes and denounces as (were it true) dishonouring to Him beyond words. It

THE ESSENCE OF CALVINISM

does not stay to ask whether a system which has had such world-wide vogue and influence among all kinds of men, not altogether without tenderness of heart, could be synonymous with a dogma easy to state with a crudeness which pillories it as revolting at once to the sensible mind and the sensitive soul. There is much need of popular illumination as to what Calvinism essentially is.

Calvinism is, of course, primarily the teaching of Calvin in its widest scope. It may seem a perverse thing to say, but Calvin, accounted among the princes of systematic theology, was not primarily a theologian, one whose nature found its chief and deepest satisfaction in constructing an edifice of theological doctrine. He was not of the race of the dry-as-dust schoolmen. What was distinctive about him was that he was first and foremost a profoundly religious man. Piety was the keynote of his character. He was a God-possessed man. Theology was of no concern to him as a study in itself; he devoted himself to it as providing a framework for the support of all that religion meant to him. It explicated and vindicated his feelings; it rationalised and articulated his experience; it gave firm foothold and handhold for what might have been evanescent emotions, or at least it made him independent of other religious support and comfort when the spring of living faith went dry. Calvin came to his work with all in his heart which gradually came out of his head. Had he not been constitutionally religious, he would never have been the kind of theologian he became. It happened that he was gifted with an intellect which made him equal to the task of giving religion, as experienced by him, embodiment in a systematised theology congenial to the logical character of a mind which believed in the divinely ordained orderliness of things and expected to find a concatenated series of propositional doctrines corresponding to a harmonious, unchaotic body of religious feelings and emotions. As evidence of what was deepest in Calvin might be adduced the fact that in the first edition of the Institutes dogma, *pur et simple*, plays a minor part, the emphasis being on the things which go to nourish the spiritual and moral life. It was only as he became aware of the looseness of conduct associated with libertinism of thought that in later editions he gradually elaborated and urgently claimed assent to what was essentially dogmatic. It is notable, too, that in his children's Catechism there is no mention of predestination, and in his Church Catechism 11 sections (or one-fifth of the whole) are devoted to prayer. There spoke the real heart of the man.

Now because of this primary characteristic of Calvin, it is quite conceivable that his doctrinal system might have taken a very different shape and content, had it not been for the axiom assumed on all hands at that time—the indisputable authority of Holy Scripture as providing all the theology (taking the word in its widest sense) that need be or could be surely known. What was there, was bound to be believed. Experience must attest it and it must illuminate experience. Anything asserted without its authority was vain speculation, unnecessary, probably perilous, an impious or irreverent trespass, it may be, on ground on which it was the mind of God that foot of man should not with His consent tread. A contradiction within the Bible was unthinkable—an assumption which results in not a little expository juggling in his *Commentaries*. Calvin was not more in love with the doctrine of reprobation than his critics. But he found it in his sacred referendum, and his scrupulous honesty of mind would not let him discreetly cover it up; it was his duty as a faithful expounder of the Word to declare the whole counsel of God. If a doctrine were not to His honour and glory, it would not be there. Reprobation therefore was no erratic boulder in the sacred quarry of doctrine, intrusively alien. It must be of a piece with the whole. But for Calvin, with his estimate of man as a hell-deserving sinner and his thought of God as ever seeking His own glory, the surprising thing would have been that there should be no hint in Scripture of the rejection of men who thoroughly deserve that fate. He indeed regarded election as much more to be wondered at than rejection, for God might most justly have left mankind to its merited fate of self-incurred doom.

It needs to be reiterated that these doctrines with which Calvinism is popularly identified did not originate with

Calvin at all. He inherited them, and much else, from
Augustine, just as Luther's theology owed much to Occam.
But he was not the man to take them over from Augustine,
however much he revered him, did he not find them in
Scripture for himself. That they are there was no belated
discovery of the Church, even so late as Augustine. Controversy had busily concerned itself with them since the
dawning of the day of dogmatic thought. In the second
century, *e.g.* the letters of Octavius prove that the same
perplexities were felt about the election of God and the
same vehement objections made to the doctrine as in later
ages when in the cyclic revolution of emphasis it came once
and again over controversy's underlining stroke.

So then one might decline to find in these doctrines
the characteristic product or features of Calvinism. They
were embodied in it as they were in all other contemporary
theological systems, because the axioms of the faith left
no other alternative either to loyalty or to logic. Calvin
made use of them after his own characteristic fashion
as supports, inspirations, or admonitions. But their
absence from his system would have made no difference
in the clearness and determination with which he perceived
and pursued the aims and objects to which he gave his
life. Calvinism in fact is not essentially a systematic
body of doctrine. Its essence is revealed in that which
Calvin consistently strove to effect and actually succeeded
in effecting in no small degree—the moralisation of all
life by religion. His lifelong aim and business were to
re-wed religion and morality and establish them in indissoluble union as directors of human activity in all its spheres.
He was the apostle of the rehabilitation of the ideal of
primitive evangelical Christianity. Religion to Calvin
was not a matter of pious emotion, consequent on the
assurance of being in a state of grace. It was the acceptance of the rule of God over one's whole life. It included
dependence upon the will of God and obedience to the
will of God—not more the one than the other. A man's
conduct in all his relationships must be governed by
regard to God's will along with the ever-active sense of
direct responsibility to Him. In the provinces of home
life, social life, political life, religion must be energetically

operating to procure the dominance of truth, justice, purity, integrity. This world was meant to be the kingdom of God. It was the business of the elect to make it so; that was why they were called. Predestination was the appointment of the few good to rule over the many bad in the interests of righteousness. It was not for God's chosen to sit down idly and complacently at the feast of privilege. He had chosen them for His glory; He had chosen them for His honour, too; and the honour He sought was the establishment through them of His rule over all people that on earth do dwell. Nothing but their active participation in that work could give assurance of their election. While Calvin laid great stress on the inner witness of the Holy Spirit, he did not allow assurance to fluctuate with emotion. That was the weakness of Luther's teaching; Satan assailed him on the side of his assurance, and it took more than hard-flung inkbottles to repel his cunning assaults. Calvin suffered from no such neuralgias of doubt as to his standing with God. With far shrewder judgment, he recognised that emotion was no trustworthy criterion. To allow one's self to be troubled by its coming and going, to agonise in the fierce struggle to recover shaken certainty, was to dissipate energy which might be better employed. Was your heart steadily set to do the will of God? That was the main thing. Were you sincerely on the side of God? Did the trend of your life prove it? Then that was sufficient.

All this proves how far doctrine was from being central to essential Calvinism. Calvin himself may have thought it was; but a system-monger is not always the best judge of what is essential to his system and most valuable in it. The theory of natural selection might go to the wall without the real worth of Darwinism suffering eclipse. Calvin's doctrine of predestination might well have issued in a fatalism which induced a paralysis of ethical endeavour. It actually did the very reverse. It braced men's wills. It saturated them with aspiration. It inspired them to a strenuous and heroic activity which brought about a very miracle of moral revolution in all spheres of life and all quarters of the world. So much more was it the spirit of Calvinism which counted than its letter.

THE ESSENCE OF CALVINISM

Calvinism indeed worked as a moral purgative and stimulant wherever it gained any influence at all—and that is its greatest glory. It cleansed the Augean stables of Geneva. It entered licentious courts and touched reckless cheeks there to a strange, unwonted shame. Everywhere it awakened and made sensitive lethargic consciences. It created a refined, if vehement, piety, which blossomed into a strength and frequent beauty of high character that has since been the world's most valuable asset. Calvin's religion was reflected in his crest—a hand with a burning heart in it, and the words, " I give Thee all." That is what it meant to him, and what it meant to him he taught to others. Calvinism in a word stood for consecration, the consecration that found its ideal and example in the Christ whose tired feet climbed Mount Olivet to pray and the hill Calvary to die.

It is this fundamental and ultimate aim of Calvinism to moralise life by religion which interprets and explains the character of Calvin's own activities. It instructed his legislation. It determined his views of the relation between Church and State. The Church should be the conscience of the State, the State the organ of an evangelised conscience. As a reminder of the spirit that should infuse all life, private and public, Calvin had the letters I H S carved or stamped on all public buildings, coins, and standards in Geneva. In Scotland the same spirit fruited in projects of education (unfortunately abortive in their enlightened completeness) whose aim was to promote learning and virtue to the profit of Church and Commonwealth, as also in the endeavour to suffuse home life and social life with an ethical religion, an endeavour which found expression in the enactment of the Kirk Session of St. Andrews permitting no one to marry who could not repeat the Lord's Prayer, the Creed, and the Ten Commandments, a summary combination of the essential elements of piety, theology, and morality. It is a notable thing how closely Calvin keeps to life in his *Commentaries*. The application was the main thing with him. That is largely the reason why these expositions still retain their value. They are instinct with a constant concern for the attunement of life to the divine precepts. This fundamental principle, too, explicates his attitude to heresy. He was wonderfully patient for those days and for one in his position with all kinds of creedal vagaries around him. It was only when these threatened (in his view) the foundations of morality and orderly government and therefore of society that he became severe. But (excepting in the case of Servetus) his severity limited itself to expulsion of the offender from Geneva as a disturber of the public peace, as a discordant element in the community whose continuance there might be fraught with insidious and perilous potencies of evil. Calvin in this respect accepted and applied the principle of the Justinian code, *Cujus regio, ejus religio,* though from a different motive, the motive not of the right of the powers-that-be to command the belief of subjects, but of expediency in the interests of the public welfare, based as it was in his view on what he jealously regarded as the true religion.

Now all this, which may have seemed preliminary to our real investigation, has in reality given a large part of the answer to the question of our inquiry. Were Calvinism rightly to be identified with its body of doctrines, did the elimination of these mean the excision of its soul, then indeed it has but a slender hold on life. Already it is as a ghost peeping timidly out of the dark rooms of neglected confessions. As a system of doctrine compactly built together, it is now consigned to the attentions of vivisectionary historians. Querulous impatience clamours for the decision of the High Courts of the Churches to assign it to the custody of the Committee on Ancient Buildings and Ruins, accounted worthy of preservation as an interesting and curious memorial of a dead heroic past, whose mind moved in mysterious ways.

But that is not to dispose of Calvinism. Declare its doctrinal foundations unsound and therefore to be condemned; cast away predestination and reprobation with loathing; regard the Bible as a tract of country wherein may be found many wellsprings of truth of varying strength and sweetness amid much sandy soil and sterile country rather than as a big reservoir whose every drop has been carefully distilled from heaven. Do these things, and you may indeed have some reason to think you have consigned the body of Calvinism to lie mouldering in the grave, but the prime part has escaped you ; its soul, like John Brown's, goes marching on. For essential Calvinism, let it be again insisted, is not identical with its system of doctrine. You may discard the bulk of it (though all of it you cannot without consigning Christianity itself to the ash-heap of things done with) but still it lives on. It must and will live on so long as religion itself endures. Its dogmas were but the clothing and nourishment of a spirit which is of the ultimate essence of religion, the spirit of which Calvin himself was the very incarnation, the spirit of humble dependence upon God, of patient submission to His holy will, of whole-hearted consecration to His service, of perfect trust in His sleepless care and unchanging love. Calvinism lives in every religion which teaches and fosters these things and in every man that practises them. Where the sense of a divine providential government is deep and strong, where the eye of faith sees God sitting at the loom of time weaving with wise and loving thought, though it may be with inscrutable purpose, the web of individual lives, where piety waves aside all would-be intermediaries, seeking and finding immediate fellowship with a gracious Father-God, where the mystical in human nature is given proper recognition and due rights, restrained from extravagances by the firm rein of a cool common-sense, where men with a high gravity live life under a profound sense of responsibility and a keen realisation of its incalculable issues in eternity, where a community, a society, a people bow to the imperious claims of a Christianised conscience and seek to order their affairs under its direction, there Calvinism lives.[1]

[1] In his address on Calvinism to the University of St. Andrews, Froude says (p. 8 f.) : "I am going to ask you to consider how it came to pass that, if Calvinism is indeed the hard and unreasonable creed which modern enlightenment declares it to be, it has possessed such singular attractions in past times for some of the greatest men that ever lived. And how—being as we are told, fatal to morality, because it denies free-will—the first symptom of its operation wherever it established itself, was to obliterate the distinction between sins and crimes, and to make the moral law the rule of life for States as well as persons. I shall ask you, again, why, if it be a creed of intellectual servitude, it was able to inspire and sustain the bravest efforts ever made by man to break the yoke of unjust authority. When all

But in more ways than in these is it perpetuated. It initiated a new epoch in the spirit of communal life. The kingdom of God, which the elect are appointed to realise, is a brotherhood, and through the mutual services of brotherhood alone can it be realised. It is the special distinction of Calvin that, while he raised the worth of the individual to its highest power, each man having a line to himself in the Book of Life, he demanded that that worth should prove itself in the faithful and diligent discharge of social duties and responsibilities. Every man was in his degree directly responsible for the welfare of the body politic; he was his brother's keeper. This was the principle Calvin carried into all his work as legislator, and he has been pronounced greater as a legislator than as a theologian. It issued in Presbyterianism, whose genius is the participation of each and every member by right in the direction of the affairs of the Church. It issued in the constitution given to Geneva largely at his dictation, based on the principle of the rule of States by representative elected assemblies. It accounted for the grandmotherly legislation which he has been accused of inspiring if not actually formulating, which did not scruple or hesitate to invade the sanctuary of the home where independence claims to practise anarchism if it likes. More than anything does that which goes on within housedoors defile and poison the stream of life without. Calvin sought to deepen and vivify the sense of responsibility of the individual to society for his conduct in every relationship and activity, as father as well as citizen, in play as well as in work. Indeed he may be said to have brought to life the germ of that spirit which has now taken shape in socialism, only his was a socialism of mutual

else has failed—when patriotism has covered its face and human courage has broken down—when intellect has yielded, as Gibbon says, ' with a smile or a sigh,' content to philosophise in the closet, and abroad worship with the vulgar—when emotion and sentiment and tender imaginative piety have become the handmaids of superstition, and have dreamt themselves into forgetfulness that there is any difference between lies and truth—the slavish form of belief called Calvinism, in one or other of its many forms, has borne ever an inflexible front to illusion and mendacity, and has preferred rather to be ground to powder like flint than to bend before violence or melt under enervating temptation."

THE ESSENCE OF CALVINISM

responsibility, of communal duties based on reciprocal rights, an idealistic socialism of the spirit. It might be held that the modern era of social reform, springing from the mutual concern of the members of a community in one another's welfare, began with Calvin. Certainly it was then that the care of the social welfare first became the conscious concern and organised business of the united community.

Now Calvin was by conviction and temperament an aristocrat. The doctrine of predestination was indeed to him the divine sanction of aristocratic rule, that is the rule of the worst by the best. Yet no one has done more than he to infuse into all the veins of the world the spirit of democracy. He built other and better than he knew, like most great men. It was inevitable that that should be the outcome of his work. It could not but so fruit from his insistence upon even-handed justice that has no respect of persons and from the strong, self-assertive consciousness of individuality which he, more than any other, sowed in receptive hearts by his doctrine and by the practical demand he made upon men. The sense of personal worth, of human dignity, claimed expression, asserting its rights in institutions specifically democratic. Calvin rang the knell of autocracies. He laid the foundation stone of modern republics, as Bancroft, the historian of the United States of America, has cordially recognised in the case of that country. He paved the way for all manner of popular assemblies in all lands. Their roots creep at last to Geneva. It was principally because Calvin was such an outright uncompromising exponent of essential democracy in Church and State that his influence so quickly eclipsed that of Luther in the extent of its spread and the constructive and directive idealisms he infused into the political systems of modern civilisation. Calvinism in fact became the most powerful ferment of civic liberty which has ever worked in the world's heart. It is significant of its achievements that in the monument erected at Geneva to commemorate Calvin's tercentenary there appear statues of statesmen who at once represented Calvinism in the ages when it was fighting for existence and stood for the rights of citizenship over against aristocratic and autocratic power: William of Orange, Oliver Cromwell, Admiral Coligny, Bocksay of Hungary, Williams of America. The principle of the sovereignty of the people is the gift of Calvinism to the modern world. Calvinism no future! Why, it has laid the foundation of the future. It has cast the moulds into which the future is being poured. It struck off the last fetters which shackled the hands of civilisation and made possible that progress which has brought it farther on its way toward whatever be its goal than all the centuries that have gone before.[1]

Calvin was a man of ideals, unrealisable if you will. Among the noblest of them was his ideal of the unity of the true Christian Church in all lands. He was not riveted to Presbyterianism as the only Scripturally valid system of ecclesiastical government. He was not so straightjacketed. His candour and clearness of exegetic acumen forbade him to pronounce one constitution as alone divinely authorised. He approved of episcopacy meanwhile in other lands, where he recognised it to be more congenial to native tastes and affinities and inherited traditions. But he held the Church to be one under whatever form, so long as it was evangelically Protestant. He never hesitated to intervene in its affairs wherever the need appeared or if appeal was made to him. By that means as well as by seeking to originate a common council of the Churches, he industriously sought to promote what would have expanded into a world-embracing union of the

---

[1] John Morley (*Nineteenth Century*, Feb. 1892), says (in criticism of a statement of Frederick Harrison): " To omit Calvin from the forces of Western evolution is to read history with one eye shut. To say that Hobbes and Cromwell stand for the positive results of the intellectual revolution in Protestant countries, and that Calvin does not, is to ignore what the Calvinistic Churches were, and what they have done for moral and social causes in the old world and the new. Hobbes and Cromwell were giants in their own ways, but if we compare their power of binding men together by stable association and organisation, their present influence over the moral convictions and conduct of vast masses of men for generation after generation, the marks they have set on social and political institutions wherever the Protestant faith prevails, from the country of John Knox to the country of Jonathan Edwards, we cannot but see that, compared with Calvin, not in capacity of intellect, but in power of giving formal shape to a world, Hobbes and Cromwell are hardly more than names written on water."

Protestant Churches. His attempt could scarcely help but fail. But is his spirit not in possession again to-day? Does his ideal not hover before large and generous minds in all lands? In them the spirit of Calvin lives again and, unrecognised it may be, bodes to work yet more mightily.

One other claim may be made. Essential Calvinism will be the frontier fortress against the inroads of any philosophy which posits a God incapable of foreseeing the future, subject to mistakes, fighting a hard and not always winning battle against heavy odds of uncompromisingly hostile evil, trammelled in His endeavours by an unmanageable universe for which He is not responsible. With such a finite helper, liable to be overpowered, thwarted, outmanœuvred, in whom shall we trust? A modern Rabshakeh is given ample reason to mock. The future is left uncertain. Providence is a hallucination. Life is like a drop of water trickling down a window-pane—not even God knows where it will run next. Such a philosophy offers no guarantees for any worthy upshot of the whole perplexing business. It draws its pencil through such unauthorised and groundless anticipations as that of a great divine event to which the whole creation moves. All it can say is, Wait and see! That is the reverse of encouraging. It is crippling to high endeavour. It sets an *angina pectoris* of doubt in the breast of hope. It takes the inspiring vision from faith. It strikes intercessory prayer dumb. The surest protection against the paralysing touch of such a philosophy is the victorious assurance of Calvinism that God is supreme, indisputably Sovereign over all, that His will is done, that His Kingdom will come. That faith may set up mysteries; but mysteries we can live with if so be that we believe with our whole heart that behind them are the mercy, wisdom, and love of a Father-God to whom the isles of the sea and the stars of dreadful space are as the dust of the balance. But doubts of God's absolute power to help, to save, to perform, to carry out His will—with these we cannot live if we would be of good courage, if we would greet the unseen with a cheer. Upon the God of Calvinism rests the hope of the world.

INDEX

Academy of Geneva, 2.
Anabaptists, 67, 223.
Anathema, 222.
Angels guardian, 80.
Apocrypha, 66
Arminius, 19.
Assurance, 98, 166, 294.
Astrology, 80, 135.
Atonement of Christ, 50, 106 f.
Augustine, 28, 34, 46, 68, 94, 100, 103 f., 112, 118, 119, 141, 150, 227.

Bacon, Roger, 79.
Baptism, 150, 158, 168 ff., 206, 237.
Bells, church, 158, 207.
Berne, 191.
Berthelier, 193, 222.
Beza, 11, 122 f., 147, 277, 278, 283, 284.
Bishops, office of, 201.
Blandrata, 34.
Bolsec, 91, 186, 226.
Bourgeois, Louis, 278, 282.
Brentz, 177.
Bucer, 94, 104², 176, 239.
Bullinger, 39, 105, 150, 223.

Calvin, independence, 28, 94; learning, 3, 19 f., 35; knowledge of Heb. and Gk., 20; piety, 4 f., 32 f.; sense of beauty, 271 ff.; superstition, 287 f.; sanity of judgment, 28; attitude to ancient creeds, 35 ff.; to amusements, 4, 262; to art, 166¹, 273 f.; to democracy, 250, 253, 255, 299; to foreign missions, 153 ff.; to music, 267 f., 274 ff.; to hymns, 276; to organs, 280; to pagan philosophy, 43; to ritual and liturgies, 208 f.; to the theatre, 263; to science, 283 ff.; to speculation, 23, 41 f., 76 f.; to scholasticism, 24; to allegorising Scripture, 23 f.; as a legislator, 250 ff., 298; as a moralist, 293 ff.; as a poet, 269 ff.; as a political economist, 265 f.; as a textual critic, 73 f., prayers of, 210 ff.; on the canon, 65 ff.; confessions composed by, 38, 89 f.; catechisms, 96, 187, 292.
Calvinism, 1, 290 ff.
Canon of Scripture, 65 ff.
Card playing, 256, 262.
Caroli, 36, 37, 38.
Castellio, 62, 75, 96.
Catechisms, 36, 89, 96, 187.
Causes second, 132 f.
Celsus, 92.
Chemnitz, 177.
Christ, atonement of, 50, 106 ff.; glorified body, 174 ff.; key to Scripture, 86 f.; relation of humanity and divinity, 177 f., 236; Second Coming, 26, 179.
Church, and the community, 227; and Christ, 148 f.; and election, 149 f.; and laity, 199 f.; and the Holy Spirit, 148 f.; and Scripture, 87; and State, 107 ff.; 199, 220 f., 223 f., 295; Anglican, 199; attendance at, 205 f., 264; bells, 158, 207; marks of, 151 ff.; necessary to salvation, 148 f.; property of, 190; purity of, 152; self-government of, 198 f.; services, 205 f.; visible and invisible, 150.

INDEX

Coincidences and Providence, 139f.
Colladon Germain, 252.
Communion, private, 185.
Confession, Augsburg, 40, 59, 144, 158, 181.
    Cumberland Presbyterian, 115.
    Helvetic, 35, 81, 95, 101, 158.
    French, 122.
    Scotch, 168, 178^2.
    Westminster, 103^1, 105^1, 114^3, 123, 128, 135^1, 136^1, 150, 151, 190^1.
    of Cyril, 104^1.
Conscience, witness of, 119.
Consensus, Tigurinus, 178^2.
Consistory, 187, 192, 202, 221, 227.
Contingency or chance, 132.
Copernicus, 283 f.
Corruption, total, 98 f., 119, 237.
Council of Trent, 59.
Craig's Catechism, 103^6.
Cranmer, Archbishop, 159.
Creeds, Ancient, 35 f., 40; Apostles', 36, 38; Athanasian, 36, 38; Nicene, 36 f.; their proper nature, 40.

Deacons, 203.
Des Gallars, 18.
Discipline, 217 ff.
Duns Scotus, 49 f., 71, 180.

Elders, 192, 202.
Election, and Christ, 106 f.; and faith, 108 f.; and holiness, 110 f.; and the Sacraments, 165, 167, 168, 172.
Erasmus, 20, 154.
Excommunication, 185, 190, 193, 220 f.

Faith, 108 ff.
Fall of man, 100, 114 f., 121 ff.
Farel, 186, 192, 197^2, 205, 229.
Fathers, ancient, 34 f.
Fatalism, 121, 126.
Forgiveness, 109.
Formula of Concord, 165, 176.
Formula Consensus Helvetica, 69.
Freewill, 114 ff.
Froude, 297^1.
Funerals, 158, 206.

Geneva, 186 f., 191, 202 f., 219, 251 ff., 260 f., 262 f., 279, 295.

Gentilis, 23, 242^1.
God and law, 52; and nature, 53; and necessity, 49; and sin, 136 ff.; arbitrary will, 50 ff., 111 ff.; Fatherhood, 45 f.; foreknowledge, 102, 103^1; goodness, 47, 52; glory of, 54 ff., 101, 112, 114^2; justice, 107 f., 112 f.; permission and volition, 123; repentance, 135; righteousness, 101, 107, 109 f.; sovereignty, 46 f., 49, 102, 121, 301; unknowableness, 48 ff.
Gottschalk, 92, 106^1, 127.
Goudimel, 278.
Gratian, 188.
Greiter, Matthew, 278.
Gribaldi, 37.
Guilt, 100, 118.

Heathen, virtues of, 99.
Heaven, 175^1, 178 f.
Hell, descent into, 108.
Heresy, 36, 38, 296.
Heretics, execution of, 247 f.
Holiness, 110.
Holy Spirit, *v.* Spirit.
Hooker, 21.
Hymns, 276.

Immortality, 101, 288.
Inspiration, verbal, 72.
Institutes, 6 ff., 40, 90, 217.
Intolerance, 225 ff., 296.

John, Gospel of, 17, 18, 26.
Justification, 85, 109.
Justin Martyr, 150, 178.
Justinian, 188, 247.

Knox, John, 173, 182^1, 209.

Laity and the Church, 199.
Laying on of hands, 197^2, 202.
Le Fèvre, 94.
Legislation and Scripture, 200, 252.
Libertines, 36, 43, 44, 185, 218 f., 226.
Liturgies, 208 f.
Luther, 6 f., 49, 56, 64, 65, 66, 72, 85, 86, 87, 94, 98, 99, 105, 145, 161, 165, 172, 173, 174 ff., 188, 199, 239, 267 f., 272, 275, 277, 279, 280, 299.
Lutheranism, 2.

Marot, Clement, 275, 277.
Marriage, 206.
Melanchthon, 66, 90, 105, 121, 135, 137, 145, 157, 161, 181[5], 239, 246, 284.
Ministers, 192, 197, 201.
Miracles, 53 f., 135.
Missions, foreign, 153 ff.
Morley, John, 300[1].
Motley, 127[2].

Nationality, sense of, 187 f.
Nature, 133 f.
Necessity, 49, 117.
Newman, Cardinal, 53[1].

Occam, 49, 64[1], 68[1], 71.
Octavius, dialogue of, 92.
Ordinances, ecclesiastical, 200 f.
Ordination, 197[2].
Origen, 82, 175.
Orthodoxy, 40.
Osiander, 109[1].

Peter, the Lombard, 118.
Pighius, 91.
Prayer, 80, 135, 210 ff., 238.
Preaching, 204 f.
Predestination, 47, 88 ff., 130 f., 226, 237, 294.
Presbyterianism, 200, 203, 298.
Profiteering, 265.
Protestantism, union of, 155 ff., 300 f.
Providence, 88, 130 ff.
Psalms, 275 ff.
Psalters, Scottish, 281 f.
Punishment, eternal, 56.

Ratramnus, 93.
Reason and faith, 71 f., 80.
Reprobation, 56, 103, 106[2], 113 ff. 123 f., 292.

Sacraments, 161 ff.
Scholasticism, 24.

Scriptures, 59 ff., 292 ; allegorising, 23 f.; and predestination, 95 ; vernacular, 15.

Second Advent, 26, 179.
Seneca, 94.
Sermon, the, 205.
Servetus, 23, 186, 221, 228 ff.
Sin and penalty, 144 f.
Sin, original, 51 f., 100, 237.
Speculation, 23, 41 ff., 286.
Spirit, Holy, 64, 69, 95, 148 f., 181.
Spontaneity of sin, 118.
State and Church, 107 ff., 186 ff., 199, 220 f., 223 f., 295.
Stoicism, 46, 121, 126.
Sturm, John, 156.
Supper, the Lord's, 167 ff., 191, 207, 221 f., 237.
Sub- and supra-lapsarianism, 121 f.

Theatre, 263.
Theodosius the Great, 247.
Theology and legislation, 258.
Tokens communion, 185.
Trinity, the, 25 f., 37[1], 39[1], 83, 235 f., 247.
Union of Protestantism, 155 f., 300 f.

Visitation, pastoral, 203 f., 207[1].

Wesel, 68[1].
Wesley, Charles and John, 124 f.
Westphal, 176[1].
Will, a right, 120.
Wyclif, 68[1], 93.
Wundt, 118.

Zoll, Matthäus, 157, 162.
Zwingli, 108[1], 137, 141, 150, 164, 168, 172, 173, 199, 223, 274 f.

www.ingramcontent.com/pod-product-compliance
Lightning Source LLC
Chambersburg PA
CBHW050336230426
43663CB00010B/1881